COUNTERING TERRORISM

Countering
Terrorism

Martha Crenshaw

AND

Gary LaFree

BROOKINGS INSTITUTION PRESS

Washington, D.C.

Copyright © 2017
THE BROOKINGS INSTITUTION
1775 Massachusetts Avenue, N.W., Washington, D.C. 20036
www.brookings.edu

The Brookings Institution is a private nonprofit organization devoted to research, education, and publication on important issues of domestic and foreign policy. Its principal purpose is to bring the highest quality independent research and analysis to bear on current and emerging policy problems. Interpretations or conclusions in Brookings publications should be understood to be solely those of the authors.

Library of Congress Cataloging-in-Publication data are available.

ISBN 978-0-8157-2764-4 (pbk : alk. paper)
ISBN 978-0-8157-2765-1 (ebook)

9 8 7 6 5 4 3 2 1

Typeset in Sabon LT Std

Composition by Westchester Publishing Services

Contents

Preface

The two of us first met at a conference in 2003 and a year later helped create the National Consortium for the Study of Terrorism and Responses to Terrorism (START), a center dedicated to understanding the human causes and consequences of terrorism. We found that our connections to the study of terrorism were at once distinctive and complementary: Martha Crenshaw is a political scientist with a long track record in the study of terrorism, while Gary LaFree is a criminologist whose interest in terrorism studies is more recent and connected to general interests in collecting and analyzing historical data on criminal violence. As research on the Global Terrorism Database (GTD) matured, LaFree began thinking that it would make sense to write a general book about some of the policy lessons illustrated by the GTD. So in 2010 he approached Crenshaw with broad ideas about a policy-oriented book. She agreed to collaborate, and we began to develop the outline. From the beginning we focused on explaining why it is inherently difficult for the American government to formulate an effective counterterrorism policy. We also argued that terrorism researchers face many of the same difficulties in explaining terrorism and counterterrorism.

Over the years of work on this book, the drumbeat of terrorist threats has become even louder than it was when we first began the project. While neither of us thinks that the scourge of terrorism is going to be eliminated anytime soon, we also believe that now more than ever it is imperative to make sensible and moderate policy decisions based on a realistic appraisal of the threat.

We would first like to acknowledge the support of our respective home institutions: the University of Maryland, particularly the National Consortium for the Study of Terrorism and Responses to Terrorism (START), and Stanford University, particularly the Center for International Security and Cooperation (CISAC) and the Freeman Spogli Institute for International Studies (FSI).

Parts of the arguments developed in this book were supported by the Global Terrorism Database, which is funded by the Office of University Programs at the U.S. Department of Homeland Security and by the Bureau of Counterterrorism at the U.S. Department of State. We appreciate that our funders have steadfastly preserved our academic freedom, and the views expressed in this book are entirely our own. Margaret Wilson and Erik Dahl were members of the START research group that developed the dataset we relied on in chapter 3.

We especially want to express our appreciation for the supremely helpful comments offered at different points during the lengthy process of writing this book by the following individuals: Anja Dalgaard-Nielsen, Betsy Cooper, Morgan Kaplan, Terence Peterson, Shiri Krebs, Kate Cronin-Furman, Mark Jacobsen, William Spaniel, Itay Ravid, Erin Miller, and Alexa Andaya. Parts of the book were presented at CISAC's weekly Social Science Seminar, and we are grateful for the feedback from the participants. CISAC also generously hosted a "murder board" at Stanford for a critique of the completed manuscript, and we are in debt to our friends and colleagues Kim Cragin, Michael Stohl, Michael Kenney, Joe Felter, Lynn Eden, and Arif Alikhan for reading and responding to our work in its entirety. The two anonymous Brookings reviewers were clearly experts whose comments were constructive as well as critical. Itay Ravid, Scott Bade, Alexa Andaya, Aubrey Blanche, Kerry Persen, Kathryn Holleb, Bo Jiang, Mike Jensen, Mike Distler, and Scott Menner provided indispensable research support and administrative assistance. Bill Finan has been an encouraging and motivating editor, and it was a great pleasure to work with him as well as the excellent editing staff at Brookings.

On a personal note, we thank our spouses, Richard W. Boyd and Vicki Viramontes-LaFree, respectively, for their patience and forbearance.

Martha Crenshaw
STANFORD

Gary LaFree
MARYLAND

COUNTERING TERRORISM

CHAPTER 1

Introduction

The Context for Analyzing Counterterrorism Difficulties—
Current Threats and the State of Academic Research

W hat is it about terrorism that makes it such a challenging policy problem? The purpose of this book is to explain the characteristics of terrorism that make it inherently difficult for governments, especially the U.S. government, to formulate effective counterterrorism policies. Why is terrorism so intractable? What are the obstacles to developing a consistent and coherent counterterrorism strategy? The barriers that we identify flow from the issue itself, not the particular political predispositions of individual policymakers or flawed organizational processes. We find that scholars and policymakers face similar difficulties—the study of terrorism is often confused and contentious, and the study of counterterrorism can be even more frustrating.

Our main thesis in this book is that the conceptual and empirical requirements of defining, classifying, explaining, and responding to terrorist attacks are more complex than is usually acknowledged by politicians and academics, which complicates the task of crafting effective counterterrorism policy. Although the policymaking process, the goals of individual American leaders, and American societal and political pressures are relevant factors, our focus is on the daunting complexity, variation, and mutability of the issue itself. Moreover, the stakes are especially high since the consequences of missteps and miscalculations in responding to terrorism are potentially catastrophic. In the chapters that follow we outline some of the barriers to recognizing and responding to terrorist attacks and suggest ways to overcome the obstacles we identify. Terrorist attacks are rare, yet they encourage immediate and far-reaching responses that are not easily rolled back. Most attempts actually fail or are foiled, so that examining only successful terrorist attacks gives an incomplete picture. The actors behind terrorism are extremely difficult to identify, since there is no standard "terrorist organization." Governments and researchers often struggle to establish responsibility for specific attacks. Evaluating the effectiveness of counterterrorism is problematic. For empirical comparisons we rely to a large extent on the nearly 157,000 terrorist attacks that have occurred around the world over the past four and a half decades since 1970; they are catalogued by the Global Terrorism Database (GTD), maintained at the University of Maryland.[1]

Following this introduction, in chapter 2 we argue that the atypicality of terrorist attacks makes them difficult to study and predict and, consequently, to prepare for and counter. We examine the frequency of terrorist attacks worldwide and against Americans at home and abroad, and we demonstrate that terrorist attacks, especially those with mass casualties, are exceedingly rare, however ubiquitous they might appear. Nevertheless, the U.S. government responded to 9/11 as though it presaged the beginning of a trend. The transformative policies and institutional reorganizations adopted in the immediate aftermath of 9/11 have reshaped international and domestic security politics. It has not been easy to roll back changes made in the moment of crisis in order to adapt to a shifting threat. Democratic governments may not be capable of treating rare but highly destructive terrorist events as outliers rather than regularities.

In chapter 3 we address the complications caused by the fact that a large number of attacks against Americans at home, apparently motivated by adherence to jihadist principles, fail or are foiled (an inference drawn from an original dataset). Much of the information about terrorism that is presented to the public is the proverbial tip of the iceberg, showing only terrorist attacks that transpired rather than attempts that were thwarted. Often the difference between success and failure in terrorism is difficult to discern. In general, failed and foiled plots are more difficult to study and have less impact on public opinion and on policy than do completed attacks—with some exceptions that we will discuss. Yet developing a comprehensive response to terrorist threats requires that we not only track "successful" attacks attributed to groups and individuals but also examine who planned to accomplish what, how close they came to completion, and the intentions behind their actions.

Chapter 4 focuses on the elusiveness of the adversary. There is no single type of terrorist organization. We argue that our counterterrorist policies must be tailored to varying, complex organizational types as well as to relations among groups as they shift between cooperation and competition. The rivalry between al Qa'ida and ISIS (Islamic State of Iraq and Syria) is a case in point. We compare common stereotypes about hierarchically organized, long-lasting terrorist organizations to the range of actors that are in fact linked to terrorist attacks. On one end of the spectrum are individuals operating with little or no direct support from formal organizations; on the other, a handful of hierarchically structured, relatively long-lived entities.

In chapter 5 we take up the related issue of attribution of responsibility for terrorist attacks, a process that is frequently uncertain. Often those responsible for a particular attack are never known. Sometimes groups incorrectly take credit. In other cases one terrorist group falsely claims that an act was committed by another group. In the aftermath of a deadly terrorist attack there is often tremendous pressure to assign responsibility, understandably, because punishment is impossible without this knowledge, unless a government wishes to take the dubious path of collective punishment. Moreover, attribution can be controversial as well as indefinite, especially if there is the possibility of state involvement or the question of blame has aroused domestic political controversy.

In chapter 6 we assess the difficulties of determining how effective counterterrorism policies are. How can we tell when policies are successful in preventing or diminishing terrorism? How can the costs and benefits of different measures be calculated? Developing metrics for success has proved problematic. In fact, consensus on what success means is lacking. Conceptions of successful counterterrorism have varied considerably in the years since the 9/11 attacks.

In the final chapter of the book we summarize our main conclusions and consider their implications for developing a coherent and sensible counterterrorism policy. Terrorism can encourage outsized responses whose scope may be greater than they need to be to prevent further attacks. Overreaction by governments has been a stated goal of some users of terrorist tactics, so in these instances a disproportionate response may actually reward terrorists. On the other hand, without credible responses to terrorist threats, the risk of another catastrophic attack could increase to unacceptable levels. Certainly the public demand for an effective response will be almost impossible to resist. Finding a middle path between overreaction and underreaction is a persistent dilemma for the United States—one that is not likely to disappear in this century.

In the remainder of this introduction we provide background for the issues that will be discussed in more detail in subsequent chapters. We begin by providing historical context for the evolution of the terrorist threat in the United States, emphasizing how the general conception of terrorism has developed and how it has come to dominate the American security agenda since the 9/11 attacks. We also clarify some of the conceptual and methodological obstacles to policy-relevant academic research into terrorism and counterterrorism.

The Evolving Threat of Jihadist Terrorism in America and the West

Since 2001 violence associated with Salafi-jihadist variants of Sunni Islamism has been at the center of the American conception of the terrorist threat. The jihadist danger has understandably dominated the counterterrorism agenda, initially as a foreign threat and over time as an internal "homegrown" threat as well.[2] Domestic right-wing violence has caused more harm to American citizens at home in the same period of time, and the 1995 Oklahoma City bombing remains second after the 9/11 attack in terms of lethality within the United States.[3] However, the threat of violence from sources such as white supremacists, antifederalists, and the Christian Identity movement does not have the same resonance for the security agenda. Indeed, merely bringing up the issue or defining violence associated with right-wing causes as "terrorism" can produce a firestorm of criticism. Our purpose is not to equate or even compare the two strains of violence but to note that this dispute demonstrates yet again the contentiousness of trying to define terrorism, one of the obstacles to progress in research that we discuss later in this chapter.

Why the difference in perspective? Whereas much jihadist violence is transnational and poses a threat to national and international security, American far-right violence is a domestic problem. Domestic, localized violence is easier for the American government to control or contain, the ideology behind it is more familiar, it is organizationally and ideologically more fragmented, and in terms of overall destructiveness its effect is minor compared to that of worldwide jihadism. Images of extreme ruthlessness such as videotaped beheadings and immolations, massacres of religious minorities, mass-casualty attacks targeting schoolchildren, university students, or shoppers at a market, and extreme intolerance such as the destruction of historical antiquities and the imposition of harsh punishments for infringements of a rigid code of justice have a powerful effect on mass-media audiences. Those responsible, al Qa'ida and its affiliates and rival offshoots such as the post-2014 self-proclaimed Islamic State (known also as ISIS or ISIL), seek publicity for their deeds and are adept at advertising their message worldwide, with a social media presence that is unprecedented among violent nonstate actors. Their capacity for mobilization and communication appears to outstrip that of most other groups that have used terrorism, even if one holds technological progress constant.

In addition to their expanding transnational reach, jihadist groups undermine the domestic stability of American allies embroiled in civil conflicts. There is a real risk that states in critical regions will either collapse into chaos or come under the control of forces hostile to American interests that rule by principles antithetical to democratic and humanitarian values. This prospect became especially ominous in the summer of 2014, when ISIS moved from strongholds in Syria to seize extensive territory in Iraq, including the city of Mosul. Policymakers are fearful that jihadist expansionism will jeopardize whatever gains the United States and its allies won in Iraq and Afghanistan and in the global war on terrorism generally. They also fear continued civil conflict involving jihadist groups in Syria, Libya, Yemen, North Africa, Somalia, and Nigeria.

Both jihadist self-promotion and extensive outside media coverage magnify the threat as perceived by the public. Yet with the 9/11 shock always in the background, definitively framing the issue of terrorism, it is understandable that Americans would fear another devastating surprise attack. It is impossible to ignore the fact that before 9/11 few analysts or policymakers thought that terrorism by small conspiracies truly threatened American national security. The jihadist danger has undoubtedly been exaggerated in some quarters, but there is a sober reality behind the exaggerations, and it continues to be at the top of national and international security agendas in a way that right-wing threats are not.

The association between Islam and terrorism is also a sensitive subject to broach. The proposition that religious beliefs might be a cause of violence is often assumed rather than demonstrated, and we discuss the difficulty of establishing the causes of terrorism in the second part of this introduction. Many Muslims quite reasonably object to the idea that all Muslims should somehow be held responsible for the actions of a tiny minority who claim to be acting in their name but who are not in the least representative. Few people want to hear that their core beliefs are associated with violence, especially if those beliefs are distorted in the process of making a false equation. Yet researchers and policymakers have to deal with the fact that jihadists explicitly justify terrorism in terms of their interpretation of Islam. These adversaries are associated with or claim to act in the name of groups such as al Qa'ida or the "Islamic State." There are risks to making the connection, such as unfairly stigmatizing an entire community, but there are also risks to silence, such as neglecting the power of ideological motivations for violence.

How did the threat of terrorism move from irrelevance to American national security before September 11, 2001, to the top of the agenda for the next decade and more? How did it come to pose such an intractable policy problem? The development of the jihadist threat is characterized by a pattern of growth and decline. Each seeming downturn or setback has been reversed when new opportunities for expansion emerged. The threat has proved extraordinarily persistent, mutable, and virulent. It does not take the form of a monolithic movement, although many core ideological principles are shared. Its polycentric organizational structure may actually be a major source of its strength and adaptability, and its kaleidoscopic quality and tenacity impede coherent counterterrorist strategy.

The violent jihadist trend emerged in the context of resistance to the Soviet occupation of Afghanistan in the 1980s. This history is scarcely news, but the repercussions of that early time period are still very evident. The idea then, as now, was that jihad, interpreted as violent opposition to foreign occupation of Muslim lands, was an individual obligation for all Muslims, wherever they might live. All are considered to be obliged to defend the Muslim community from external aggression. One inspiration was Abdullah Azzam, a Palestinian cleric who became a mentor to Osama bin Laden in Pakistan. Bin Laden's narrative is well known, but the crux of the story is that he arrived in Pakistan as a wealthy and pious Saudi to aid Afghan refugees. An Egyptian physician, Ayman al-Zawahiri, also traveled to Pakistan on a humanitarian mission, although what was more relevant was his experience in organizing armed underground conspiracies to overthrow the Egyptian regime. As a result he had spent three hard years in Egyptian prisons. When Azzam was assassinated, Zawahiri apparently replaced him as the dominant influence on bin Laden. The early al Qa'ida organization was established to keep track of the volunteers in the assistance program.

In retrospect it is ironic that at the time all were legitimate figures in the eyes of the West and certainly in the countries they came from. Both Azzam and Zawahiri traveled to the United States to raise money for the cause. "Foreign fighters" from countries such as Saudi Arabia, Algeria, or Egypt volunteered to aid the mujahideen. The Reagan administration generously supported the anti-Soviet resistance, including supplying the Stinger missiles that were lethally effective in defeating the Soviet Union. Pakistan, restored to American good graces after being isolated as a result of its nuclear ambitions, was the conduit for both military and humanitarian aid to the mujahideen.

The Soviet withdrawal in 1989 was a victory for both the United States and the Afghan resistance. But American attention turned elsewhere, and Afghanistan slowly collapsed into civil war. Bin Laden returned to Saudi Arabia determined to change the Saudi regime—not necessarily to overthrow the monarchy but to induce the country to reject Western influence. After Iraq invaded Kuwait in 1990, bin Laden supposedly volunteered to defend Saudi Arabia and was bitterly offended when his offer was dismissed and American troops were invited instead. By 1991 bin Laden had become such an irritant that he was expelled from the country.

He relocated to the Sudan, an extremist sanctuary designated by the U.S. State Department as a state sponsor of terrorism in 1993. There bin Laden at first seemed content with managing his business enterprises, including local construction projects that ensured his welcome. Simultaneously, however, his wealth and his far-flung organizational contacts in al Qa'ida allowed him to support violent opposition in Muslim territories around the world, in Somalia, the Balkans, Chechnya, and the new former Soviet republics in Central Asia—struggles that were not necessarily anti-American, although bin Laden later claimed to have helped drive the United States from Somalia.

This activism led Saudi Arabia to revoke his citizenship in 1994. In 1996 the Sudanese government was induced to expel bin Laden. It is not clear where bin Laden was expected to go, but the most obvious destination was Afghanistan, a transfer he accomplished just as the Taliban was poised to come out on top in the civil war.

In 1997, from Afghanistan, bin Laden issued a call for jihad against the United States. In 1998 a public declaration of a "Holy War against the Jews and Crusaders" signaled his alliance with Zawahiri's Islamic Jihad group and the beginning of the terrorist campaign that resulted three years later in the devastating 9/11 attacks. The amalgamated al Qa'ida turned its attention from the "near enemy"—local regimes that stood in the way of the Islamist revolution sought by jihadists—to the "far enemy," the United States and its allies. Without the support of "far enemies," "near enemies" presumably could not resist the jihadist challenge. The assumption that outside powers blocked change at home was neither new nor unique; in the 1960s and 1970s revolutionaries in third world countries saw the United States as the main obstacle to socialist revolution, and extremist Palestinian factions saw it as the mainstay of Israel.

The August 1998 bombings of the American embassies in Kenya and Tanzania opened the beginning phase of jihadist terrorism against the West. For the next three years neither American nor UN pressure, including sanctions, could compel the Taliban to turn bin Laden over for prosecution. Nor would Pakistan sever its connections with the Taliban. From his sanctuary in Afghanistan bin Laden continued to plot attacks against American interests. In October 2000 a second try succeeded in ramming an explosives-laden boat into the U.S. Navy destroyer *Cole* in the port of Yemen. Over the summer of 2001 warnings of impending terrorist attacks became more urgent, and several plots were disrupted, but the 9/11 destruction of the World Trade Center and part of the Pentagon came as a terrible and stunning surprise.

The ensuing defeat of the Taliban and occupation of Afghanistan by American military forces should have ended the threat from al Qa'ida. But the leadership slipped across the border into Pakistan, where bin Laden hid until 2010 and Zawahiri hid until at least 2016. Control from the top weakened, but the movement diffused transnationally. Powerful local and regional affiliates and associates proliferated, especially in Iraq after the 2003 invasion by the U.S.-led coalition. There was no repetition of terrorism on the scale of 9/11, which was an extremely rare event. However, attacks and threats were steady and persistent, including deadly bombings of trains, subways, and buses in Madrid and London, nightclubs in Bali, weddings in Jordan, United Nations headquarters in Iraq and Algeria, tourists in Tunisia and Morocco, and journalists in Paris and Copenhagen. In 2006 the discovery of potentially deadly plots against transatlantic airliners bound for the United States showed that al Qa'ida had not lost interest in mass-casualty attacks against civil aviation.

One reason for the post-2001 resurgence was that the "global war on terrorism" in all its aspects—secret prisons, extraordinary renditions, imprisonment of "unlawful combatants" at Guantanamo Bay, the Abu Ghraib scandal, the use of torture, as well as the preemptive use of military force, developing into a reliance on drones to remove the leadership of enemies even outside of war zones—was easily interpreted by jihadists as a war on Islam rather than a war on terrorism. The invasion of Iraq in 2003 provided a powerful boost for jihadists—an unintended consequence, to be sure, but not surprising. Now Western military forces occupied a second majority-Muslim country, this time in the heart of the Arab Middle East. Iraq bore no responsibility for the 9/11 attacks. The stated purpose of the invasion, removing "weapons of mass destruction" and later installing democracy, was unpersuasive to the local and transnational constituencies attracted to jihadist causes, especially as the weapons program turned out to be nonexistent. The fact that democracy enabled the Iraqi Shia majority to prevail over the formerly powerful Sunni minority only reinforced sectarian tendencies, which were exploited by al Qa'ida's Iraqi branch, which formed in 2004.

The core leadership of al Qa'ida was stateless, but the organization's affiliates held local power bases from which they challenged their home governments and sometimes the West. These groups represented the diversity and geographical dispersion of the jihadist movement. The rise of Lashkar-e-Taiba in Pakistan reflected growing militancy within Pakistan as the Taliban remained active and the Afghan conflict spilled over the border. Groups originally formed to fight India in Kashmir became more committed to global jihad. Pakistani militant groups such as the "Pakistani Taliban," known by its acronym TTP (Tehrik-e-Taliban), also allied with the Afghan Taliban, or al Qa'ida, or both. In addition, Jemaah Islamiyah in Indonesia, the Abu Sayyaf Group in the Philippines, al-Shabaab in Somalia, and al Qa'ida in the Islamic Maghreb in Algeria anchored a loosely affiliated anti-Western jihadist alliance in Asia and Africa.

In 2004 and 2005 Western perceptions of the terrorist threat began to shift, largely as a result of the bombings of mass transit infrastructure in Madrid and London, which led to recognition that "homegrown" terrorism and "self-radicalization" of young Muslims living in the West, as opposed to terrorists who attacked from outside, posed a new danger. The Madrid train bombers represented a mix of foreign and domestic backgrounds, which was alarming enough, but the four young perpetrators of the 2005 London bus and subway bombings were British citizens of immigrant backgrounds who to all appearances led ordinary lives. In 2007 the New York Police Department's report on "the homegrown threat" from "unremarkable" citizens or residents signaled American awareness of a changing threat landscape.[4]

In Iraq after 2003 American and allied military forces faced a Sunni insurgency composed of a number of different groups among which the precursor of the post-2014 ISIS, al Qa'ida in Iraq (AQI), founded in 2004 by Abu Musab al-Zarqawi, was the most ruthless. Its hallmark was suicide bombings of both American and Shia targets; among its most consequential actions were the bombing of UN headquarters in Baghdad in 2003 and of the Golden Mosque in Samara in 2006, the latter leading to a full-fledged sectarian civil war. It distributed videos of the beheadings of hostages, including the American contractor Nicholas Berg, in 2004. However, its chief mandate was driving coalition forces out of Iraq and establishing an Islamic state, not internationalizing the jihadist mission. In 2006 after Zarqawi's death in an American air strike, al Qa'ida in Iraq changed its name to the Islamic State of Iraq (ISI). Moreover, the combination, in Iraq, of the American military surge in 2007 and a shift of allegiance by some Sunni tribes (the Arab Awakening) led to the marginalization of ISI, whose brutality alienated potential supporters, just as al Qa'ida central leaders feared. This split between the two centers widened in successive years, until the final break over jihadist representation in the Syrian civil war.

Over time the al Qa'ida affiliate that came to be seen as the gravest danger to the United States was not the Iraqi branch but al Qa'ida in the Arabian Peninsula, or AQAP. In 2009 AQAP was launched in Yemen when a local jihadist group incorporated a Saudi contingent that had failed to gain traction at home. AQAP was distinctive in directing its attention to targets abroad as well as in Yemen. AQAP organized several clever and potentially lethal plots, the most notable of which was its inaugural effort, the attempt to bomb an airliner in Christmas 2009. The convicted bomber, twenty-three-year-old Umar Farouk Abdulmutallab, was a Nigerian who had concealed plastic explosives in his underwear but had failed to detonate them properly. Although unsuccessful, the fact that al Qa'ida had orchestrated an attack on a U.S. aircraft with 290 people on board was extremely unsettling—especially since it seemed to be such a close call. Had the young Nigerian's effort succeeded it would have been the first al Qa'ida–directed attack on American soil since 2001. In 2010 AQAP tried to ship explosives-filled packages to the United States and also launched an English-language magazine, *Inspire,* as a tool to recruit Americans to strike at home. Both plots demonstrate that understanding the intent behind terrorism requires analysis of incomplete attempts as well as completed attacks. That AQAP was led by the influential American cleric Anwar al-Awlaki was further evidence of its danger to the United States, and his boldness led to his death in a drone strike in Yemen in 2011. But his ability to reach out to English-speaking audiences and to inspire acts of terrorism at home lived on after his death in the many videos featuring him that are available online.[5]

With Anwar al-Awlaki's demise American counterterrorism officials undoubtedly breathed a sigh of relief. Withdrawal of coalition troops from Iraq in December of the same year reinforced the optimistic expectation that jihadist terrorism would subside as the war in Iraq and foreign military intervention ended. Unfortunately, also in 2011, another opportunity for jihadist revival presented itself in the outbreak of the Syrian civil war. The Islamic State of Iraq was eager to join the fight to overthrow the Assad regime but found its services rejected by al Qa'ida in favor of another affiliate, the al-Nusra Front. ISI, however, strengthened sufficiently to sweep back into Iraq, quickly occupying first Sunni areas northwest of Baghdad and then the northern part of the country, including Iraq's second largest city, Mosul. Sunni discontent with the government of Nouri al-Maliki predictably played a part in this success, but the rapidity of the accomplishment was still astonishing. When it moved into Syria, ISI had already grandiosely renamed itself the Islamic State of Iraq and Syria or the Levant (ISIS/ISIL). In June 2014, in Mosul, the organization declared itself to be the Islamic State and the successor caliphate of the caliphate that had been dismantled after the fall of the Ottoman Empire. The Islamic State leader, Abu Bakr al-Baghdadi, became the caliph, and all Muslims worldwide were called on to swear allegiance to him and, in fact, to relocate to the new caliphate. Its establishment increased the ideological appeal and the recruiting power of ISIS. The popularity of ISIS reached new heights—and its break with al Qa'ida was final. Local and regional jihadist affiliates seemed to be switching loyalties in the power struggle between the two centers of jihadism.

Iraqi security forces proved distressingly incapable of the defense of the country, and when ISIS adopted the tactic of beheading Western hostages and distributing horrifying videos of the killings, the United States was compelled to send a limited number of American special forces troops back to Iraq. The administration also reversed an earlier decision not to arm the Syrian rebel groups who could be considered moderate. Air strikes against ISIS mounted steadily after August 2014, and the United States found itself in the awkward position of being on the same side as Iran and Russia in trying to combat

Sunni jihadists, although on opposite sides with regard to the Assad regime.

In the meantime the security situation in Afghanistan deteriorated steadily as the deadline for American withdrawal approached, and Pakistan seemed no more capable than ever of defeating or containing its own militants. The 2008 attacks on civilian targets in Mumbai, led by Lashkar-e-Taiba with the assistance of elements of Pakistani intelligence, showed both the limits of Pakistani government control and the speed with which cross-border terrorism could provoke an international crisis. A Pakistani Taliban attack on schoolchildren in Peshawar demonstrated the Pakistani Taliban's power as well as its ruthlessness. Pakistan promised a mobilization against extremism, but the results were meager. Instability in Afghanistan and in the region led the U.S. government to announce a delay in the withdrawal of forces from Afghanistan.

By 2015 jihadist terrorism seemed a more serious threat to Western countries than ever, as the year opened with a devastating attack on a Paris satirical newspaper perpetrated by French citizens of immigrant origin, responsibility for which was claimed by AQAP. At the close of the year, the threat of domestic terrorism inspired or directed by ISIS reached new heights with new attacks in Paris and San Bernardino, California. On the evening of November 13, 2015, a team of terrorists coordinated attacks in Paris and a northern suburb, including suicide bomb attacks on a large stadium, followed by suicide bombings and mass shootings at cafés, restaurants, and a concert hall. The attackers killed 130 people and wounded 368 more, many of them seriously. Seven of the attackers also died. ISIS claimed responsibility for the attacks. The authorities discovered that all the known attackers were EU citizens, and at least one of them was a member of the ISIS organization in Syria who traveled back and forth.

A little over two weeks later, fourteen people were killed and twenty-two seriously injured in a mass shooting in San Bernardino, California. The perpetrators, Syed Rizwan Farook and Tashfeen Malik, a married couple living in the city of Redlands with their six-month-old daughter, targeted a San Bernardino County Department of Public Health training event and holiday party. Farook was an American-born U.S. citizen of Pakistani descent who worked at the health department. Malik was a Pakistani-born lawful permanent resident.

Both were killed in a shootout with police. There was no indication of direct contact with ISIS, although pledges of allegiance to ISIS were discovered in a last-minute Facebook post by Malik.

In March 2016, suicide bombings at the Brussels airport and at a metro stop near European Union headquarters killed thirty-five people, including three of the attackers. ISIS again claimed responsibility, and police investigations in Belgium and France revealed strong connections between those who had plotted both the Brussels and Paris bombings. Both assaults appear to have been directed by ISIS through a complicated underground network that included French and Belgian citizens. Early assumptions that ISIS was focused on building a caliphate and not attacking the "far enemy" were being proved wrong.

Terrorism inspired but not directed by ISIS reached a new level in the United States in June 2016, when an attack in Orlando by Omar Mateen left forty-nine dead and became the deadliest mass shooting in American history. Coming in the middle of the presidential campaign season, it intensified an already rancorous political debate over the dangers of homegrown violent extremism and the links between terrorism and immigration as well as religion. France experienced similar shock and horror on July 14 when a Tunisian immigrant with no apparent ties to any organization drove a heavy truck into crowds watching Bastille Day fireworks in Nice. The result was eighty-four deaths. The fears of Western governments that some of a growing number of foreign fighters—young Western citizens drawn to anti-Assad jihad in Syria or to the defense of the territory defined by ISIS as its caliphate—would return to commit acts of terrorism at home at the direction of a foreign-based jihadist group seemed justified by the Paris and Brussels attacks. The call to jihad, welcomed in the 1980s, when jihad meant attacking the Soviets in Afghanistan, had become a domestic threat. Added to this concern was the fear that terrorists would conceal themselves among the ranks of refugees, as Europe was overwhelmed to the point of crisis by refugees fleeing the conflicts in Syria, Afghanistan, and elsewhere.

In conflict zones, terrorism showed no signs of ending. The Taliban appeared to be on the ascendant again in Afghanistan. ISIS also established a presence in Afghanistan, claiming responsibility for deadly terrorist attacks such as the suicide bombing of a protest demonstration in Kabul in July 2016 that killed scores of people. The Pakistani Taliban or its factions continued to attack civilian targets with impunity.

In the Middle East, Russia entered the war in Syria on the side of the Assad regime, and the United States engaged further by sending more special forces advisers into Syria, in addition to those assisting the Kurds and Iraqi government forces in Iraq. Although ISIS suffered losses in fighting on the ground, its terrorist potential in the region was undiminished. In July 2016, during Ramadan, ISIS claimed credit for the truck bombing of a market that killed over three hundred people, the deadliest terrorist attack in Baghdad since 2003 but only one of dozens of lethal assaults on Iraqi civilians since the declaration of the ISIS caliphate.[6] Civil war raged in Yemen, pitting Saudi Arabia against Iran, and ISIS gained strongholds in Libya. Tunisia, the only democratic survivor of the Arab spring, suffered two major incidents of ISIS-related terrorism against tourists. Turkey experienced ISIS terrorism in the summer of 2016 as well, including a bombing at the Istanbul airport that killed over forty people. Against the drumbeat of an ongoing set of violent attacks around the world first orchestrated by al Qa'ida and later by ISIS, along with their affiliates, punctuated by a series of domestic plots and attacks by their individual followers in the United States and allied countries, the pressure on American policymakers to fashion effective counterterrorism policies only intensified in the fifteen years after 9/11. Yet the challenges of providing reliable, objective recommendations based on empirical scientific evidence remained daunting. We review the state of policy-relevant research on terrorism and counterterrorism in the remainder of this chapter.

Challenges in Studying Terrorism and Counterterrorism

Research on terrorism and counterterrorism has made considerable progress since the early 1970s, and not only in terms of number of studies undertaken. Despite barriers to the development of basic research that could support sound policy, terrorism and counterterrorism are the subjects of a lively ongoing debate engaged in from many different disciplinary perspectives, including political science, international relations, history, criminology, economics, anthropology, sociology, and psychology. Here we outline some of the issues in this debate and identify problems that continue to impede research—conceptual and theoretical on the one hand, and empirical and data-based on the other. Since the purpose of this book is to explain why counterterrorism is so difficult to analyze and combat, in the chapters that follow we take up many of the specific obstacles to constructive analysis, but we emphasize some central dilemmas here.

Conceptual Problems in Studying Terrorism

We identify three areas that have proved troublesome for the academic analysis of terrorism: crafting a definition, specifying causes, and evaluating outcomes. The first problem is the absence of a universally accepted and rigorous definition of terrorism that distinguishes it from other forms of political violence. The meaning of the term remains contested and controversial. Rather than using objective criteria, some popular or politicized accounts not only employ a subjective interpretation of the term "terrorism" but also use the more generic appellation "violent extremism." The Obama administration substituted "violent extremism" for "terrorism" in an effort to distance its counterterrorist policies from the Bush administration's war on terrorism and perhaps also to avoid the pejorative connotation of the term "terrorism," but the administration has been criticized in some quarters for singling out Muslims and in others for refusing to refer to Islam in discussing jihadist terrorism.

Clearly, the moral relativism of the commonplace saying that "one person's terrorist is another person's freedom fighter" further complicates analysis. Rather than rehearsing all the arguments in this debate, we propose that this banal truism confuses ends and means. Our definition of terrorism is "a method or strategy of violence, not tied to any particular political actor or type of actor."[7] That is, terrorism can serve different political ambitions; it is not tied to one ideology or group. The end does not necessarily dictate or justify the means. The definition we develop further and use for many of our data illustrations throughout the book emphasizes politically motivated violence or the threat of violence by nonstate actors, although states can also be involved.

It is still useful to think of terrorism in terms of the meaning given to it by nineteenth-century anarchists: "propaganda of the deed." The act of violence in itself communicates a political message to a watching audience. Because terrorism aims to shock and surprise—and because the number of followers its cause can muster is usually small—it typically targets victims who are unprepared and undefended. It is more symbolic than materially consequential. Thus civilians are chosen deliberately; they are not "collateral damage" incurred when the real target is the adversary's military potential. The method of attack is also selected in order to be painfully outrageous and disturbing, such as the videoed beheadings by al Qa'ida in Iraq and ISIS in Iraq and Syria and its Libyan imitators. In addition, the term "terrorism" usually implies a systematic campaign of violence, not an isolated act.

The issue is complicated further by the relationship between terrorism and insurgency. Lines quickly become blurred. In the Afghanistan war the United States developed the idea of a distinction between counterterrorism (CT) and counterinsurgency (COIN). CT aimed at destroying and defeating the militant organization, for example, via drone strikes against leaders and key operatives. COIN aimed at winning over a population tempted to support insurgents, who presumably both seek and require popular support and material resources that terrorists do not. The assumption is that insurgents must mobilize a population against the government in power, whereas terrorists do not necessarily need popular support in order to challenge the government. In reality the same organization can engage in both terrorism, whether domestic or transnational, and insurgency—the Taliban, ISIS, and AQAP are cases in point. These groups aspire to govern; although they use terrorism they are not stateless transnational organizations or ideological phantoms. They are entities capable of holding territory and imposing their own form of order. They operate openly in the areas they control, so they have a dual identity as an underground conspiracy and an aboveground government. A bifurcated policy does not take this duality into account, although one aim of counterterrorism policy is to deny safe haven to terrorists. In addition, a two-track policy of CT and COIN neglects the fact that actions taken to defeat terrorism (such as drone strikes) can encourage popular mobilization and buttress an insurgency because civilian casualties are inevitable, however unintentional.

There is a similar lack of agreement on an overarching causal theory of terrorism. Even if there were a standard definition of terrorism, the answers to why are not obvious, and without a diagnosis it is hard for government to find a good remedy. The response many terrorists or militants or violent extremists would give is "We had no other choice," implying that terrorism is the weapon of the weak, of those who lack power and thus other means of expressing their opinions or influencing the outcome of the political process. But absence of alternatives is by no means a sufficient explanation for some people to become terrorists, even if it is sometimes the case. For example, committed jihadists claim to require violence to fulfill a religious duty—an imperative even if other means to this end are available. Furthermore, terrorism has emerged in political contexts, such as Nigeria, where citizens in opposition to the government have the vote.

One of the first approaches to causation was to look at macro-level societal conditions or the characteristics of the regimes in which terrorism occurs or against which it is directed.[8] The onset of terrorist campaigns has been linked to poverty, inequality, discrimination, demographics, unemployment, democracy or the lack of democracy, apocalyptic ideologies, fundamentalist religions, the presence of American troops or American economic interests, Western cultural influence, globalization, to name just some conditions that might make terrorism likely. A problem for this line of analysis, however, is that large numbers of people live under or are affected by these conditions, but very few resort to terrorism. As President Obama said in his concluding remarks at the 2015 Conference on Combating Violent Extremism held in Washington, these are conditions that are not necessarily direct causes of violence or determining factors, but they can be exploited by groups intent on fomenting disorder.[9]

Thus underlying conditions considered in the aggregate are not sufficient in themselves to explain terrorism, and it is not even clear that they are necessary. For example, the users of terrorism on the revolutionary left in the 1960s and 1970s were often the children of privilege, and many of those in Western Europe, the United States, and Canada lived in robust democracies with ample opportunity for peaceful expression of opposition. Terrorism was often the spin-off of protest movements as they subsided. Sometimes it was the work of separatists doomed to be a permanent minority in a majority voting system—still the overwhelming majority of separatists rejected violence. Similarly, most jihadists are not the most underprivileged members of their societies.

This puzzle concerning societal causes of terrorism led other scholars to consider the opposite end of the spectrum of causation: the characteristics of individuals who embrace terrorism. The current interest in radicalization processes falls in this category of inquiry. How do individuals come to favor the use of violence in the service of a cause? Can individuals be converted to radical beliefs through exposure to propaganda contained in Internet communications? Many different motivations influence an individual's decision to use violence. Motivations can range from frustration and disaffection to a sense of romantic adventurism. It is clear that psychopathology is not viable as a cause, and there is often nothing out of the ordinary in behavior or expressed attitudes that would distinguish potential recruits from their peers who are indifferent to the appeal of terrorism. Relatives, friends, and neighbors often express astonishment that persons who appeared mild-mannered and ordinary turn out to be killers. There is no uniform terrorist profile.

Another approach to understanding the causes of terrorism takes the middle level of analysis, focusing on the group within a society. In general, few of the individuals who engage in terrorism fit into the category of so-called lone wolves although the number of individuals acting alone and inspired by jihadism may be increasing. A point of agreement among scholars is that the group dynamics behind terrorism are important, no matter what the ideology—far right, far left, jihadist, separatist, or any other. Often friends and relatives join together, and even if individuals join separately they become bonded to a group—small or large, structured or informal. The contemporary focus on Internet communications, important as they are to publicizing the cause and putting would-be recruits in touch with organizers and each other, should not distract from the reality that there are still tightly knit conspiracies of individuals who have face-to-face contact with each other, as in the Paris attacks in 2015 and the Brussels bombings in 2016, where two of the suicide bombers were brothers. One consequence of this dynamic is that members can come to identify so strongly with the group that conformity and compliance become paramount values. Peer pressure under conditions of secrecy and danger, added sometimes to the exhilaration and risk of fighting, binds members to each other and to their leaders. Thus the ostensible "cause" of ideological ambition—to establish an Islamic caliphate or independence from foreign occupation, for example—may not be the actual driver of individual behavior. This suggests that a policy response based on the assumption that terrorism is exclusively designed to achieve long-term political objectives rather than short-term emotional satisfaction may backfire. Researchers and policymakers need to understand both aspects of terrorism: the collective reasoning and the cultures of militant organizations.

In either case, whether terrorism is a strategic choice by an organization or a means of maintaining an organization for purposes of social solidarity and collective identity, one of the reasons for choosing it as a method is its apparent effectiveness as a political instrument: it is expected to produce the desired results, thus ensuring group survival. If this is the case, then the best way of dealing with terrorism is to make sure that it does not work. The long-standing U.S. policy of no concessions to terrorist demands is based on this assumption. This is a deceptively simple answer, however.

For one thing, it is extremely difficult to measure terrorism's effectiveness. Terrorism is almost never the sole method used by any political actor to achieve its aims, so it is hard to specify what terrorism has accomplished as opposed to what other political or social activities have contributed to the outcome. Moreover, it is hard to distinguish the effects of terrorism from those of other outside factors such as government blunders or circumstances beyond anyone's control. Consider the use of terrorism by the Front de Libération National (FLN) during the Algerian War of the 1950s and 1960s. Mass attacks on civilians are often thought of as a modern jihadist tactic, but the FLN launched the era of urban terrorism during the famous Battle of Algiers in 1956 to 1957. Certainly France withdrew and Algeria became independent, but to what extent did terrorism produce victory? Even some of those sympathetic to the FLN felt that terrorism was counterproductive—it provoked such a harsh repression from the French that the cause of the revolution was set back for years.[10]

Consider another more recent case: al Qa'ida in Iraq, the precursor of ISIS. The brutal tactics of its leader, Zarqawi, compelled Zawahiri himself to criticize Zarqawi directly. The harsh methods of AQI alienated other Sunnis and contributed to the tribal resistance that became the Arab Awakening, which in turn supported the success of the surge in American troops. As noted earlier, had the Syrian civil war not given ISIS a new lease on life (and had the Maliki government been more willing and able to incorporate its Sunni citizens) it might have faded away.

Further complicating matters, short-term tactical advantage should not be confused with long-term strategic success. That is, in the immediate aftermath of a major attack terrorism will almost certainly garner publicity, name recognition, "branding," and a place on national and international security agendas. It can also be remunerative; kidnappings by jihadist organizations in the Middle East and Africa have earned large ransoms in recent years. But can the success of terrorism go beyond short-term gains to the accomplishment of fundamental political goals?

In some quarters the answer is "yes." For example, some research has found that campaigns of suicide terrorism compel foreign occupying powers that are democratic, and of a different religion from that of the occupied population, to withdraw from conflicts where they have intervened.[11] The reason is supposedly that governments are sensitive to public opinion pressuring them to withdraw. Examples are said to be the Israeli withdrawal from Lebanon and from Gaza. However, it is not clear that terrorism drove these decisions or why suicide terrorism would be more effective as a form of coercion than other forms of terrorism. It seems logical to think that numbers of victims, destructive impact, or identity of targets would matter more. Also, democracies may not be unduly susceptible to coercion.

Other scholars answer "no": terrorism only pushes democracies to be more resistant to terrorist demands.[12] This view is that by itself, terrorism, particularly against mass civilian targets, cannot produce fundamental concessions. Instead, it hardens public attitudes. In fact, suicide terrorism would be more likely than other forms to produce a hardline response, since its use signals unwillingness to compromise. Indeed, the American and French response to ISIS terrorism has been military escalation. The provocative quality of terrorism could also explain its usefulness for spoilers in a peace process.[13] This observation is worth remembering, because if the intent of terrorism is to provoke and antagonize an adversary, then the hardening of the opponent's attitudes is a success.

In conclusion, the issue of effectiveness is more complicated than a simple yes or no answer would indicate.[14] Militant organizations need to survive if they are to profit from the achievement of long-term goals, such as driving out a foreign occupier or establishing a new political order. The group has to win the overall fight and come out on top of a power struggle among likeminded groups who seek the same general goal. Thus, ISIS competed with the al-Nusra Front to be the lead jihadist organization in Syria. Short-term gains are essential to long-term gain. Seen in this light, terrorism can be a form of "outbidding in extremism," because intergroup competition produces an escalation of violence as each actor tries to "outbid" the others for popular support and resources as well as produce the long-term goal. Of course, the assumption that extreme violence rather than moderation attracts the support of constituencies may not reflect reality. As noted with regard to Iraq, militant organizations can overreach to the point of exceeding the bounds of tolerance of their potential supporters.

Data Problems in Studying Terrorism

The premise of this book is that understanding terrorism presents unique challenges for policymakers. We noted the familiar but misleading commonplace "One man's terrorist is another man's freedom fighter." The U.S. State Department lists Hamas as a Foreign Terrorist Organization, but many regard it as a legitimate political party that won major democratically held elections. Although many in China regard the ethnic Uighurs who were detained by the United States at the Guantanamo Bay Detention Camp as terrorists, much of the rest of the world appears to disagree.[15] Indeed, many of the most prominent nonjihadist terrorist groups in the world—including the Shining Path in Peru, the ETA in Spain, the Irish Republican Army (IRA) in Northern Ireland, and the Revolutionary Armed Forces of Colombia (FARC)—have conceived of themselves as freedom fighters and had a loyal constituency who might have denounced terrorism but were, indeed, relying on these groups to advance their political agenda. This fundamental difference in viewpoints explains in large part why international organizations such as the United Nations have not succeeded in adopting a universally accepted definition of terrorism.

As noted, defining terrorism is no less complex for researchers than it is for policymakers, and the definition of terrorism represents a data problem as well as a conceptual problem. In an influential survey of terrorism researchers, Alex Schmid and Albert Jongman found 109 different definitions of terrorism.[16] Indeed, the first chapter of many prominent books on terrorism is devoted to exploring and defending competing definitions. The official definition used by the Global Terrorism Database (GTD), which we rely on for data throughout this book, is "the threatened or actual use of illegal force and violence by non-state actors to attain a political, economic, religious, or social goal through fear, coercion, or intimidation."[17]

We find it useful to use the GTD data to illustrate our arguments, but in fact each part of the definition raises numerous complications when it is applied to real-world phenomena. For example, this definition includes the assumption that terrorism may involve the threatened as opposed to the actual use of violence: individuals who seize an aircraft and say they will blow it up unless their demands are met may threaten violence without actually using it. At the same time, the GTD has never included idle threats such as bomb threats made by phone that turn out to be hoaxes or threats against the life of world leaders that are never acted upon. In addition, the requirement that these events be limited to the actions of nonstate actors to be defined as terrorism means that the GTD excludes the considerable violence and terrorism that is directly carried out by governments or their militaries. Although this exclusion seems justifiable given the practical impossibility of gathering accurate information on the political violence used by states, in practice it is often difficult or impossible to distinguish perpetrators operating entirely as nonstate actors from those intending to support a particular regime or government, from those receiving actual material support from a regime or government. And the requirement that a terrorist act by definition must have a direct political goal means that the GTD excludes ordinary criminal violence that resembles terrorism. In practice it is often difficult to distinguish political from criminal motivation.

The consequence of collecting terrorism data on the basis of varying definitions and operational coding rules is potentially great. For example, the Worldwide Incidents Tracking System (WITS), used between 2004 and 2010 by the U.S. government's National Counterterrorism Center (NCTC), took a very inclusive approach, reporting nearly 70,000 terrorist attacks in the seven years from 2004 to 2010.[18] For the same period, the GTD included less than 24,000 attacks. Much of the difference is explained by attacks that claim no casualties. For example, the GTD does not routinely include the hundreds (perhaps thousands) of primitive rocket attacks launched annually from the Palestinian territories toward Israel if those attacks do not kill, injure, or do property damage.

On the other side of the inclusiveness spectrum, the researchers John Mueller and Mark Stewart argue that most estimates of worldwide terrorist attacks as well as attacks on the United States are a wildly exaggerated exercise in what they call "chasing ghosts."[19] They would greatly reduce the number of attacks that are included in the GTD. In particular, they argue that by definition terrorist attacks are infrequent and sporadic; when attacks become extensive and frequent the activity should no longer be called terrorism but rather war or insurgency. For example, Mueller and Stewart would exclude attacks by ISIS because it "occupies territory, runs social services, and regularly confronts armed soldiers in direct combat" and therefore ISIS should be considered an insurgency rather than a terrorist organization.[20] They make similar arguments for groups like the Liberation Tigers of Tamil Eelam (LTTE) in Sri Lanka and for political violence in Algeria during the 1990s. As we discuss later, a great many attacks included in the GTD are drawn from countries such as Iraq and Afghanistan, where there is an insurgency or outright civil war. Moreover, the GTD includes a large number of cases from ISIS as well as groups like the LTTE and the Armed Islamic Group (GIA) and Islamic Salvation Front (FIS) in Algeria. In fact, our point here is not to offer a definitive resolution to these conceptual differences but rather to highlight the extent to which they complicate counterterrorism policies.

Further, as we will see in greater detail in chapter 3, conceptual issues are also important in terms of defining the success of attacks.

The GTD defines success according to its tangible effects rather than the larger goals of the perpetrators, which are usually unknown. In practice this means that assessing success often depends on understanding the type of attack. For example, in the GTD, an unexploded bomb in a building is considered unsuccessful, whereas a bomb exploding in a building is considered a success even if it does not bring the building down. In order for an assassination to be designated as "successful," the target of the assassination must be killed. "Unsuccessful" armed assaults are those in which the perpetrators attack but do not hit their targets or are apprehended on their way to commit the assault. And aerial hijackings are "successful" if the hijackers assume control of the craft at any point and unsuccessful otherwise.

Adding to the challenge of arriving at a defensible operational definition of terrorism that is a useful "data container" is the considerable difficulty of collecting valid data on terrorism, however defined. In academic research, data on illegal violence have traditionally come from three sources, corresponding to the major social roles connected to criminal events: "official" data collected by legal agents, especially the police; "victimization" data collected from the general population of victims and nonvictims; and "self-report" data collected from offenders.[21] Victimization surveys have been of little use in the study of terrorism. Despite the attention it gets in the global media, terrorism is much rarer than more familiar types of violent crime. This means that even with extremely large sample sizes, few individuals in most countries will have been directly victimized by terrorists. Moreover, because victims of terrorism are often random—they happened to be in the wrong place at the wrong time—they are unlikely to know or even encounter the perpetrators, making it difficult to produce details about offenders. And finally, in many cases, victims of terrorism are killed by their attackers, making it impossible for them to relate their experiences. For all of these reasons, terrorism data that rely on the reports of victims are likely to be of limited use.

Self-reported data, where researchers collect information on terrorist acts from those who committed the acts, have been more fruitful than victim data, but they also face serious limitations. Most active terrorists are, obviously, unwilling to participate in interviews. Even if they are willing to participate, getting access to known terrorists for research purposes raises evident logistical challenges. As Ariel

Merari explained some years ago, "The clandestine nature of terrorist organizations and the ways and means by which intelligence can
be obtained will rarely enable data collection which meets commonly
accepted academic standards."[22] In general, data that rely exclusively
on the accounts of perpetrators, even when available, are often biased and incomplete, although they can yield useful insights.

Although governments in some countries have collected official
data on terrorism (for example, the U.S. National Counterterrorism
Center), data collected by governments are regarded with suspicion
by many, either because they are influenced by political considerations
or because of the fear that they might be so influenced. Moreover, although vast amounts of detailed official data on common crimes are
routinely produced in most countries by the various branches of the
criminal justice system, this is rarely the case for terrorism. For example, the majority of offenders suspected of terrorism against the
United States are not legally processed for terrorism-specific charges,
but rather for other related offenses, such as weapons violations and
money laundering.[23] Thus, Dzhokar Tsarnaev, the surviving bomber
in the 2013 Boston Marathon bombing case, was charged not with
terrorism but with thirty individual counts involving the use of weapons
of mass destruction, bombing, possession and use of firearms, mali-
cious destruction of property, and carjacking. This case was relatively
easy to classify as a terrorist attack because the incredible publicity it
received provided an abundance of information, but less well-known
cases around the world are often not easy to classify as terrorism on
the basis of media reports alone. Even within the United States it is
not always possible to get a clear idea of perpetrator intent.

Finally, much primary data collected by officials working for
intelligence agencies are not available to researchers working in an
unclassified environment. Government secrecy is an impediment to academic research. For example, most of the documents seized in the raid
on bin Laden's residence in Abbottabad remain inaccessible to academic researchers. Congress called for their declassification and release, and some selected documents were made available in the spring
of 2015. Similarly, some other primary source documents held by the
government have been declassified, translated, and released to researchers, even if not comprehensively. The Combating Terrorism Center at
West Point and the Conflict Records Research Center at the National

Defense University (which closed in June 2015) are or were sources of documents that the American government captured during the war on terrorism and the invasion of Iraq. Admittedly the government recognizes its tendency to overclassify as secret and is working to reduce the number of documents that are classified, but progress appears to be slow.[24]

Another impediment to primary research, such as interviews with actual or former terrorists, is located within the institutions of academia, in the form of institutional review boards (IRBs). These university bodies are charged with seeing that researchers at their institutions do not endanger or violate the rights of individuals who might be interviewed or surveyed or about whom information might be collected. Prison interviews—where they can be obtained, not an easy task—are particularly problematic. IRB concerns are not without foundation. The Boston College Belfast Project was a case where researchers promised confidentiality to interviewees but could not protect their sources when the courts intervened.[25]

In response to the limitations of data from victims, self-reports or primary accounts, and official data on terrorists and terrorist attacks, for nearly half a century researchers have relied on open-source, unclassified terrorist-event data. Terrorism event databases generally use news reports from electronic and print media to collect detailed information on the characteristics of attacks.[26] This dependence on media coverage obviously has drawbacks: underreporting in some parts of the world, overreporting in others, and possible biases of various sorts.

The Global Terrorism Database is currently the most comprehensive of the event databases used by researchers. The GTD relies entirely on unclassified sources, primarily electronic media articles, to identify and systematically record the details of terrorist attacks. These include individual news outlets such as the Associated Press, Reuters, Agence-France Presse, the BBC, and the *New York Times,* as well as existing media aggregators such as Lexis/Nexis, Factiva, and the Open Source Center. At present, the data collection process begins with a universe of over 1.6 million articles published daily worldwide, in order to identify the relatively small subset of articles that describe terrorist attacks. The GTD team accomplishes this using customized search strings to isolate an initial pool of potentially relevant articles, followed by more sophisticated techniques to further refine the search results. In order to maximize the efficiency of the data collection process, they use natural language processing techniques to automatically identify and remove duplicate source articles by measuring similarities between pairs of documents. In addition, they have developed a machine-learning model using feedback from trained GTD staff that classifies the remaining documents as either likely or not likely to be relevant to terrorism. This model is continually refined using input from the research team regarding the accuracy of the classification results. At present, 10,000 to 15,000 articles are manually reviewed to identify attacks for each month of data collection. Once the attacks have been identified, domain-specific research teams record data on over 120 variables pertaining to the location, perpetrators, targets, weapons, tactics, casualties, and consequences of each attack.

As we discuss in more detail in chapter 3, the GTD excludes planned plots or conspiracies that were thwarted by officials before the perpetrators took kinetic action to carry out the attack. The GTD team refers to this as the "out the door rule": events are only eligible for inclusion in the database if the perpetrators were out the door and on their way to execute the attack. The GTD also excludes planned attacks that were never actually initiated, for example, if the would-be perpetrators abandoned the plot before it was executed or the bomb makers died in an explosion while building the bomb. This latter scenario is fairly rare, but has happened on several occasions, including the 1970 explosion at a townhouse in Greenwich Village in New York City, where a bomb under construction in a basement blew up, killing three members of the Weather Underground.

Conceptual and Data Problems in Studying Counterterrorism

Although we discuss counterterrorism in greater detail in subsequent chapters, we consider here some of the general problems of studying it with standard scientific methods. Counterterrorism is a highly contentious political issue, even more so than terrorism itself. It is thus hard to address without making implicit or explicit value judgments, something scholars typically want to avoid. It became especially controversial and partisan after the launch of the "global war on terrorism" by the Bush administration in 2001. Other difficulties are related to the problems of studying terrorism itself, which we outlined earlier. For example, the lack of a widely accepted explanation for the causes of terrorism makes it difficult to propose solutions.

Another complication for research, as well as for public understanding, is the expansive scope of actual and potential counterterrorist policy. As we consider in more detail in chapter 6, many diverse measures can be considered counterterrorism, from restricting financing, to winning hearts and minds and "countering radicalization" through delegitimizing counternarratives, to "decapitation" of groups by killing leaders by means of drone attacks, to preemptive military force and invasion and occupation. This expansiveness can lead skeptics to ask what government activity is *not* counterterrorism in a post-9/11 world. In addition, counterterrorism has a place on both domestic and foreign policy agendas, which is appropriate considering the nature of the threat, and it falls under the jurisdiction of multiple agencies at all levels of the American government. It is a problem for international cooperation and foreign assistance programs as well as for local policing and transportation security. Join to this complexity the political temptation to add the label "counterterrorist" to almost any regulatory or legislative proposal, and the result is a mishmash of policies and institutions. In chapter 2 we analyze some of the notable changes made to the organization of the U.S. government for the conduct of counterterrorism in the immediate aftermath of the 9/11 attacks.

Scholars also disagree about the nature of the strategic interaction between governments and terrorist challengers. A concern is whether scholars are asking the right questions, such as whether a "substitution effect" operates. That is, if governments harden their defenses against particular forms of terrorist attack, will terrorists adapt and shift to softer, unprotected substitute targets, or will they keep trying against the same hard targets even if they repeatedly fail? How well do terrorists learn from their mistakes and their successes? Evidence can be found for both propositions, and the debate remains inconclusive.

Similarly, what are the effects of the use of military force against terrorists? On balance, is the utility of drone strikes in dismantling organizations (removing leaders, impeding communication, or discouraging recruits) greater than their disadvantage in alienating publics? This dilemma is related to the distinction between terrorism and insurgency mentioned earlier in this chapter. As we shall see, academic analysis can be found to support either side in this debate. A related issue is whether terrorism can be deterred, either by denial or by the threat of retaliatory force. Instances of retaliation are actually rare, but scholars still struggle to understand the effect of military force on the calculus of extremist organizations. We refer in chapter 6 to some of the problems of empirical research in this area, due as much to data issues as to theoretical gaps.

Other unresolved questions have more relevance to conciliatory policies. When is it helpful to negotiate with terrorists? Will public opinion in democracies accept such initiatives? If scholars are right that terrorism only hardens public attitudes, rather than inducing concessions, how is compromise possible? Under what conditions should governments give in to ransom demands in hostage-taking situations? Do concessions always encourage more terrorism?

For all these reasons, scholarly studies of the effectiveness of counterterrorism policies so far have been limited in providing specific guidance for policymakers. Researchers lack a standard of what constitutes success and failure in counterterrorism as well as objective measures of progress toward goals. The search for convincing metrics of effectiveness has not yet yielded usable results. In addition, it is clear that the effects of all counterterrorism measures are highly context-dependent, making it difficult to generalize or to predict outcomes in specific cases. It is hard for scholars to be definitive. All alternatives seem to have serious risks and downsides; unintended consequences may be the rule rather than the exception.

Thus many accounts of counterterrorism policy offer either descriptive surveys or polemical treatises. Most commonly, these studies provide either a narrative history of policy (informative if objective and unbiased) or a condemnation or defense of policy, especially post-9/11 policy. Some researchers may be too driven by the policy agenda, while others may resist studying counterterrorism precisely because it is such a hot topic. There are periods of excessive attention to one aspect of policy in the news or controversies such as the components of the global war on terrorism or counterradicalization or effects on civil liberties rather than an effort to identify and evaluate options for a comprehensive and balanced policy. It is tempting to focus on highly salient and contentious issues such as intelligence failures. There are serious studies of intelligence failures especially with regard to the 9/11 surprise attack, but they offer little advice as to how such mistakes (if they were avoidable mistakes) could be corrected in the future.[27] Being critical of government is of course part of what many scholars regard as an obligation if one is to be independent.

Academic studies are beginning to move beyond critiques of specific policies and institutions to consider counterterrorism in terms of broader theoretical and comparative frameworks.[28] There is an interesting parallel: bureaucracies dealing directly with terrorism, such as what is now the State Department's Bureau of Counterterrorism, were rarely part of the policymaking process when it came to high-profile threats before 9/11. Terrorism was considered something of a sui generis phenomenon. And this compartmentalization was also the tendency in academia.

In many ways obtaining accurate data on counterterrorism measures is even more difficult than collecting valid data on terrorism. Whereas the organizations that employ terrorism are often actively looking for open-source media attention, and indeed obsessively and adroitly disseminate information about themselves through multiple media channels, governments are rarely so forthcoming. Governments are especially secretive about their covert operations with regard to terrorism, and their reactions are often classified and unavailable to the public. Following the 9/11 attacks, levels of secrecy on the part of the U.S. government have been especially high. For example, even though President Obama promised more transparency about the drone program, it remains highly secret. The public knows little about the criteria for target selection. Even documents taken directly from open sources by government agencies such as the FBI are frequently classified "For Official Use Only," making them off limits for academic research intended for public dissemination. Given this reality, it is hardly surprising that no worldwide data on government responses to terrorism currently exist.

Conclusion: Policy Challenges of Countering Terrorism

In this introductory chapter we have provided historical context for the evolution of the terrorist threat that has dominated the American security agenda since the attacks of 9/11. We also outlined conceptual and empirical obstacles to policy-relevant academic research into terrorism and counterterrorism. In the remainder of this book we dissect the unique characteristics of terrorism and counterterrorism to explain why there are no simple solutions in this policy arena. We begin this explication in the next chapter by considering one of the defining features of mass-casualty terrorist attacks—their rarity.

CHAPTER 2

Overresponding to Rare Events

The Problem of Uncommon Threats
with Irreversible Consequences

In this chapter we demonstrate how rare extremely destructive terrorist attacks like the coordinated assault on the United States on September 11, 2001, really are. We then examine both the research and policy implications of responding to uncommon yet horrendous events. In fact, a large part of the destructive potential of terrorism revolves around the human and material costs that can be imposed on a society by a relatively small number of shocks. The essayist Nassim Nicholas Taleb refers to the 9/11 attack as a "black swan" event—a term that he coined for an event that falls outside the realm of regular expectations, has an enormous impact, and yet, with the benefit of hindsight, is treated as if it were predictable.[1] The source of the expression is the observation that before they visited Australia, Europeans assumed that all swans were white, an assumption that at the time was supported (for Europeans at least) by their own experience. In addition to 9/11, Taleb regards the dissolution of the Soviet Union, the start of World War I, the rise of the Internet, and the development of the personal computer as black swan events.

An important implication of black swan events is that however unpredictable and rare, they encourage outsized responses that literally change the course of human history. This is an especially important concern in the case of terrorism, where producing overreaction by governments is often a major goal of those using terrorist tactics. The pervasive fear that 9/11 was only the opening salvo in a series of impending attacks encouraged a hasty response—the mistaken but understandable belief that it was not the rare event that it turned out to be but the beginning of a sustained and devastating campaign of recurring similar events.

Two critical characteristics of the 9/11 attack that shape its singular position in world history are, first, the great loss of human life that resulted and, second, the fact that it was an international attack—carried out against the United States by individuals from other countries who acted in the name of a nonstate organization that had grandiosely declared war on the United States. The iconic significance of the targets—the World Trade Center, the Pentagon, and probably the nation's Capitol—added to the shock. And the attacks came as a near complete surprise.

We begin this chapter by examining how uncommon these features of the 9/11 attacks actually were and still are. We rely on the Global Terrorism Database (GTD) maintained by the National Consortium for the Study of Terrorism and Responses to Terrorism (START) at the University of Maryland (described in the preceding chapter). We show that terrorism is rare, terrorist attacks with mass casualties are exceedingly rare, and catastrophic attacks on U.S. territory are rarer still.

We then consider the research and policy implications of these rare events. Researchers refer to events whose distributions are highly skewed—where the vast majority of events in a distribution have very low values such as 0 or 1 and very few have high values—as long-tail distributions. We explain long-tail distributions and consider some of the methods researchers have developed for examining them. We then consider in more detail the policy implications of these long-tail distributions.

Overall in most parts of the world terrorism is a relatively rare phenomenon. For example, in 2012, the Global Terrorism Database reported 15,417 worldwide fatalities from terrorism; meanwhile, the United Nations reported a total of 437,000 homicides worldwide for the same year. So around forty times as many people died as a result of homicide as from terrorism.[2] Similarly for the United States, whereas the GTD recorded a total of 18 terrorist attacks in the United

States in 2010, the Federal Bureau of Investigation for the same year reported that there were nearly 13,000 homicides and over 360,000 robberies in the United States.[3] One of the major challenges in responding to terrorism is that a handful of unusual cases—or even a single case—have a disproportionate effect on setting the agenda for preventing and responding to what are actually more common phenomena.

The impact on public policy of rare but heinous attacks may be uniquely serious for populist democracies like the United States. As we mentioned in chapter 1, some scholars have been extremely critical of U.S. policy in the wake of 9/11, arguing that the media and partisan politicians have exaggerated threats and hyped the risk of terrorism.[4] We suggest that although the controversy surrounding counterterrorism is not without foundation, one reason for extreme reactions may be the perception that rare events could have been predicted.[5] There is a corresponding tendency to see them not as unusual but as initiators of a recurring series of events. Something that was extremely irregular is seen as a regularity. Thus, prevention of a repetition of the rare event becomes a policy priority, even if it is not likely to happen again and even if, in fact, the threat is likely to change as a result of the government's own actions.

The Infrequency of Mass-Casualty International Terrorism

The GTD provides a useful way of developing a comprehensive overview of how rare an attack on the scale of 9/11 actually was. If we take the thousands of terrorism attacks included in the GTD from 1970 to 2015, how many resulted in fatalities? How many of those attacks with fatalities produced a large number of fatalities? And how many attacks produced a large number of fatalities in the United States?

Counting Fatal Terrorist Attacks

One of the most surprising statistics drawn from the GTD is that many of the recorded terrorist attacks do not result in fatalities. Of the nearly 156,772 attacks in the database through 2015, only 51 percent

(79,411 attacks) resulted in at least one fatality. For more than 49 percent of attacks the media sources we use to record cases did not report any deaths.[6] When we present information from our database to the public it is common for someone in the audience to hear a statistic like this and ask, "But if no one was killed, how can this be terrorism?" Indeed, how can it be the case that so many of the attacks recorded in the GTD involve no deaths? To begin with, many terrorist attacks are not directed at human targets but at property. The GTD includes all incidents that entail some level of violence or immediate threat of violence, including violence intended to damage or destroy property. For example, the environmental and animal rights groups Earth Liberation Front and Animal Liberation Front typically target businesses or animal test laboratories. In other cases attacks against property are intended to include fatalities but fail to do so. For example, the GTD includes cases where perpetrators sabotage railway equipment or rail lines with the apparent intention of causing derailments. In many cases, when buildings or facilities are targeted, whether people are killed or injured is a matter of chance. This was the case in an April 9, 2008, bombing of a woman's hairdressing salon in the Gaza Strip in Palestine. The salon was completely destroyed, no group claimed responsibility, and no casualties were reported. The attack could easily have caused human casualties as well as property damage.

Other attacks are aimed at killing civilians, but they fail. The intention is clear but the attack is unsuccessful. Although the GTD does not include plots or conspiracies (which we will discuss in more detail in chapter 3), it does include attacks in which the perpetrators were on their way to execute an attack but either failed to carry it out or were somehow thwarted in its implementation. Examples of failed attacks that had the potential to be highly lethal include the 2001 unsuccessful attempt of Richard Reid, the so-called "shoe bomber," to detonate explosives hidden in his shoes on American Airlines Flight 63 from Paris to Miami, and Umar Farouk Abdulmutallab's effort in 2009 to ignite explosives concealed in his underwear on board Northwest Airlines Flight 253 from Amsterdam to Detroit.

In other cases, attacks were actually carried out with the apparent intent of killing people but only ended up causing injuries. Again, according to the GTD, nearly 28 percent of all attacks that did not produce deaths did produce injuries. In some cases, the total number of injuries ran into the hundreds. Altogether, we identified 13 attacks in which more than 100 people were wounded although no one was killed. The attacks that injured many but produced no fatalities often relied on biological or chemical weapons. One high-profile example is the 1984 case in which over 700 people became ill when a leading group of followers of the guru Bhagwan Shree Rajneesh intentionally contaminated salad bars in The Dalles, Oregon, with salmonella in a bizarre attempt to incapacitate voters and influence a local election. A more recent example is a 2009 toxic gas assault on a girls' school in Afghanistan that injured nearly 100 students and staff; the perpetrators were suspected to be members of the Taliban.

In other cases groups actually provide warnings to civilians before striking in order to reduce or eliminate fatalities. This was a common practice for both the Basque separatist group, the ETA, in Spain and the Provisional Irish Republican Army (PIRA) in Northern Ireland and Britain as well as the Weather Underground in the United States. For example, in February 2006, a bomb was left in a bag by ETA members outside of a construction company near Bilbao, Spain. An advance warning was given which allowed police to evacuate an individual living on the premises and while the blast caused property damage there were no casualties. Similarly, in a 1985 case an unknown caller phoned an abortion clinic in New York City and informed the receptionist that a bomb was set to go off. The clinic was evacuated and indeed twenty minutes later the bomb exploded. Finally, in 1998 a group called the Revolutionary Nuclei in Greece called in a warning to the local Athens police threatening an attack on the Higher Council for the Evaluation of Civil Servants, a government agency responsible for hiring civil servants in Athens. Shortly afterward the bomb exploded. Two police officers cordoning off the streets around the building were slightly injured, but there were no fatalities.

Thirty years ago these types of warnings and other apparently self-imposed constraints led the terrorism researcher Brian Jenkins to suggest that "terrorists want a lot of people watching, not a lot of people dead."[7] In the years since 2001 doubt has been cast on this assumption, and Brian Jenkins himself qualified his judgment. And it is still the case that about half of the attacks in the GTD (50.6 percent)—produced at least one fatality. But how often do we observe mass casualty attacks?

Worldwide Fatalities

In table 2-1 we list the ten deadliest terrorist attacks in the GTD from 1970 to 2015 and the year, the location, and the perpetrators of each one. We can see that the 9/11 attacks on the Twin Towers are still the deadliest attacks in the GTD. But what is perhaps most striking about the table is that four of the ten deadliest attacks took place in 2014 and all four were claimed by the Islamic State of Iraq and Syria (ISIS). Three of the ISIS attacks took place in Iraq and a fourth, in Syria. Taken together, these four attacks claimed the lives of nearly 3,200 victims. If we add the al Qa'ida 9/11 attacks we can conclude that half of the ten deadliest terrorist attacks in the world since 1970 can be attributed to ISIS and al Qa'ida.

The second deadliest attack in the GTD took place when ISIS assailants abducted nearly 1,700 soldiers from Camp Speicher in Tikrit, Iraq.[8] Media sources concluded that there were at least 1,500 fatalities (the number recorded in the GTD), but also speculated that the number may well have been higher. Indeed, reports indicated that only two people escaped from ISIS. ISIS claimed responsibility for the attack and stated that it was in revenge for the killing of the ISIS leader Abdul-Rahman al-Beilawy. While we list this attack behind the 9/11 attacks on the Twin Towers, in fact the GTD treats the 9/11 attacks as four separate but "coordinated" attacks on each of the World Trade Center towers (thus, 2,763 fatalities split between the two towers), on the Pentagon, and on United Airlines Flight 93 that crashed in Pennsylvania. If we follow this logic, then the recent attack in Tikrit would be the deadliest since 1970.

The other three 2014 ISIS attacks rank as the fourth, sixth, and seventh deadliest in the history of the GTD. On June 10, 2014, a group of assailants stormed Badush prison in Iraq, separated the Shiite and Sunni prisoners, released the Sunni inmates, and killed 670 Shiite prisoners. This was one of six coordinated incidents on the same day and one of three similar attacks targeting jails and prisons in the area. A little less than three months later, on August 3, 2014,

TABLE 2-1. The Ten Deadliest Attacks in the World, 1970–2015

RANK	YEAR	LOCATION	ATTACKERS	FATALITIES
1	2001	New York, United States	al Qa`ida	2,763
2	2014	Saladin, Iraq	Islamic State of Iraq and Syria (ISIS)	1,500
3	1994	Gikoro, Rwanda	Hutus	1,180
4	2014	Nineveh, Iraq	Islamic State of Iraq and Syria (ISIS)	670
5	2004	Bedi, Nepal	Communist Party of Nepal—Maoist (CPN-M)	518
6	2014	Raqqah, Syria	Islamic State of Iraq and Syria (ISIS)	517
7	2014	Nineveh, Iraq	Islamic State of Iraq and Syria (ISIS)	500
8	1978	Abadan, Iran	Mujahedin-e Khalq (MEK)	422
9	1987	Homoine, Mozambique	Mozambique National Resistance Movement (MNR)	388
10	1996	Kivyuka, Burundi	Tutsi	375

Source: Authors' compilation, based on Global Terrorism Database.

assailants attacked Yizidi (an ethnically Kurdish religious community) civilians in Sinjar, Iraq, killing an estimated 500 people. The attackers also kidnapped an estimated 300 women. Reports claimed that at least 27 of the abducted women were sold into marriage. An unknown number of hostages were released and the fate of the remaining victims is unknown. The GTD attributes responsibility to ISIS. Two weeks later, on August 19, 2014, ISIS assailants attacked Tabqa Air Base in Syria. In the confrontation that followed, 346 assailants and 171 soldiers were killed (517 was the official GTD estimate). However, 150 soldiers were also abducted in the attack and their fate is unknown.

The third deadliest attack in table 2-1 took place in Rwanda in 1994 when 1,180 Tutsis were killed by Hutu attackers. The Tutsi-Hutu conflict also produced another extremely deadly attack in Burundi in 1996—this time with the Tutsis attacking the Hutus.[9] The final two extremely deadly attacks occurred in Nepal in 2004 and Mozambique in 1987. The Communist Party of Nepal—Maoist took 518 lives in Nepal in 2004. The Mozambique National Resistance Movement killed 388 in 1987.

As horrible as these events were in terms of the tragic toll on human life, it is also important to put these deadly acts in context. A database that includes nearly 160,000 terrorist attacks from around the world over nearly fifty years contains only 18 attacks that claimed more than 300 lives. And these numbers decline substantially when we consider only those attacks aimed at U.S. territory and U.S. targets abroad.

Attacks against U.S. Targets at Home and Abroad

Given our central focus on counterterrorism policy for the United States, we next consider the frequency of terrorist attacks aimed at U.S. targets in general and specifically on the United States itself. In table 2-2 we list the top ten deadliest terrorist attacks against U.S. targets, both at home and abroad.

As expected, the coordinated attacks on the Twin Towers again top the list. The next most deadly attack on a U.S. target was the airline bombing that took place over Lockerbie, Scotland, in December 1988. A bomb detonated Pan American World Airways Flight 103 flying from London Heathrow Airport to New York's John F. Kennedy International Airport, killing 243 passengers, 16 crew members, and 11 people on the ground. In 2003 Muammar Qaddafi admitted Libya's responsibility for the Lockerbie bombing and paid compensation to the victims' families, although he maintained that he never personally gave the order for the attack and Libya's responsibility is still highly contested.

The next deadliest attack targeting Americans was the Beirut barracks bombing of October 1983 that occurred in a double suicide bombing during the Lebanese civil war, when two truck bombs struck

TABLE 2-2. The Ten Deadliest Attacks against U.S. Targets, 1970–2015

RANK	YEAR	LOCATION	ATTACKERS	FATALITIES
1	2001	New York, United States	al Qa`ida	2,763
2	1988	Lockerbie, U.K.	Unknown	270
3	1983	Beirut, Lebanon	Hezbollah	241
4	1998	Nairobi, Kenya	al Qa`ida	224
5	2001	Arlington, United States	al Qa`ida	189
6	1995	Oklahoma City, United States	Individuals (Timothy McVeigh, Terry Nichols)	168
7	1974	Athens, Greece	PFLP-GC	88
8	1983	Beirut, Lebanon	Hezbollah	63
9	2001	Shanksville, Pennsylvania	al Qa`ida	44
10	2004	Baghdad, Iraq	Jama'at al-Tawhid wal-Jihad	41

Source: Authors' compilation, based on Global Terrorism Database.

separate buildings housing U.S. and French military forces—members of the Multinational Force in Lebanon[10]—killing 241 American and 58 French servicemen. The organization Islamic Jihad (the precursor of Hezbollah) claimed responsibility for the bombings. At the time, this attack represented the deadliest single-day death toll for the U.S. Marine Corps since the Battle of Iwo Jima in World War II, the deadliest single-day death toll for the U.S. military since the first day of the Tet Offensive during the Vietnam War, and the deadliest single attack on Americans overseas since World War II. It was also the single worst military loss for France since the end of the Algerian War. The blasts led to the withdrawal of the international peacekeeping force from Lebanon, which had been stationed there since the withdrawal of the Palestine Liberation Organization following Israel's 1982 invasion of Lebanon.

Next deadliest (fourth on our list) were the August 1998 U.S. embassy bombings in the East African capitals of Dar es Salaam, Tanzania, and Nairobi, Kenya, where simultaneous truck bomb explosions took the lives of 224 people. The date of the bombings marked the eighth anniversary of the arrival of American forces in Saudi Arabia, and the attacks brought Osama bin Laden and Ayman al-Zawahiri to the attention of the American public for the first time. Fazul Abdullah Mohammed would be credited with being the mastermind behind the bombings.

Two of the next deadliest attacks against U.S. targets include the other coordinated attacks from 9/11: on the Pentagon in Arlington, Virginia, and the plane that crashed in Shanksville, Pennsylvania. The Oklahoma City bombing in 1995 was number six. Another of the remaining deadliest attacks against U.S. targets took place in Beirut on April 18, 1983, when a suicide bomber struck the U.S. embassy, killing 63 people, including embassy and CIA staff members, several soldiers, and one Marine. The other two deadly attacks in the top ten include a 1974 attack in Athens by the Popular Front for the Liberation of Palestine and a 2004 attack in Baghdad by the group Jama'at al-Tawhid wal-Jihad (which would eventually morph into the Islamic State in Iraq and Syria).

Finally, on June 12, 2016, Omar Mateen, a 29-year-old security guard, shot and killed 49 people and wounded 53 others in an attack on a gay nightclub in Orlando, Florida.[11] He was killed by Orlando police after a three-hour standoff. Although the GTD data for 2016 were not yet available when this book was being finalized, it now looks like the case will be included. It does not appear that Mateen received in-person assistance or training from any terrorist organization. However, Mateen became a person of interest to the FBI in May 2013 after he made comments to co-workers about being a member of Hezbollah and having family connections in al Qa'ida, and that he had ties to the Fort Hood shooter and the then-suspects of the Boston Marathon bombing.[12] In response, Mateen said that he made these comments in response to "a lot of harassment" and frequent derogatory epithets made by police and co-workers, who taunted and made jokes about him being a possible Muslim extremist.[13] A July 2014 FBI investigation was opened after Mateen was linked to Moner Mohammad Abu Salha,[14] an American radical who committed a suicide bombing in Syria. Mateen was interviewed three times in connection with the two investigations. Both cases were closed after finding nothing that warranted further investigation. In a 9-1-1 call shortly after the Orlando attack began, Mateen swore allegiance to the leader of the Islamic State of Iraq and the Levant (ISIL), Abu Bakr al-Baghdadi. He later told a negotiator he was "out here right now" because of the American-led interventions in Iraq and in Syria, and that the negotiator should tell the United States to stop bombing ISIL.[15] If the case is included in the GTD it will replace the 9/11 attack on the aircraft over Shanksville, Pennsylvania as the ninth deadliest attack on an American target since 1970.

The attack on Orlando is a fresh reminder of the violent destructiveness of terrorism. And again, our point is not to diminish the brutality or destructiveness of these attacks in any way, but to point out that over a period of nearly half a century no terrorist attacks on U.S. targets around the world except for the 9/11 attacks have claimed more than 300 lives. Only eleven attacks took more than 30 lives. We next narrow our focus to examine only terrorist attacks on U.S. territory.

Attacks on U.S. Territory

The number of total fatalities is far lower when we restrict our analysis to attacks that occurred in the United States. In table 2-3 we show the ten deadliest terrorist attacks against U.S. targets on U.S. soil. Again, the 9/11 attacks on the Twin Towers top the list. In fact, three of the four deadliest terrorist attacks on U.S. soil were produced by the coordinated attacks of 9/11. In addition to the Twin Tower attacks (counted here as a single attack), the attack on the Pentagon ranks as second deadliest and the downed plane in Shanksville, Pennsylvania, ranks as the fourth deadliest. However, as we have just seen, the June 2016 shootings in Orlando are likely to replace the plane crash in Shanksville, Pennsylvania, as the fourth deadliest terrorist attack on American soil since 1970. The Oklahoma City bombing is the third deadliest. No other domestic attack against the United States from 1970 to 2015 claimed more than twenty fatalities.

Four of the six remaining deadliest attacks on U.S. soil were perpetrated by individuals. The fifth deadliest attack on the U.S. homeland

TABLE 2-3. The Ten Deadliest Attacks against U.S. Territory, 1970–2015

RANK	YEAR	LOCATION	ATTACKERS	FATALITIES
1	2001	New York City	al Qaʾida	2,763
2	2001	Arlington, Virginia	al Qaʾida	189
3	1995	Oklahoma City, Oklahoma	Individuals (Timothy McVeigh, Terry Nichols)	168
4	2001	Shanksville, Pennsylvania	al Qaʾida	44
5	2015	San Bernardino, California	Individuals (Syed Rizwan Farook, Tashfeen Malik)	16
6	1999	Littleton, Colorado	Individuals (Eric Harris, Dylan Klebold)	15
7	2009	Killeen, Texas	Individual (Nidal Hasan)	13
8	1975	New York City	Croatian Nationalists	11
9	2015	Charleston, South Carolina	Individual (Dylann Roof)	9
10	1973	New Orleans, Louisiana	Individual/Republic of New Afrika (Mark Essex)	8

Source: Authors' compilation, based on Global Terrorism Database.

was the San Bernardino shootings on December 2, 2015, that killed 16 people, including the two attackers, Syed Rizwan Farook and Tashfeen Malik. The April 1999 Columbine High School shooting, which claimed the lives of fifteen people in Littleton, Colorado, ranks as sixth deadliest.[16] Two armed high school students with no major group affiliations shot and killed twelve fellow students and one teacher before committing suicide. The November 2009 shooting at Fort Hood in Killeen, Texas, perpetrated by Major Nidal Malik

Hasan, killed thirteen people in Killeen, Texas, and ranks as seventh deadliest. Hasan opened fire on fellow soldiers with two semiautomatic pistols capable of firing up to twenty rounds without reloading before military police forces shot and apprehended him.

Finally, ninth on our list is the June 17, 2015, church shooting in Charleston, South Carolina, by a white supremacist, Dylann Roof, who killed nine people during a prayer service. The morning after the attack, police arrested Roof, who later confessed that he committed the shooting in hopes of igniting a race war. Roof is to be indicted on federal hate crime charges, and has been charged with nine counts of murder by the State of South Carolina. If convicted, he could face a sentence of death or thirty years to life in prison.

The two remaining deadliest attacks on U.S. soil occurred in New York and New Orleans. The December 1975 bombing of New York's LaGuardia Airport by suspected Croatian nationalists killed eleven people and ranks as the eighth deadliest. The January 1973 shooting at the Downtown Howard Johnson Hotel in New Orleans claimed the lives of eight people and ranks as the tenth deadliest.[17] The shooting began when Mark Essex, a member of the Black Panthers movement, broke into the hotel and killed Robert and Elizabeth Steagall, a white couple staying at the hotel, and set their room on fire. Essex also shot and killed the assistant and general managers of the hotel as well as a deputy police superintendent and two patrolmen of the responding police department before he was shot and killed on the roof of the hotel by sharpshooters in a military helicopter. Essex had links to the Republic of New Afrika, a secessionist movement that sought to create an independent African American–majority country in the southeastern United States.[18]

What is perhaps most striking about table 2-3 is the incredible diversity of the deadliest terrorist attacks on U.S. soil over the past four and one-half decades. Included with the iconic attacks of 9/11 are five attacks by individuals as diverse as a former military enlistee with right-wing extremist views (McVeigh), a husband-wife team from California who were apparently inspired by foreign terrorist groups (Farook and Malik), two deeply troubled Colorado teenagers (Harris and Kleibold), an Army psychologist with vague ties to radical Islam (Hasan), and a white supremacist with no major connections to any specific terrorist oganization (Roof). If we update the list through mid-2016 we add the case of Omar Mateen, who killed forty-nine people in a gay bar that he had frequently visited as a patron. Rounding out the top ten are attacks by Croatian Nationalists and Black Panthers.

French philosopher Michel Foucault leads off his book *The Order of Things* with a quote from Argentine author Jorge Luis Borges who quotes a "certain Chinese encyclopedia" as including a list which divides animals into an improbable assortment of categories including "a) belonging to the Emperor . . . (f) fabulous . . . (h) included in the present classification . . . (and) (l) having just broken the water pitcher . . . ."[19] Foucault's point is that it is impossible to think of these diverse categories as all belonging to the same descriptive list. Indeed in looking at the ten deadliest terrorist attacks on American soil, we might reach a similar conclusion; finding underlying patterns here may be a bit like trying to identify the commonalities among a random group of individuals who happen to be on an elevator in a big city! We will return to this theme of just how diverse terrorist attacks have been throughout the book.

The other striking feature of table 2-3 is that if we remove the coordinated attacks of 9/11, the Oklahoma City bombing, and now the Orlando shooting spree, no terrorist attack on the U.S. homeland in nearly a half century has claimed the lives of more than twenty people. These findings enforce the rarity of mass casualty terrorist attacks, especially on the U.S. homeland. It may also be worth noting that many of the top ten deadliest attacks in the United States are relatively recent. Two of them happened in 2015 and once the GTD is updated through 2016, the revised list will also include the Orlando shooting. Six of the deadliest attacks happened since 2000. Perhaps this explains in part why Americans remain very concerned about the threat of terrorist violence.

Research Implications of Rare Events

The previous sections demonstrate that terrorist attacks are rare, and attacks on the United States and its citizens and interests abroad are rarer still. This fact raises unique analytic challenges for both policymakers and researchers, and it makes prediction nearly impossible. Most basically, while the small numbers of cases for most countries at most points in time are an obvious benefit from a policy standpoint, they also limit the possibilities for generalizations—especially those based on statistical analysis. There are simply too few data. Small sample sizes no doubt explain why much statistical research on terrorism to date has focused on long-lived and exceptionally active groups such as the IRA and ETA. Even an incredibly influential group such as al Qa'ida has so few attacks that statistical analysis is constrained. The GTD includes a total of fifty-nine attacks for al Qa'ida Central, including only eleven attacks since 2008.[20] In general, this is too few cases to be useful for most complex statistical models used by social scientists.

Moreover, statistical analysis of terrorism is limited not only by the fact that sample sizes for most types of terrorism are quite small but also by the highly irregular occurrence of terrorist attacks over time. In general, many characteristics of terrorism fit into a particular type of distribution called a long-tail distribution that has some unusual statistical properties.

Long-Tail Distributions

Most common statistical analyses in the social sciences are based on the assumption that the distribution of underlying events form a "normal curve." This generally resembles a bell-shaped distribution with an average (mean) in the center and symmetrical "wings" gradually diminishing on either end, or tail, of the curve (forming the eponymous "bell" form). Without getting into too much complexity, bell-shaped distributions can be linked directly to the central limit theorem, which gives them certain properties that make them useful and convenient for statistical analysis. For these reasons, the normal curve distribution is widely used for analysis in both the natural and social sciences as a simple way of modeling complex phenomena. For example, height is distributed as a normal distribution with an average mean for men in the United States of 70 inches, one standard deviation above the mean at 73 inches, and one standard deviation below the mean at 67 inches. This means that most men (about 68 percent, assuming a normal distribution) have a height within

3 inches above or below the mean (67 inches to 73 inches)—one standard deviation—and almost all men (about 95 percent) have a height within 6 inches above or below the mean (64 inches to 76 inches)—two standard deviations. In general, the probability of encountering a value that is far from the mean in a normal distribution—more than a few standard deviations away—declines very rapidly. In the height example, three standard deviations account for 99.7 percent of the sample of all adult men in the United States, assuming the distribution is normal.

By contrast, long-tail distributions arise when a particular distribution has only a few extremely high (right-tail distributions) or extremely low (left-tail distributions) outcomes. When we find such distributions, many of the most common statistical methods in the social sciences do not produce robust results. Among such distributions, the *power law distribution* has attracted a good deal of attention in recent years both because it sometimes produces surprising results and also because of the ubiquity with which it appears across a wide range of social and physical distributions.[21]

In statistics, a power law is a functional relationship between two quantities, where one quantity varies as a power of another. For example, consider the area inside a square in terms of the length of one of its sides: if the length is doubled, the area under the square is quadrupled. These kinds of outcomes have some unique characteristics. Imagine a distribution that looks at the total population living in each square mile of the United States arranged from square miles with no inhabitants all the way up to New York City, which has 27,000 inhabitants per square mile. This distribution would show that the vast majority of square miles in the United States have relatively few inhabitants. Indeed, according to the 2010 U.S. census, the average population of the United States per square mile is just over 87. So the distribution of population per square mile in the United States is going to have a very large number of areas with relatively small numbers of people per square mile and then a very long tail to take into account cities like New York and Chicago. It turns out that the urban population of the United States per square mile is a power law distribution. In fact, power law distributions describe a bewildering assortment of other distributions, including size of e-mail address listings at universities, the number of acres burned in California forest fires, and the net worth in U.S. dollars of the richest people in the United States.[22] Computer scientist Aaron Clauset and his colleagues argue that some aspects of global terrorist attacks are also best described as power law distributions.[23]

Implications for Analysis

Thus, developing statistical models of terrorist attacks inherently involves more limitations than is the case with events that occur more routinely and are distributed more normally. Looking at the entire world from 1970 to 2015, the GTD counts 156,772 terrorist attacks. This is no doubt an undercount of the true number of events but likely is a decent representation of the events that were most consequential in terms of political significance. But depending on the specific interests of the investigator, the number of cases relevant for analysis is usually much smaller. As we have seen, just over half of the cases in the GTD resulted in fatalities. A much smaller proportion were mass-casualty attacks. Because different terrorist organizations generally have different motives, histories, and backgrounds, many analytical questions must be addressed at the group level. And here we see that even extremely dangerous groups such as al Qa'ida have conducted relatively few attacks thus far. Moreover, the characteristics of terrorist organizations change a good deal over time, so for some types of analytic questions it may be misleading to include the full time series. The data analyzed here included 2,337 discrete terrorist organizations for the forty-three years included in the database. Thus, depending on the research question asked, the available number of cases on a particular group may severely limit our ability to produce statistically supported generalizations. In other words, it is hard to identify trends and patterns in terrorism.

Beyond the sheer number of cases available for researching specialized policy questions using statistical methods, we find a bewildering array of variation within the cases included. In other words, within the general category of "terrorist acts" there are significant differences. Again, 9/11 provides the clearest example. Including a terrorist attack that involved four coordinated subparts and eventually killed nearly 3,000 people in the same analysis as an attack that claimed no lives may be problematic, even if we can argue that the same definition of terrorism applied to both cases.

Policy Consequences of the 9/11 Black Swan Event

Our discussion shows just how unusual the 9/11 attack actually was in terms of U.S. and even world history and how difficult it is to predict acts of terrorism, especially highly destructive ones. But despite its uniqueness, it is difficult to overstate the 9/11 attack's political impact. A first reaction to such a rare but incredibly painful attack was an attempt to understand why experts and policymakers, and especially the intelligence agencies, did not see it coming. Anguished questions flooded public discourse. Could the attacks have been predicted? If not, why not? What went wrong? Why was the United States so surprised? Who was to blame? A second reaction was an ambitious and costly omnibus effort not only to understand how and why the attacks occurred but, even more, to prevent a repetition. It was based on the frightening assumption that 9/11 was only the opening assault in a long campaign that would feature equally if not more destructive events. This assumption in turn grew out of confusion about the adversary's capabilities and intentions.

Memories have faded, so it is easy to forget the extent to which the immediate aftermath of 9/11 was a time of high anxiety and alarm, and orderly decisionmaking suffered as a consequence. The expansive response included not only President Bush's launching the global war on terrorism with all of its extensions and ramifications but also reorganizing and redirecting the government to better coordinate, conduct, and expand the national counterterrorism mission. The measures taken strengthened executive branch power, an example of which was secret orders to conduct electronic surveillance such as bulk collection of the telephone records of American citizens who had no connections to terrorism. None of these far-reaching initiatives—neither the war on terror, nor bureaucratic reorganization, nor expansion of the state's powers—would or could have been undertaken without the terrible shock of 9/11. It is also hard to imagine the invasion of Iraq in 2003 absent the 9/11 attacks—the momentum propelling the decision began immediately after 9/11. Not only the 9/11 attacks but the counterterrorist measures initiated in response provoked political clashes that were not resolved over the next decade and indeed have still not been resolved. Often political responses were originally modest in scope but grew into vast and complex policy and institutional transformations. In the end, many of the extraordinary measures taken in haste became permanent, even though they were not always the best-adapted responses to an evolving threat.

Failure to Foresee

No one foresaw the rare event of the coordinated attack of 9/11 in part because it was outside the bounds of the expectations policy-makers and experts had developed over some thirty years of experience with terrorism against the United States.[24] Although some policy analysts and a few fiction writers had speculated for years about various sorts of extreme terrorist possibilities, there was no way to say which of the imagined schemes might prove both attractive and feasible for actual terrorists such as al Qa'ida. The range of scenarios for what terrorists *might* do was almost endless, from poisoning public water supplies to detonating nuclear explosives in large cities. If counterterrorist thinking before 9/11 was linear, based on projecting trends of the past into the future, then the most likely attack on an aviation target involved smuggling explosives onto aircraft either on the persons of passengers or in checked cargo luggage. This prospect was what agencies such as the Federal Aviation Administration prepared for. When the authorities thought of hijackings, they planned to negotiate a mutually acceptable outcome. Hijackings were seen as efforts to bargain with governments, with airline passengers as the bargaining chips. Hostages were valuable commodities. Airlines followed the strategy of doing what the hijackers instructed and leaving resolution of the problem to the authorities. Thus 9/11 was not an instance of government leaders ignoring evidence-based predictions from the scientific and expert community, as was apparently the case with responses to Hurricane Katrina and the Fukushima earthquake and tsunami disaster in Japan.

In light of these conceptions about terrorism, correct anticipation of an attack required good tactical warning, that is, the detection of a signal of a plot in progress that was sufficiently precise to be operational (providing "actionable intelligence," meaning that the plot could be intercepted in timely fashion). The warning of an impending attack had to be not only specific enough to permit the authorities to thwart the attack in real time but also compelling enough to overcome established preconceptions about likely terrorist threats. The projected attack also had to be potentially deadly enough that top government leaders would make preventing terrorism a priority over other national security threats.[25] A vague description of such an unlikely plot as 9/11 would surely have seemed preposterous and incredible, even though the plot was set in motion as early as 1998. There was no precedent for one hijacker, let alone four hijackers, trained to pilot commercial aircraft and accompanied by "muscle" teams capable of seizing control of the airplane without using guns or explosives. The necessity for detailed information about the plot meant that most of the blame for failure to predict and prevent fell on the intelligence agencies, the CIA and the FBI, and to a certain extent the National Security Agency. Both the Clinton and Bush administrations also received their share of criticism for not stressing the threat of terrorism before 9/11. If terrorism had been more of a priority on the national security agenda, presumably there would have been better preparedness throughout the government and perhaps more attention paid to the clues that seemed obvious with hindsight.

Both the original failure and the investigations into the causes of that failure were a source of enduring political controversy. Over the years of second-guessing and rancorous debate the desire to avoid a repeat of the past led to unwillingness to be blamed for any future attack—thus to an approach to terrorism that is acutely sensitive to potential failure to anticipate.[26] It seemed that avoiding blame became a lasting obsession in Washington—underscoring the possibility that a populist democracy like the United States may be especially susceptible to the politicization of terrorist threats.

The official investigations into what went wrong were centered in two government institutions: the long-established congressional committee structure and the 9/11 Commission, newly appointed to respond to the crisis at hand and also following the American precedent of creating independent commissions to figure out what went wrong after what are perceived as intelligence failures.[27] In addition, in the academic and think-tank worlds social scientists and terrorism experts turned their attention to the question. For instance, former counterterrorism czar in both Clinton and Bush administrations,

Richard Clarke, published his memoir and his views on the events surrounding 9/11 the same year as the 9/11 Commission report appeared.[28] Few people were willing to say that the details of the attacks were not likely to have been predictable at all—and that detecting the plot once set in motion might have required not just skill but luck. The fact that opportunities were undeniably and tragically missed still does not mean that predicting the attacks was simple. Clarke recognized that it would be facile to say that the government could have stopped the attacks; in his view, if the nineteen hijackers had been intercepted there would have been a later attack unless al Qa'ida was removed from the scene.[29] But the catch-22 was that without an attack of the overwhelming magnitude of 9/11 the political determination to take risks to pursue al Qa'ida was lacking. The debate over who was to blame continued years after 9/11 as those who were accused of negligence or carelessness felt the need to defend their records and the reputations of the agencies where they worked, and the results of the official investigations were roundly criticized. In fact, two years after its publication the chairmen of the 9/11 Commission criticized their own report, asserting that stonewalling by the executive branch had blocked their access to critical information.[30]

In February 2002, five months after the attacks, the leadership in both the House and the Senate authorized each chamber's Select Committee on Intelligence to conduct a joint investigation into the performance of the intelligence community. One reason for the delay was the government's intense focus on prosecuting the war in Afghanistan to capture or kill bin Laden and destroy the Taliban, which by harboring bin Laden had enabled the planning of the 9/11 attacks. The two select committees produced a joint report of their inquiries that expressed majority and minority views, an unclassified version of which was published in July 2003. It took the intelligence agencies—the very subject of the report—seven months to declassify even the "unclassified" portion, much to the dissatisfaction of Senator Lindsey Graham of South Carolina, who lambasted what he saw as the Bush administration's obsessive concern with secrecy.[31] Fallout from the original investigation as to what had gone wrong included a broadening of the issues that came under the microscope, such as excessive classification of information. Positions on the new as well as the original issues increasingly took on a partisan cast.

The Bush administration first resisted the desire of many in Congress to establish an independent bipartisan 9/11 Commission, which finally happened only in November 2002. The administration said that it preferred to wait to decide until after the release of the congressional report. However, following a trend that began after the midair bombing of Pan Am 103 in 1988, the families of the victims joined together to form an influential interest group to press for a more comprehensive investigation into the causes of the failure to anticipate and prevent the attack. The 9/11 Commission's final report was submitted to the president and Congress on July 22, 2004. As had been prearranged, it was immediately published by W. W. Norton as an inexpensive paperback, which quickly became a bestseller. By 2005, Norton had sold over a million copies. It had not had to pay for the rights to publish the report, but it announced that it would donate $600,000, about 10 percent of the profits, to three charities: the Center for Catastrophe Preparedness and Response and the International Center for Enterprise Preparedness, both at New York University, and the Paul H. Nitze School of Advanced International Studies, part of Johns Hopkins University but based in Washington, D.C.[32]

The 9/11 Commission publication stood in contrast to the significantly redacted joint inquiry report, although the commissioners did chafe at secrecy restrictions imposed by the executive branch, and some twenty-eight pages were redacted because of classification issues. Complaints about lack of transparency persisted for years. The twenty-eight redacted pages were finally made public in July 2016.

The extent of the effort involved in the reports is impressive. The two official inquiries together conducted 1,700 interviews of individuals and reviewed stacks of documents: the joint congressional inquiry reviewed a million documents, and the 9/11 Commission staff of seventy-eight reviewed two and a half million pages of documents. In total, nineteen public hearings and at least thirteen more closed meetings were held. In addition some government agencies such as the FBI conducted their own reviews. The financial cost of the investigations is hard to calculate. The official budget of the 9/11 Commission alone was $15 million, but this is a low figure when compared to the costs of other official investigations into disasters, such as the space shuttles *Challenger* and *Columbia*.

So, what did go wrong? Were the various investigators able to produce a diagnosis? The consensus appeared to be that a key internal problem was lack of communication within and between intelligence agencies, so that critical pieces of information were not passed on or assimilated into existing knowledge. The result was that dots were not connected, and suspicions were not acted on. Important clues were noted by astute officials at lower levels—and indeed by some in the private sector—but the signals were missed at higher levels because they did not arrive on the right desks and because their meaning lay in their being parts of a larger pattern. Overlooking the puzzle of unlikely candidates presenting themselves for commercial flight training is one example of missed opportunities to detect the plot. But without a pattern, even the most imaginative analysts cannot put the pieces of the puzzle together. It is part of the definition of black swan events that they do not fit a pattern.

At higher levels of government, there was insufficient appreciation of the destructive potential of terrorism, as compared to other national security threats. Similarly, the general scholarly community in international relations and foreign policy, as opposed to experts on terrorism per se, did not consider terrorism by nonstate actors to be a serious threat to national security unless it involved "weapons of mass destruction"—in particular, nuclear weapons. More interest on the part of the White House in the destructive potential of terrorism could have produced heightened watchfulness in the FBI and CIA and intensified efforts to bring down the al Qa'ida apparatus, including destroying its bases in Afghanistan and putting more pressure on Pakistan to persuade or coerce the Taliban into turning over bin Laden. American allies, too, might have been persuaded to look more closely at al Qa'ida's global connections. The Clinton administration had discussed escalating the use of military force against al Qa'ida beyond cruise missile strikes, including arming drones, but concluded that the public would not support such a risky enterprise—nor was the military in favor of ground intervention. The long hiatus between the Clinton and Bush administrations, due to the disputed 2000 election outcome, was also an untimely distraction.

Rapid and Massive Responses to 9/11

The stunning shock of 9/11 provoked a fundamental and enduring reorientation not just of American counterterrorism policies and institutions but also of American foreign policy—and that well before any diagnosis of the problem was completed, in fact, months before a congressional investigation was even launched. All of these sweeping initiatives proved both contentious in the short and the long run and were hard to reverse. It was difficult for national leaders to back away from the positions, first, that the United States both could and must win a war against terrorism, even though victory was projected far into the future, and second, that extraordinary measures were justified by the gravity of the threat. The government firmly resisted the charge that the threat was exaggerated.[33] In the following sections we explain how quick reactions to one extremely rare event altered both the structure of the U.S. government and global politics.

The War on Terrorism. Within days of 9/11 President Bush unilaterally declared a global war on terrorism. It became the top national security priority, a policy implemented not just by the Department of Defense but also by the CIA. As a consequence of this, the agency took on more and more military functions. A bill for the Authorization for the Use of Military Force (AUMF) was introduced to Congress on September 14, 2001, and was signed into law on September 18. Still in effect in 2016, it authorizes the president "to use all necessary and appropriate force against those nations, organizations, or persons he determines planned, authorized, committed, or aided the terrorist attacks that occurred on September 11, 2001." In the House, only Representative Barbara Lee voted against it. She expressed apprehension about the overly broad powers—a "blank check"—the AUMF conferred on the executive when the facts were still not clear and the consequences of whatever actions might be undertaken could not be foreseen.[34] On February 7, 2002, the administration declared that suspected terrorists captured during the war on terrorism would be held as "enemy combatants" at Guantanamo Bay Detention Camp rather than treated as prisoners of war or ordinary criminals, thus depriving the detainees of specified rights in either military or civilian justice systems. At Guantanamo they—and the country—entered a gray zone largely outside the laws of war and U.S. domestic statutes dealing with terrorism and crime.

President Bush called on nations to be either for us or against us in the global war on terrorism. There could be no neutral ground. The use of military force in preemptive self-defense was explicitly justified. Stephen Walt, a theorist of international relations, reflected a general scholarly opinion in saying that the September 11 attacks had triggered the most rapid and dramatic change ever in the history of American foreign policy.[35]

Although some scholars have argued that the use of military force as retaliation for terrorist provocation is a defining feature of post–Cold War international politics, military responses to terrorism originating from outside the country are extremely rare, especially responses directed at nonstate actors.[36] So not only was 9/11 a rare event, so, too, was the American reaction. The United States had used limited air power earlier—against Libya in 1986, against Iraq in 1993, and against Sudan and Afghanistan in 1998. But the government had refrained from retaliation on numerous other occasions (for example, following the bombing of the Marine barracks in Beirut in 1983, the midair bombing of Pan Am 103 in 1988, the Khobar Towers attack in 1996, and the U.S.S. *Cole* bombing in 2000).

After 9/11, however, the official position of the United States was set immediately by framing the threat as a war against "terrorism of global reach."[37] The war metaphor was both diagnostic and prescriptive, because it defined the situation and recommended a response. It was also familiar, because the United States had routinely declared "wars" on poverty, crime, and drugs.[38] The implications of defining the task ahead as a "war" were clear: the United States could not lose. The enemy must be destroyed or defeated through military force.

The war metaphor was further reinforced by concrete historical analogies, linking the war on terror to World War II and to the cold war, thereby enhancing its legitimacy and its importance as well as intensifying the national sense of crisis and urgency.[39] Comparisons to the surprise attack at Pearl Harbor and the miscalculations at Munich before the beginning of World War II became commonplace. The president used rhetoric such as "axis of evil" and "Islamic fascists" to identify and describe the enemy. The United States was said to be combatting totalitarianism, making "appeasement" unacceptable. In 2002 President Bush observed, "We're not facing a set of grievances that can be soothed and addressed. We're facing a radical ideology with inalterable objectives: to enslave whole nations and intimidate the world. No act of ours invited the rage of the killers—and no concession, bribe, or act of appeasement would change or limit their plans for murder."[40]

Thus the initial strategy for the global war on terrorism was based on unilateralism and preemptive use of military force ("anticipatory self-defense") to forestall 9/11-type threats, although its contours were subsequently softened as time passed. The international community and the United Nations supported going to war in Afghanistan. A defiant Taliban had repeatedly refused to surrender bin Laden, although he had declared war on the United States, organized a series of attacks on American targets outside U.S. territory, and plotted attacks in the United States. NATO invoked the collective security provisions of its charter for the first time and joined the offensive.

The Bush administration's ambitions were not restricted to Afghanistan; they extended to overthrowing the Iraqi regime, ostensibly on grounds of Saddam Hussein's possession of weapons of mass destruction and failure to comply with UN inspections of his suspected nuclear program. The charge was bolstered by the claim—which later turned out to be false—that he had contacts with al Qa'ida and might provide it with nuclear weapons or materials that could be used to make weapons. As this rationale for the war was undermined by the failure to find evidence that Saddam was concealing a nuclear program, the goal of invasion and regime change in Iraq shifted to spreading democracy throughout the Middle East and ending tyranny everywhere (discussed further in chapter 6).

The war on terror had other far-reaching foreign policy consequences by removing many normative and legal limitations on the conduct of counterterrorism. As noted, these included the decision to declare terrorist adversaries "unlawful enemy combatants" and to establish a special prison for them at Guantanamo Bay. There military tribunals replaced the civil court system that had been used successfully to prosecute earlier terrorists, including Ramzi Yousef. Reliance on harsh interrogation methods such as waterboarding stemmed from a desperate need for information to prevent the follow-on attacks that were expected. As these secret methods were exposed to the public, charges of torture followed. Extended covert operations were also part of the war: secret renditions of suspects, establishment of secret "black" prisons to hold them, and extensive involvement of the CIA in these clandestine activities. Over time the CIA became more like a military organization, and the Department of Defense became more like an intelligence agency.

Expanded Executive Power at Home. The Patriot Act was introduced on October 23, 2001, and signed into law three days later. It was actually a second attempt at domestic counterterrorism legislation; the administration first proposed a bill on September 19, with the anticipation that Congress would approve it by September 21—a "demand for haste" that Senator Russell Feingold called both "inappropriate and dangerous" in his remarks explaining why he would vote against the Patriot Act (the only senator to do so).[41] Section 215 of the Patriot Act was immediately employed by the Bush administration to begin a classified program of collecting telephone metadata by presidential authorization, a program that was concealed from the public for a decade.[42] In addition, the act substantially expanded the power of the police to obtain evidence in terrorism cases and authorized intelligence and criminal justice investigators to share the information collected. All surveillance operations were expanded. With its new powers, the FBI shifted from its traditional emphasis on drug laws and traditional crimes toward counterterrorism. After passage of the Patriot Act, the FBI also undertook major efforts to integrate its criminal investigations with foreign and domestic intelligence operations. The Patriot Act also broadened the scope of what could be considered material support for terrorism to include "expert advice or assistance," and it extended the grounds for excluding immigrants with ties to terrorist organizations as well as their spouses and children.

Following on the Patriot Act, the Enhanced Border Security and Visa Entry Reform Act became law in May 2002. It increased the number of immigration inspectors and investigators, required universities to monitor foreign students, and tightened the oversight of visa applications of citizens from countries labeled as sponsors of terrorism. Universities must report the addresses of foreign students and their major fields of study and notify the Immigration and Naturalization Service (INS) if they leave school. (Two of the 9/11 hijackers were in the country on student visas. The Justice Department concluded that the INS had not followed its own procedures in these two cases.) In June 2002 the INS introduced the National Security Entry-Exit Registration System (NSEERS) to screen male visitors over the age of sixteen coming from specifically designated countries, all majority Muslim with the exception of North Korea. Both entry into the country and activity while in the United States were monitored. Some visitors already in the United States were also required to register and comply with the terms of the program or face severe penalties.

Opponents criticized many aspects of the program, and the "special registration" component was dropped quickly, in 2003. Opponents also alleged that the program was ineffective as a tool for stopping terrorism anyway because it targeted individuals solely on the basis of their national origin or religion, and not on the basis of specific evidence of criminal or terrorist activity. The *New York Times* reported in 2003 that out of roughly 85,000 individuals registered through the NSEERS program in 2002 and 2003, just 11 were found to have ties to terrorist organizations. The number of individuals screened through NSEERS and subsequently removed on the grounds of participation in terrorism-related activities is unknown; this information has not been made publicly available by the Department of Homeland Security (DHS).[43] In 2004 the U.S.-VISIT program required visa holders to be photographed and fingerprinted before entering the country.

The Reorganization of the Government for the Prevention of Terrorism. The idea of reorganizing domestic counterterrorism agencies was not new in 2001, because lack of coordination within the federal government and across federal, state, and local government and the resulting lack of accountability had long been recognized as problems. The 9/11 attacks provided a window of opportunity for significant change. As the investigations into what went wrong concluded, sweeping revisions to the government's bureaucratic apparatus followed, with some recommendations following logically from the diagnosis, some not, and many going well beyond counterterrorism. Some initiatives began as limited reforms but expanded through the political process into vast reorganizations of administrative effort. Most comprehensive, of course, was the establishment of the Department of Homeland Security. In addition, the intelligence community was officially united under a newly created position, Director of National Intelligence, including the establishment of a new National Counterterrorism Center under its authority. The United States had not undertaken such a large-scale government reorganization since the aftermath of World War II, when the Department of Defense and the Central Intelligence Agency were established.

The process that culminated in the establishment of the DHS, an amalgamation of more than twenty agencies and 180,000 employees from disparate corners of government, began immediately after 9/11, in late 2001. The legislation that created the Transportation Security Administration (TSA), which was later incorporated into DHS, came almost immediately, a little over two months after 9/11, when the president signed into law the Aviation and Transportation Security Act (ATSA) on November 19, 2001. For the first time the United States mandated federalized passenger and baggage screening at the nation's airports. Enhanced security measures now required passengers to arrive at airports hours before flying and submit their shoes, jackets, laptop computers, and bodies (via x-rays) for inspection after shuffling slowly through marked lanes to inspection and x-ray machines. Sharp instruments such as pocket knives and nail scissors were banned from carry-on luggage. The same legislation required that passenger airplanes flying in the United States henceforth have reinforced cockpit doors to prevent intruders from gaining access to flight decks.

In October 2001, President Bush created an Office of Homeland Security within the White House that was designed to coordinate domestic terrorism efforts. The president argued that this office was sufficient for coordinating government-wide homeland security activities. However, some members of Congress and some policy experts recommended a new federal agency or full cabinet department to integrate and heighten antiterrorism efforts. When reports surfaced in May 2002 of the failure by FBI leaders to take seriously lower-level reports that might have headed off the 9/11 attacks, compounded by failure of the FBI and the CIA to communicate with one another, the president decided to change course. In June 2002 the White House proposed a cabinet-level Department of Homeland Security and on November 25, 2002, little more than a year after 9/11, Congress passed and the president signed a substantially modified bill called the Homeland Security Act that established the Department of Homeland Security (DHS).

In January 2003, Tom Ridge, the governor of Pennsylvania, became its first secretary. The twenty-two departments and agencies folded into DHS were: U.S. Customs Service, the Immigration and Naturalization Service, the Federal Protective Service, the Transportation Security Administration, the Federal Law Enforcement Training Center, Animal and Plant Health Inspection Service, Office for Domestic Preparedness, the Federal Emergency Management Agency, the Strategic National Stockpile and the National Disaster Medical System, the Nuclear Incident Response Team, the Domestic Emergency Support Teams, the National Domestic Preparedness Office, the CBRN Countermeasures Programs, the Environmental Measurements Laboratory, the National BW Defense Analysis Center, the Plum Island Animal Disease Center, the Federal Computer Incident Response Center, the National Communications System, the National Infrastructure Protection Center, the Energy Security and Assurance Program, the U.S. Coast Guard, and the U.S. Secret Service.

Because the threat was seen as coming from outside the United States, the creation of DHS brought together several former border and security agencies under one umbrella, now called Immigration and Customs Enforcement (ICE). In combining the resources, jurisdictions, and functions of the U.S. Customs Service, the Immigration and Naturalization Service, the Federal Protective Service, and, later, the Federal Air Marshals Service, ICE became Homeland Security's largest investigative bureau. ICE's responsibilities included securing the nation's long, porous borders with Mexico and Canada. Agents also tracked weapons smuggling and shipments of equipment that could be used to produce weapons. Increased numbers of plainclothes federal air marshals now flew aboard passenger airlines to deter terrorists, and interdiction teams coordinated air and land responses to border threats. ICE's Student and Exchange Visitor Information System (SEVIS) automated and centralized tracking of foreign students during their stays in the United States.

The congressional report on 9/11 was released in July 2003 and the 9/11 Commission report in July 2004. Both investigations into the failure to prevent the 9/11 attacks concluded that lack of coordination among the intelligence agencies that dealt with external terrorist threats was a critical problem. Like other initiatives such as DHS, the process of reform began as an executive branch mandate articulated by President Bush in his 2003 State of the Union address, in which he called for the creation of a Terrorist Threat Integration Center (TTIC) to link the FBI, the CIA, the DOD, and the new DHS. It was first established within the CIA. The venture became much more complex with the passage of the Intelligence Reform and Terrorism Prevention Act of 2004, which created a new national-level institution, the National Counterterrorism Center (NCTC). Its purpose was to coordinate the work of the many agencies with terrorism portfolios, including not just the CIA but also the State Department and the National Security Agency. The legislation also stipulated that the appointment of the NCTC director would require the advice and consent of the Senate. Further complicating bureaucratic matters, NCTC was placed within another new agency, the Office of the Director of National Intelligence (ODNI). The NCTC director thus reports to the president as well as to the Director of National Intelligence (DNI).

Rolling Back the Crisis Response: Enduring Legacies

When it comes to terrorism, measures taken in the heat of the moment are extremely difficult to reverse when the crisis fades and the perception of the threat changes.[44] This rigidity is unintended and unanticipated, and it weakens the government's capacity to adapt. Many critics of the Bush administration's response to terrorism expected the government to change course after Obama's election in 2008 and his reelection to a second term in 2012. As presidential candidate and as president he had been highly critical of his predecessor's policies, and he had promised to roll back many of them. Yet although some alterations were made, the legacy of the immediate post-9/11 policy shift persisted. It might also have been expected that the death of Osama bin Laden in 2010 would have brought an end to the post-9/11 era, but ISIS emerged as a likeminded and even more ruthless rival to al Qa'ida. The United States appeared to remain in the grip of the "one percent doctrine" as described by journalist Ron Suskind and attributed by him to Vice President Dick Cheney: if there is even a 1 percent chance of a threat of the magnitude of 9/11 policymakers must act as if it is a certainty.[45]

Thus the war on terror did not end; the Obama administration resisted using the "global war on terrorism" language but continued to say that the nation was at war.[46] As we will see in more detail in chapter 6, the struggle nominally became one to counter violent extremism, at least in much of the administration's rhetoric, but the use of military force remained central to American policy. American troops formally withdrew from Iraq in 2011, and their numbers were reduced in Afghanistan. However, a complete exit from Afghanistan had to be delayed because of the escalating threat from the Taliban; ultimately the war in Afghanistan became the longest in the nation's history. In addition, special forces units remained posted around the world's hot spots, and in 2015, following the astonishing rise of ISIS and in light of Iraq's inability to defend itself, units returned to advise Iraqi security forces as well as to assist the Peshmerga, units of Kurdish fighters. As civil war escalated in Syria, the United States launched airstrikes and deployed advisers to try to defeat ISIS. American air power, both drones and bombers, became critical to counterterrorism worldwide.

In fact, drones became the mainstay of the Obama administration's foreign counterterrorism operations. Operated by both DOD and CIA, they were used to remove key leaders of terrorist networks not just in ongoing conflicts such as Afghanistan and Iraq, where U.S. forces were engaged, but also in Pakistan, Yemen, and Somalia, and possibly elsewhere. Responding to criticisms of lack of transparency, in 2013 the Obama administration pledged to concentrate the control and direction of drone operations in the Department of Defense, thus presumably ensuring greater accountability for decisions and operations. However, the shift away from CIA management did not begin until the summer of 2016. In July 2016 the Obama administration released statistics on the official count of combatant and noncombatant deaths from drone strikes, although the number of noncombatants was lower than most nongovernment sources had estimated.[47] In August 2016 the Obama administration also declassified the May 2013 Presidential Policy Guidance document on the use of drones, in response to a Freedom of Information Act request from the American Civil Liberties Union.[48]

The Obama administration rejected the use of torture and reliance on secret foreign "black" prisons, policies that the Bush administration had begun to move away from by 2006. However, congressional opposition made it impossible to fulfill the promise to close the prison at Guantanamo Bay. Both the Guantanamo detention center and the black prison sites were consequences of the Bush administration's failure to consider what would be done with captured terrorist suspects in the war on terror. By mid-2016 the number of the almost 800 enemy combatants who had been imprisoned at Guantanamo after 2001 had been reduced to around 60. Most detainees were released without trial, evidence being either lacking or tainted. From fiscal 2002 through fiscal year 2014, the cost of "Gitmo" to the United States was almost $5 billion.[49]

The Patriot Act was criticized from the outset, and its opponents were vocal. Critics of its negative impact on civil liberties immediately began to try to reduce the powers of surveillance of private citizens that the act gave the executive branch and to restrict its expansive definition of actions that would constitute terrorism or support for terrorism as well as the treatment of Muslim immigrants as inherently suspicious. The act contained sunset provisions, with the first set of expirations set to begin in 2005 when the legislation would have to be renewed. Challenges in the courts were brought by groups such as the American Civil Liberties Union and the Humanitarian Law Project. In addition, various new pieces of legislation were introduced in Congress to restrict the Patriot Act's scope, but none were passed.

Do sunset provisions work when it comes to legislation on terrorism? Even though in 2013 the disclosure of the secret collection of telephone records disturbed many on both the left and the right, and despite intense debate and discussion, the Patriot Act was repeatedly reauthorized by Congress and the president up through June 1, 2015. There were no meaningful improvements or reforms through legislative initiative. Expiration dates were sequentially extended. The Justice Department on its own authority made some changes that accorded with suggested reforms, such as provisions regarding the use of national security letters and roving wiretaps to acquire information. Similarly, the DHS acted on its own initiative to end the controversial NSEERS program in 2011. The DHS explained that it was redundant in light of post-9/11 improvements in intelligence gathering and the tracking of immigrants, but the agency also recognized that the generic designation of people by country of origin should be replaced by a focus on individuals representing specific threats.

Do challenges through the courts affect counterterrorism law? The Patriot Act had been modified somewhat over time as a result of legal challenges. The Supreme Court first took up a legal challenge to the Patriot Act in 2010, when it upheld a broad reading of the material support provision, one of the main charges on which individuals were prosecuted. Federal courts on occasion held specific provisions of the Patriot Act unconstitutional, especially the government's search powers and the "expert advice and assistance" part of the material support provision. But the act's basic outlines remained unchanged.

In June 2015 the USA Freedom Act replaced the Patriot Act. As of November 2015, it restricted the bulk collection of telephone records by the National Security Agency (the original Patriot Act's controversial Section 215), but its implementation remained open to question. It also provided for greater transparency of rulings made by the Foreign Intelligence Surveillance Courts, which had become the authorizing body for metadata collection.

Conclusions about the Policy Implications of Rare Events

Any account of counterterrorism policy in the early twenty-first century must depend heavily on an assessment of the consequences of the 9/11 attacks. Much of the domestic and foreign policy of the George W. Bush administration following 9/11 was a direct reaction to the event, despite its uniqueness. The war on terror came to define Bush's presidency. The Obama administration was constrained in its freedom of action by the choices of its predecessor as well as the continuity of the threat, even though that persistence was partially due to the extent and nature of the original response. The threat shape-shifted over time, becoming both discontinuous and cumulative, with old and new elements mixed together.

The United States reacted initially by doing everything in its power to prevent a repetition of a 9/11-type attack—one that came from outside the country's borders and involved an extremely clever and complicated plot that required extensive planning over a period of years and depended on the recruitment of a very special set of individuals centered around Mohammed Atta. Perhaps it was impossible to have known then that al Qa'ida did not have a follow-on attack in process. On reflection, post-crisis, it was also clear that once the element of surprise was lost, there could not be an exact repeat of the 9/11 attacks. The fate of United Airlines Flight 93 showed that once passengers were aware of the possibility that hijackers could and would fly a commercial aircraft into a target, they could block the attempt. Failed and foiled airline bombing attempts in 2006 and 2009 also demonstrated that passengers would not remain passive, even though the plots also showed that the strictest aviation security policies could still be circumvented by agents of external groups. Hardening cockpit doors was also a simple but effective solution to a 9/11-type threat.

Nevertheless, American involvement in Iraq, Syria, and to a lesser extent Afghanistan both increased the attractiveness of the United States as a target and contributed to the evolution of the threat that we summarized in chapter 1. While the threat was dynamic, the policies and institutions put in place hurriedly after 9/11 remained mostly static; newer responses such as "soft power" initiatives to counter radicalization and violent extremism at home and abroad were overlaid awkwardly on the foundations of the old "hard power" responses.

Perhaps less obvious, the most vocal challenges to the policies of both the Bush and Obama administrations were also set to a large extent by the lessons of 9/11. In fact, many popular assumptions about terrorism are influenced or directly formulated in response to 9/11—including the image of terrorism that audiences frequently pick up from Hollywood and the entertainment industry, that the number of terrorist attacks was rapidly increasing in the years before 9/11, that most attacks originate outside U.S. borders in the Middle East, that successful attacks rely on complex planning and sophisticated weaponry by tightly organized conspiracies, and that attacks are incredibly and increasingly lethal. A rare event has defined official and public perceptions of terrorism and the response itself ever since.

CHAPTER 3

The Tip of the Iceberg

Accounting for Failed and Foiled Terrorist Plots

Tactically successful terrorist events are rare occurrences, but they represent the tip of an iceberg when it comes to all planned attacks. Most attacks planned by terrorists fail for reasons internal to the plot or are foiled by external intervention. For example, in the past fifteen years since the 9/11 attacks there have been around a hundred jihadist-linked plots to attack American targets in the United States, but only eight of those plots resulted in the deaths of their intended victims. A comprehensive picture of the threat must include an analysis of what violent jihadist adversaries planned to do as well as what they actually managed to accomplish. Examining failed and foiled as well as successful plots is essential to avoiding selection bias in research methodology. It is also essential to understanding adversaries' intentions as well as capabilities. Nor can the validity of public concern be judged without an evaluation of what extreme jihadis aspired to do. A balanced view of plots, successful and unsuccessful, is essential to understanding public appreciation of the threat. The potential danger posed by plots can be exaggerated, but at the same time the threat is hardly nonexistent. This chapter puts the threat in perspective by close analysis of plot realities.

Furthermore, a realistic appraisal of the threat at home as well as of the fear it engenders in the public is needed if we are to propose a sound counterterrorism strategy. Some foiled attacks—such as the

2006 liquid explosives plot (a plan to detonate liquid explosives carried on board seven airliners traveling from the United Kingdom to the United States and Canada) and the Christmas bomber attempt in 2009 (by the so-called underwear bomber)—have generated extensive public policy reaction. Such thwarted attacks probably have had more impact on American policymakers than earlier terrorist successes such as the 1993 World Trade Center bombing because, as we described in the last chapter, the threat is perceived not only in terms of the shadow of 9/11 but also in light of expectations about the performance of the vast post-9/11 counterterrorism bureaucracy. The public and news media are more sensitive to the threat and to the response as well as fearful of the future. Periods of relative quiet are punctuated by spectacular terrorist successes, and audiences are primed to react to them in a way that they were not before the high-profile black swan event of 9/11. In fact, merely listing numbers of individuals somehow linked to extremism, however ill-defined or varied in terms of behaviors that are said to reflect violent intent, may raise alarms. Thus it may take only an occasional completed act of terrorism or news of a plot, however vague or unlikely to succeed, to remind audiences of the risk, raise anxiety levels, and fuel public demands for government action.

Assessing jihadist plots to use violence against the United States also matters because the methodologies for assessing the seriousness of these attempts is controversial. The question of the reliability of such assessments touches on issues of overreaction and the effectiveness of counterterrorism strategies in preventing terrorism (discussed in more detail in chapter 6).

Summary statistics—especially comparisons of terrorism to other causes of death and injury such as car accidents, falls at home, lightning strikes, or bee stings—lead academic researchers such as John Mueller and Ian Lustick to argue that the threat of jihadist terrorism is vastly exaggerated—"overblown" per Mueller.[1] Such critics argue that most terrorist plots are trivial or insignificant, and that the dangers that counterterrorist policies pose to the liberty, privacy, and sense of well-being of American citizens outweigh their effectiveness in stopping terrorism. Risa Brooks, a political scientist, also cautions firmly against overemphasis on violent jihadist proclivities among American Muslims.[2]

On the other hand, government officials are much more likely to see foiled plots as potentially deadly and consequential and to value counterterrorist policies as essential to their suppression. Their judgments often credit American authorities with having prevented a series of potential disasters. Overall, government secrecy makes it hard to ascertain the validity of competing claims, and this lack of certainty enhances controversy over how plots were foiled and whether they represented real danger in the first place. For example, the critical 2014 report by the Senate Select Committee on Intelligence agreed that the plots that the CIA claimed to have foiled through use of enhanced interrogation techniques were potentially consequential, but questioned the claim that the use of torture had made it possible to intercept and disrupt them.[3] The CIA response to the report countered that the information thus acquired did produce unique and valuable intelligence, but the agency also admitted to having failed to perform a comprehensive analysis of effectiveness, especially in comparison to using alternative methods of eliciting information.[4] The agency pledged to systematically and objectively evaluate future counterterrorism measures. Officials who were involved rose to the CIA's defense. For example, former CIA head of both the Clandestine Service and the Counterterrorism Center Jose Rodriguez argued forcefully that the interrogation techniques were effective in halting highly deadly and feasible terrorist plans worldwide in the immediate aftermath of 9/11.[5] Former CIA deputy director Michael Morell, who commissioned the CIA review, asserted that there was "no doubt in [his] mind" that these techniques were effective.[6]

For bureaucratic reasons government agencies have good reason to be apprehensive about the political consequences of failed or foiled plots, as the 2009 Christmas bombing example showed. The Project on National Security Reform, a nonpartisan research and policy organization in Washington, financed by Congress, issued a critical report in February 2010.[7] According to the report, the National Counterterrorism Center (NCTC) had proved to be less than successful in integrating and directing a national effort, and long-standing tensions between the NCTC, the State Department, and the CIA remained unresolved. The decisionmaking process was still decentralized, which diluted responsibility and accountability. In May 2010 the unclassified version of a Senate Intelligence Committee report summarizing its investigation of the Christmas bombing attempt stressed systemic failures across the entire intelligence community.[8] The committee cited the NCTC specifically as inadequately organized to carry out its mission, and it expressed disappointment in the lack of progress in counterterrorism implementation nine years after the 9/11 attacks. Whether or not the decision was related to the report, President Obama fired Director of National Intelligence Dennis Blair soon thereafter. Interestingly, Blair had recently given a speech that expressed a healthy dose of realism: "The standard for success in countering violent extremism has to be incredibly high, because the stakes are incredibly high. And I will tell you that no one is harder on us than [we] ourselves about the times that we fall short. But I cannot promise you that the Intelligence Community will be able to discover and to stop every attack by a violent extremist group like al-Qaida."[9]

Despite the importance of plots, academic research and appraisal has often excluded them from analysis. For example, the Global Terrorism Database (GTD) does not include plots that have not developed to the point where a specific action toward carrying them out has taken place (as we pointed out in chapter 1). Thus, the GTD includes cases where suicide bombers actually don vests and undertake suicide missions but excludes cases where perpetrators building suicide vests blow themselves up by accident. However, researchers are beginning to collect data on terrorism that includes plots at earlier stages. For example, Thomas Hegghammer and Petter Nesser developed databases on jihadist plots in the West.[10] Erik Dahl's work included plots as well as attacks on U.S. targets within and outside the homeland.[11] And finally, research by Jeff Gruenewald and his colleagues presented comparisons between total plots that targeted the United States and completed attacks.[12]

In this chapter we provide an overview of our data and analytical framework and discuss what can be learned about targets and methods, perpetrators, and plot outcomes. We address the specific problem of the link between foreign fighters and plots against the U.S. homeland. We find that genuine "lone wolves" are actually rare, that bombs are more often associated with foiled plots, while shootings are more likely to result in fatalities, and that returned foreign fighters have not so far posed a serious threat. Most U.S. plots are foiled, and most of those foiled plots involve government informants who enter the plot at an early stage.

Data on Failed and Foiled Plots

In order to get a better understanding of these often neglected cases, the analysis in this chapter is based on an original dataset, the Failed and Foiled Plots (FPP) dataset.[13] Our approach to counting plots that did not result in actual attacks differs from other recent efforts to collect data on terrorist plots but complements them and adds additional variables and details. The research team collected data from public sources on failed and foiled jihadist attempts to use violence against the territories of the United States and key allies since the first bombing of the World Trade Center in 1993. We may have missed information known only to intelligence agencies, even though we think that in the United States most cases are brought to public view through news media coverage of arrests and trials. Thus if anything our account underestimates rather than overestimates plots as opposed to completed attacks.

The primary unit of analysis is the plot itself. We focus in this chapter on the United States, although the failed and foiled plots project also collected data on countries that are members of the European Union and the North Atlantic Treaty Organization as well as Australia and New Zealand, which permits comparison between the United States and other Western democracies. In addition, what happens in these countries is often interpreted as a warning signal of what is likely to happen in the United States. For example, the deadly 2005 London bus and subway bombings led to fear of similar homegrown terrorism in the United States, which materialized with the 2013 Boston Marathon bombings.

Our subject in this chapter is threats to the U.S. homeland rather than to U.S. interests and citizens abroad, although the two are obviously related. As described in chapter 1, there are two vectors of attack on the United States: agents of a foreign group who are trained and directed from the outside, and "home-grown" or "self-radicalized" terrorists. Striking examples of the former are the 9/11 attacks and, more recently, outside the United States, the November 2015 attacks in Paris and the March 2016 bombings in Brussels that were mounted by ISIS from Syria, with the aid of a network of local citizens.

Acts of "home-grown" or "self-radicalized" terrorism are performed by individuals who are inspired by the ideology of a foreign group but not under its control nor even known to its leaders. The appeal is usually broadcast generally through social media and other Internet sources, such as the English-language online publications of al Qa'ida and ISIS, that are accessible to anyone. The two attack vectors converge when organizations such as al Qa'ida or ISIS attract sympathizers through Internet communications and then recruit them directly into the organization through personal contact or encrypted communications. This combination of electronic and personal contact is part of what makes government and the public so sensitive to the prospect of domestic terrorism by returned foreign fighters.

A Framework for Analyzing Failed and Foiled Plots

Our research identified 113 jihadi-linked plots to use terrorism against the territory of the United States between February 1993 (the date of the first bombing of the World Trade Center) and July 2016. Seventeen of these incidents produced casualties among both victims and perpetrators, but the rest did not cause physical harm. How did we identify plots, which are the key units of analysis? A plot involves a plan or scheme to commit violent action. Usually targets and methods are specified in the plan, although these may be general categories. It is not necessary for would-be perpetrators to have acquired weapons for a plot to exist. Plots often have multiple component parts, as did the 9/11 attacks and the 2015 Paris assaults. A plot can involve a coordinated group of perpetrators or an individual acting alone, although multiple targets and methods may be involved in any given plot.[14] Deciding whether to define sequences of events or intended events as one plot or as several independent plots takes into account time intervals between intended or actual attacks, geographical location of the targets, and the apparent intent of the perpetrators. Knowledge of the details of the plan is thus essential, although sometimes hard to glean from public sources.

Our dataset of plots is restricted to concrete plans to use violence in or against the U.S. homeland, including attempted bombings of airliners flying to the United States. It excludes travel abroad to fight or train in local conflicts, financial contributions to jihadist organizations, and membership in an officially designated Foreign Terrorist Organization. These activities may of course coincide with plans to use violence but they are not necessarily or always connected. Many individuals are convicted of terrorist offenses under the "material support" provision of current antiterrorism law, which goes well beyond plans to use violence.[15] Early in their implementation a legal critic of the material support provisions complained, "The government is using them as catch-all offenses that can be invoked in widely varying situations where individuals engage in conduct that may contribute in some way to the commission of terrorist offenses. The government is also using these offenses as a basis for early intervention, a kind of criminal early-warning and preventive-enforcement device designed to nip the risk of terrorist activity in the bud."[16]

Thus, we do not simply include all individuals accused of links to extremism but look also at the details of charges and convictions as well as press reports. Our analysis is concerned with individuals and groups who intend and prepare for direct harm to people on American soil and on American airliners flying to or from the United States. The territories and airliners of other Western democracies provide a basis for comparison.

We consider as perpetrators all the individuals who take an active role in the plot, including making plans, acquiring and deploying weapons, conducting surveillance, or providing funds with direct knowledge of their intended purpose. The key consideration is that the members of a group are involved in the same plan of action and are in communication with each other as the plan develops. They are not simply imitating others, following a similar line, or inspired by the same ideologues. Complicating matters, the same perpetrator or group of perpetrators can be responsible for several independent plots or a single plot with multiple interdependent components. There may be many or few perpetrators, including so-called "lone wolves." With the dramatic exception of the 9/11 attacks, most plots against the United States do not involve large numbers of conspirators. Plots in Europe, in contrast, are more likely to be developed by larger groups and to be transnational—involving citizens of different countries such as France and Belgium.

A possible 2012 plan by al Qa'ida in the Arabian Peninsula (AQAP) to place another bomb on an airliner, a follow-on to the failed 2009 Christmas bombing, provides an illustration of how difficult it can be to ascertain the existence of a terrorist plot.[17] U.S. authorities seized an explosive device in transit somewhere in the Middle East, outside Yemen, that was constructed by the same expert bomb maker as the one in the Christmas bombing. However, there was apparently no indication that AQAP had selected a target or method of placing the bomb (many details of the plot were not revealed to the public). The timing appeared to coincide with the anniversary of bin Laden's death, making the idea of a bombing plausible, but the White House denied explicitly that there was a credible plot that posed any threat to the public. Taking this statement into account and lacking further information, we did not include this in our plot dataset.

By "acting in the name of jihadist causes" we mean that there is evidence that the perpetrators or would-be perpetrators intended their actions to serve the ends of violent jihadist ideologies. Obtaining conclusive evidence of individual motivation is notoriously difficult, especially since the perpetrators themselves may not know why they acted. We relied on public statements made by perpetrators (such as videotaped statements distributed by the groups that claim them or Facebook postings), intercepted communications among perpetrators (used by government authorities in court, for example), witness reports of statements made before or during an attack or attempt, or perpetrators' trial testimony explaining motivation. Most American perpetrators have been convicted in a court of law of the actions in question; if perpetrators are charged or indicted but subsequently not convicted they are not included in the dataset. In some cases foreign countries apprehended the perpetrators, as occurred in the 2006 London liquid-explosives plot. The perpetrators are rarely acting as agents of a recognized organization, although we note credible links between perpetrators and organizations as well as claims of responsibility by known groups. This distinction allows for the possibility that there were links between an individual and a group but the group did not claim responsibility, which is a puzzling question in itself.

We identify the perpetrators by name, residence (U.S. city and state where available), citizenship, and country of origin, if not identical to the country of citizenship. We also note whether the perpetrators are Muslims, and if so, whether they are converts to Islam or are Muslims from birth. A few self-declared American jihadis are not Muslims.

The plots we analyze are classified in terms of categories of outcomes, as well as in terms of number of perpetrators involved, their targets and methods, and the physical consequences (number of victims). There are plots that failed because of something the would-be perpetrators did, a factor internal to the plot—either they made a mechanical mistake or they had a change of intention.[18] For example, constructing an explosive device is technically difficult and the procedure can go wrong, as it fortunately did in the case of Faisal Shahzad's failed Times Square car bombing attempt in 2010. Saajid Badat, the accomplice of the shoe bomber, Richard Reid, did not follow through with the plan to bring down transatlantic airliners in December 2001—he changed his mind. There may be many more cases of failed plots than publicly available information indicates, so we may be undercounting these cases.

Next, some plots were foiled owing to external intervention by members of the public, friends, family, or government authorities, usually the FBI or local or state law enforcement, sometimes with the assistance of the intelligence agencies of foreign governments.[19] We also ask at what point in its development the plot was abandoned, fizzled out, or was thwarted. If foiled, we ask how: Through the use of surveillance? Placing informants? Intervention in the field, such as law enforcement agents arresting someone approaching the target with a weapon? Did private individuals tip the government off? We ask whether the government that directly interrupted the plot had assistance from a foreign government. How important was cross-national intelligence sharing to interdiction?

Some plots were physically completed but did not necessarily result in tangible and visible effects—for example, would-be perpetrators placed a bomb at their chosen target but it failed to explode, as occurred in the 2010 Times Square attempt. These plots might be either failed or foiled. Perhaps the bomb maker was inept, which says something about terrorist capabilities as well as the technical obstacles to constructing explosives. Perhaps the government intervened and provided or substituted inert explosives, which says something about the effectiveness of specific counterterrorist measures. These plots reveal the perpetrator's intentions to do harm even though they were not successful in a material or kinetic sense. We would place the shoe bomber, Richard Reid, in 2001 and the underwear bomber, Umar Farouk Abdulmutallab, in 2009 in this category, as their destructive efforts were blocked at the last minute by fellow airline passengers, and it is also not entirely certain that the devices would have actually detonated.

Last, some plots are tactically successful, although they are in the minority. For the purposes of this analysis we define plots as successful if they were physically completed and resulted in tangible effects—there was violence or harm as a result of the action. This convention follows the logic of the GTD. We do not judge success in terms of whether the perpetrators attained their objectives in a larger political sense and could thus be considered effective in using terrorism—something that is very difficult to know and has provoked much debate among academics.[20] For example, a plot might have been intended to kill hundreds of people but fortunately killed many fewer; thus it might constitute a failure in the eyes of the perpetrators, but we would count this as a success in the narrow sense we are using here. In addition, even a foiled plot such as the 2009 Christmas bombing attempt can produce a dramatic public impact that constitutes a significant success from the terrorists' point of view despite the immediate outcome. As Anwar al-Awlaki explained in claiming credit for the bombing attempt for AQAP:

> With Allah's grace, the hero mujahid martyrdom-seeker, brother Omar Al-Farooq, carried out a quality operation on an American plane that took off from the Dutch city of Amsterdam to the American city of Detroit, while they were celebrating the Christmas holiday on Friday December 25, 2009, which broke through all modern advanced technological equipment and security barriers in world airports, with courage and determination, not fearing death, placing his trust in Allah, breaking with his great act the legend of American and international intelligence,

demonstrating its frailty, rubbing their noses in the dust, and making all they have spent upon security technologies a waste for them.[21]

We also coded the stages of plot development: (1) communication of intent, by telling someone face-to-face, posting messages on Facebook or other websites, or e-mailing someone (sometimes involving searching for useful information on the Internet); (2) attempt to acquire capability, for instance, by purchasing or stealing weapons or the materials necessary to build a bomb, engaging in exploratory travel, or recruiting accomplices; (3) practice or training specifically for an attack, such as training in the use of weapons or explosives, training that might take place abroad; (4) elaboration of an actual plan with detailed target and method selection; (5) final physical implementation stage, such as travel to the target with the weapon. The final stage is also called the "out-the-door" phase, such as when a bomb is physically placed at the target destination.

These distinctions between different phases of plot development permit us to ask at what stage the plot was foiled or failed, if it was. We consider a plot to be foiled when the government discovered it and took steps to prevent its successful execution, which might include substituting inert explosives in a device or providing a gun that will not fire. Foiling a plot at stage 5 would usually mean intervention in the field, that is, the authorities or the public intercepted it at the last minute. These plots that are stopped at the "out-the-door" phase are the most likely to be included in the GTD. We can also ascertain the stage at which an informant entered a plot. We found that these plot development stages did not necessarily follow each other sequentially. For example, plans might be made and targets selected after detailed reconnaissance but before weapons and capabilities are acquired. The al Qa'ida operative Dhiren Barot's scheme to bomb the New York Stock Exchange, the International Monetary Fund headquarters, and the World Bank, discovered in 2004, is a case in point: Barot had made elaborate plans, including reconnaissance videos, before acquiring the means of attack.

Failed and Foiled Plots in the United States

In figure 3-1 we show the trends in the 113 plots against the U.S. homeland included in the FFP database. There were high points in these U.S. plots in 2003, 2010, and 2015. Why? The U.S.-led war in Iraq was launched in 2003. In 2010 al Qa'ida in the Arabian Peninsula was established, and the influence of the American ideologue Anwar al-Awlaki began to spread. AQAP, a merger of al Qa'ida's Saudi and Yemeni branches, showed extraordinary determination in launching efforts to attack American territory. The likely explanation for the large increase in plots in 2015 is the dramatic rise to power of ISIS in Syria and Iraq and the appeal of the caliphate and ISIS's self-promotion to amateur self-starters in the West. Both al Qa'ida and ISIS have called on their supporters or adherents to undertake independent individual terrorist initiatives. An increase in plots suggests the groups' success in this, coinciding with large numbers of individuals in the United States being linked generally to extremism.[22] The November 2015 Paris attacks signaled that ISIS had shifted from consolidating power in its nominal caliphate to directly striking its adversaries at home: the attack followed closely on the crash of a Russian charter plane in the Sinai peninsula on October 31, which ISIS claimed to have sabotaged. The successful San Bernardino attacks in December 2015 seem to have been a particularly deadly example of ISIS influence via social media, although the connection is not certain. The frequency of extremely deadly ISIS-connected attacks around the world in 2016 continued this trend.

Targets and Methods

Where are the preferred targets of jihadist terrorist plots in the United States? Targets were located in twenty-three different states and the District of Columbia. It is not surprising that almost a fourth of all plots were planned to occur or did occur in New York. If New Jersey is included the figure is close to 30 percent. Another 17 percent of all plots are aimed at targets in the District of Columbia and Virginia. Next in order of attractiveness as targeted locations are Florida, Texas, California, and Illinois. Targets track somewhat with location of perpetrator residence, as about half of the 149 perpetrators whom

FIGURE 3-1. U.S. Jihadist Terrorist Plots, February 1993–July 2016

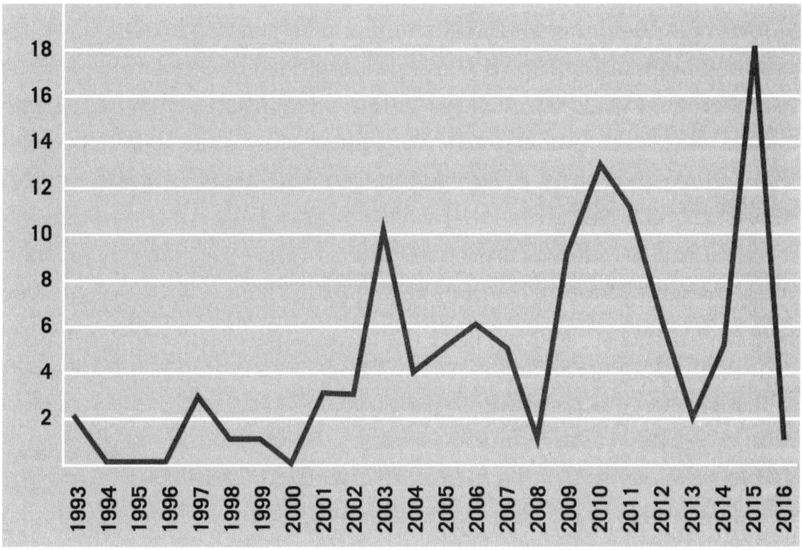

Source: Authors' compilation, based on the Failed and Foiled Plots Database.

we could identify as having a U.S. residence were from New York or New Jersey. Florida and California ranked next.

Aside from location, what types of targets are chosen? Private citizens and property and military institutions and personnel are most common, together accounting for about a third of the plots.[23] Airports and aircraft, general government, and business targets are the next most frequent targets.[24] If transportation and aviation targets are combined into one category, they account for about one fourth of the plot targets. Since 2011 police have been targeted more often, perhaps because military targets are now on alert for attacks, and police are a more available and accessible substitute.[25]

The majority of attacks and plots involve bombings, followed by armed assaults, which number fewer than half the total of attacks or attempts involving explosives. Worldwide and over time terrorists show a strong predilection for bombings.[26] Why would this be so? It could be that the introduction of undercover informants into extremist groups by counterterrorism agencies is often the source of the explosives used by the perpetrators. Most plots involving informants also involved the use of explosives. The study by Jeff Gruenewald and others concurs that those who planned attacks but failed or were foiled generally intended to use bombs, and they speculate that these results may be partly due to the successful infiltration of groups that are plotting attacks, post-9/11, by undercover FBI operatives or informants.[27] The authors show that 33 percent of plots were foiled by FBI operatives and 23 percent with assistance from FBI informants. A possible consideration here is that any sort of bomb is defined as a weapon of mass destruction under federal law, whereas guns are not. The penalties for deployment of the former are severe. The law provides that suspects "convicted of conspiring, attempting, threatening, or using a Weapon of Mass Destruction may be imprisoned for any term of years or for life, and if resulting in death, be punishable by death or by imprisonment."[28]

On the other hand, the study by Gruenewald and others finds that in general shootings are more common causes of death in terrorist attacks: 45 percent of the resultant deaths involved firearms.[29] Their finding is reinforced by the June 2016 Orlando nightclub shootings and the December 2015 San Bernardino shootings, in addition to the 2009 Fort Hood shootings, which combined left 76 victims dead. Gruenewald and others also confirm our finding that the 1993 World Trade Center bombing and 2013 Boston Marathon bombings were the only successful homicide events related to extremist jihadist plots that were committed with conventional explosives.[30] All of the other deadly jihadist inspired attacks since 1993, excepting 9/11, were shootings.

As we observed earlier, the 9/11 attacks accounted for the vast majority of fatalities and injuries associated with jihadist terrorism in the United States since 1993. Leaving aside this exceptional case, our figures show 93 victim deaths in a total of thirteen plots from 1993 to mid-2016. Approximately half of these fatalities (49) were due to the 2016 Orlando mass shooting. There have also been close to 1,400 injuries in these 13 lethal attacks plus in three others that did not result in the deaths of victims. The 1993 bombing of the World Trade Center accounted for the majority of injuries, about 1,000, as well as 6 fatalities, and the Boston Marathon bombings caused 264 injuries and 3 fatalities.

Perpetrators

What can this dataset tell us about the characteristics of the perpetrators and would-be perpetrators of jihadist terrorism in the United States? Roughly two thirds of the plots we analyzed involved only one perpetrator. The first reaction of the reader might likely be that the "lone wolf" explanation of contemporary terrorism is correct—terrorism has devolved into sporadic and largely unpredictable actions taken on individual initiative, and it is no longer mainly the product of sustained and systematic group activity even though these individuals might share a common allegiance to jihadist principles and answer the same appeal to action.[31] However, most of the individual plots we identify were infiltrated by law enforcement at their earliest stages, and informants or undercover agents convinced perpetrators that they were part of a larger group, indeed that they were an important asset to the cause. The plot then developed with the participation of the informant or agent, who might provide ideological and moral support and assistance in acquiring weapons and organizing other logistics such as transportation, planning, and target selection. The Gruenewald study also finds that mental illness was an antecedent factor in many fatal lone-wolf attacks, which might make the perpetrators more gullible or dependent on a co-conspirator.[32]

Our finding is that nine cases of jihadist-linked terrorism in over twenty years of plots involved what we would define as true lone wolves, individuals who acted without direct outside guidance or assistance, face-to-face interaction with fellow conspirators, or interactions with informants whom they mistakenly believed to be like-minded followers of the jihadist cause.[33] All the lone-wolf attempts or attacks that we catalog followed the 9/11 attacks. It is difficult to generalize since the number of perpetrators and plots in question is so small. The perpetrators have few characteristics in common, but all were citizens or residents of the United States. Three were converts to Islam. None of them exhibited noticeable religiosity except for Major Hasan. Five of their targets were military or police. Also, almost all lone wolves completed their attacks, and most were lethal. A plot need not involve a large number of perpetrators to be deadly; the 2016 Orlando shooting left 49 dead. We list two perpetrators for close to a fifth of all plots. Only two people, a married couple, were involved in the attacks in San Bernardino in December 2015, and two brothers in the Boston Marathon bombings in April 2013. The six other plots that also succeeded in causing fatalities involved only one perpetrator.

Who were the lone individuals? Omar Mateen claimed to be acting out of allegiance to ISIS to carry out the Orlando mass shootings in 2016, although his motivations were not clear. The nightclub he targeted was popular with the LGBT community, which may have been his actual motive. Mateen was an American citizen whose parents emigrated from Afghanistan. He had been investigated by the FBI but no evidence was found of jihadist links so he was not under surveillance. In January 2016 Edward Archer, also an American citizen, a convert to Islam, shot and wounded a Philadelphia police officer. He claimed to be acting in the name of Allah and ISIS but his motives were obscure, and no direct links were immediately evident. In July 2015, Muhammad Youssef Abdulazeez killed five American military personnel in two related shooting attacks on a recruiting center and U.S. Navy Reserve center in Chattanooga, Tennessee. Abdulazeez was an engineer who was a naturalized American citizen of Jordanian-Palestinian background. He was apparently influenced by Anwar al-Awlaki but was reported to have had drug and alcohol problems. Zale Thompson, who attacked New York police officers with a hatchet in 2014, was a recent convert to Islam who had consulted Islamist websites but did not state a particular reason for his attack.[34] Naser Abdo, an AWOL soldier himself, plotted to use a bomb to kill American soldiers near Fort Hood, Texas, in 2011.[35] In court, Abdo, a teenage convert to Islam, claimed to be protesting American military crimes against Muslims, and he expressed admiration for Nidal Hasan. In 2010 Yonathan Melaku shot at military buildings in northern Virginia; the prosecutors agreed that he did not intend to harm people.[36] He was a naturalized citizen, originally from Ethiopia, and a Marine reservist. He was arrested at Arlington National Cemetery, apparently intending to deface graves. He claimed to be protesting the wars in Iraq and Afghanistan, but there was a question of mental illness. In June 2009, Abdulhakim Mujahid Muhammed fired on a military recruiting center in Little Rock, Arkansas, killing one soldier and wounding another.[37] Born Carlos Bledsoe, he had converted to Islam while in college and spent time in Yemen, which may be where he was radicalized. He had been interviewed by the FBI but was not under surveillance. He claimed to be a member of al Qa'ida but there was no evidence of contact. Major Nidal Malik Hasan, who was responsible for the Fort Hood shootings in November 2009, was a follower of Anwar al-Awlaki and sought his advice generally via e-mail but was not directed by his instructions as, later, Umar Farouk Abdulmutallab seems to have been. Hasan was unusual in being a serving Army officer and a psychiatrist. At his trial, Hasan stated that his motivation was to defend the Taliban leadership in Afghanistan.[38]

Mohammed Reza Taheri-azar is a puzzling case, indeed on the margins of meeting our requirements for inclusion in the database, since his ideological leanings are obscure. In 2006 he drove a Jeep into a crowd at his alma mater, the University of North Carolina, Chapel Hill. An Iranian who had lived in the United States since he was two, he claimed to be retaliating for the killing of Muslims and America's "immoral behavior."[39] A similarly ambiguous case is that of Hesham Mohamed Hadayet, who in 2002, killed two people at the Los Angeles airport El Al Airlines check-in counter. A resident of Irvine, California, who had lived in the United States for ten years, Hadayet was fervently anti-Israel and possibly a former member of the Egyptian Islamist group Gama'a al-Islamiyya. His motive was never established since he was killed on the scene by El Al security officers.

Three-quarters of the perpetrators of U.S. plots whose residences are known lived in the United States. Excluding the 9/11 hijackers, over 80 percent of perpetrators were U.S. residents. The most common states of residence were New York, New Jersey, Florida, and California. Almost half of the perpetrators were U.S. citizens. If we remove the World Trade Center cases of 1993 and 9/11, well over half of perpetrators were U.S. citizens; some also had dual citizenship. The next largest groups are citizens of Great Britain and of Saudi Arabia; the large 9/11 group accounts for the high number of Saudis. Overall, about 70 percent of perpetrators were Muslims from birth; close to a quarter of perpetrators were converts to Islam. About 6–7 percent were not Muslims. Dhiren Barot, for example, was born in India, and was raised as a Hindu in the United Kingdom. He converted from Hinduism to Islam as a young man in the United Kingdom. He subsequently trained with al Qa'ida in Pakistan, entered the United States in 2000 on a student visa, and conducted extensive target surveillance before returning to the United Kingdom in April 2001. He was arrested in 2004, and in 2006 a British court sentenced him to a lengthy prison term for conspiracy to murder. As noted earlier, he had developed extremely detailed plans for multiple simultaneous attacks in New York and London but had not yet acquired weapons or explosives to carry out the plots.

Which foreign terrorist organizations direct the plots and attacks? Here we are not referring to claiming the act or praising it after the fact but to bearing specific responsibility for its organization, insofar as the public record shows. Two thirds of the American plots we traced could not credibly be linked to the direction of a known organization. Those for which we could ascertain links were mostly tied to al Qa'ida and its Yemeni proxy, AQAP. Of these twenty-seven plots linked to al Qa'ida and AQAP, only four were completed. Of those, only the 9/11 attacks (which we code as one plot) resulted in casualties. We identified three plots that could be linked to ISIS or its predecessor, the Islamic State of Iraq.

We also asked whether a known group claimed credit for the attack or the attempt, regardless of our ability to establish a concrete connection. Groups sometimes claim credit for plots they had nothing to do with, or they do not accept responsibility even though the association seems unquestionable. Sometimes the claim is ambiguous. In the U.S. cases, claiming credit is rare: only six plots were "officially" claimed. Plots that resulted in completed attacks are the 1993 and 9/11 World Trade Center and Pentagon plots and the Orlando and San Bernardino shootings in 2015 and 2016. Plots that did not result in completed attacks were also claimed occasionally. These include the 2009 Christmas bombing attempt, the 2010 Times Square bombing attempt (linked to the Pakistani Taliban), the printer shipment plot in 2010, and the attack on the First Annual Muhammed Art Exhibit and Contest in Garland, Texas, in 2015. ISIS claimed credit for this shooting, in which one school security officer was wounded and the two shooters killed, but it is improbable that the attack was actually directed by the organization. The leader in the plot was Elton Simpson, who converted to Islam while attending high school in Phoenix, Arizona. He had been arrested previously for trying to travel to Somalia and had been sentenced to probation and a fine. He had subsequently been in contact with an ISIS recruiter via Twitter, but the attack plan appeared to be his own. The recruiter was subsequently killed in an American drone strike. (The challenge of reliably attributing attacks is discussed in chapter 5).

Why is responsibility for attacks or plots so rarely claimed? Whether or not the plot results in a completed attack does not seem to make a difference, although our sample is quite small. Possible explanations are that organizations do not claim credit because they hope to escape retaliation or do not need to make public statements since audiences can infer their responsibility from the act itself. Another hypothesis is that groups that are competing with other organizations for the same constituency will be more likely to claim credit in order to boost their status against rivals. In recent years ISIS seemed to accept specific responsibility if the perpetrator made a public statement of allegiance to ISIS but was also willing to take credit generally for attacks that its calls to arms might have inspired.

Plot Outcomes

Success in the sense of a completed attack is rare, whether or not the result is associated with a chosen method. Around a fifth of the plots can be considered at least partially successful; for example, one part of a plot might be foiled while another reaches completion. However, the majority of jihadist plots in or against the United States were foiled, most of those were foiled by the authorities, and most of those were foiled as the result of surveillance or the use of informants. Very few attempts failed completely on their own because of some mistake or loss of resolve on the part of the perpetrators. At least fourteen plots were foiled by the public. In the latter group are the "Christmas bomber," Umar Farouk Abdulmutallab, and Richard Reid, the "shoe bomber"; both were tackled by alert fellow passengers on the aircraft they meant to bring down, even if their bombs would probably have fizzled anyhow. Occasionally, employees of businesses where perpetrators tried to purchase guns or material for explosives have turned them in. Tips to the authorities from members of the public account for only half of the plots foiled by the public.

Fifteen of the foiled plots were intercepted when a foreign government provided assistance, demonstrating the importance of intelligence cooperation and information sharing. For example, in 2010 AQAP's efforts to send two Hewlett-Packard printers with bombs concealed in the ink cartridges to Chicago via FedEx and UPS were thwarted by a tip from the Saudi government. The governments that have provided such assistance with foiling plots are the United Kingdom (eight plots), Saudi Arabia (three), Pakistan (three), and one plot each for Thailand, Lebanon, Russia, France, the United Arab Emirates, and one additional unspecified "Asian country."[40]

As noted earlier, our project defined and identified five distinct plot stages: the perpetrators' initial communication of intent; attempts to acquire capabilities; practice and training for an attack; development of a plan with specification of target and method; and the final implementation stage (the "out-the-door" phase, such as placing a bomb at the target).[41] Almost half of foiled American plots are discovered, and in effect interrupted, by the authorities at the initial stage of the perpetrator's communication of intent. Outside the United States, it is more likely that a plot will be foiled at the stage of attempt to acquire capability or, somewhat less common, to lay out a plan or even in the final implementation stage. Only around 10 percent of American foiled plots are discovered at the last minute, in the final implementation or "out-the-door" stage.

This observation regarding early discovery is consistent with the finding that most attempts are foiled by the use of surveillance and informants, who enter the plot early and often participate in the planning and acquisition of weapons. Apparently few if any plots were foiled because of the analysis of the metadata collected by the National Security Agency.[42] The arrest may not come immediately after discovery of the plot, but there is little to no possibility that perpetrators will be able to carry out their plans once they are revealed, and we do not find any instance of perpetrators eluding the authorities once the latter knew of the plots. In fact, in order to secure a conviction in court the authorities often allow perpetrators to believe that they have carried the plot to conclusion. We find that perpetrators seem to blurt out their intentions to undercover agents or informants with some frequency, leading us to ask how the agents or informants who were paid or hoped to be paid happened to be present. In one case, a would-be perpetrator called attention to himself by going about asking how to buy an al Qa'ida flag. There are also some sting operations.

Sometimes perpetrators were stopped for other offenses or crimes—for example, speeding, robbery, or trespassing—and were discovered to be in possession of weapons or some other evidence that they were planning violent acts.

This early interception is reassuring, but it can also raise questions of entrapment. No entrapment defense has succeeded in terrorism cases in American courts to date, but the use of informants, especially paid informants rather than undercover law enforcement agents, is controversial.[43] Critics charge that law enforcement has stepped across a boundary into actively participating in the plot and also that reliance on informants and sting operations alienates the Muslim communities whose support is essential to preventing terrorism and thus undermines efforts to counter violent extremism and radicalization. It is impossible to know whether the aspiring perpetrators would have been able or willing to carry out the plots without assistance, so everything depends on the credibility of law enforcement officials, especially the FBI and Department of Justice. Most perpetrators of foiled plots possessed little situational awareness and had poor knowledge of basic security practices or tradecraft. However, we could say the same thing about many of the plotters who accomplished their plans.

Foreign Fighters

The "foreign fighter" phenomenon has aroused intense concern, especially after the ISIS declaration of a caliphate in 2014 motivated sympathizers in the West to join the struggle. For purposes of our analysis we define foreign fighters as individuals who attempt to join insurgencies and military actions outside their country of residence, for example the conflicts in Afghanistan, Iraq, Syria, or Libya. A study by Patrick James, Michael Jensen, and Herbert Tinsley found that in a search against more than 30,000 unique news sources that make up the LexisNexis Academic electronic database the term "foreign fighter" only became a term of widespread media use in the middle of 2014.[44] In the United States apprehensions about foreign fighters were heightened in September 2015, when Ali Saleh, a twenty-two-year-old resident of Queens, New York, was arrested after making several failed attempts to join ISIS. At the same time a congressional task force issued a report emphasizing the threat of foreign fighters returning to attack at home.[45]

By the end of 2015 Saleh's story was no longer unique. In recent years, dozens of individuals, many seduced by ISIS's finely tuned social media–enhanced propaganda machine, have attempted to travel to Iraq and Syria to join the terrorist group, causing FBI Director James Comey to proclaim that stopping the flow of fighters to foreign combat zones was among the "highest priorities" for the intelligence community.[46]

An attraction to fighting that was welcomed in the days of resistance to the Soviet occupation of Afghanistan is now distrusted, but the number of foreign fighters is hard to establish with any certitude, and only a small number of these foreign fighters have returned home to commit acts of terrorism (and of these none in the United States as of the summer of 2016). Thomas Hegghammer estimated that the supply of foreign fighters from the West between 1990 and 2010 was 945 individuals.[47] The Soufan Group, a New York–based security consulting firm, found that from the start of the war in Syria in March 2011 through December 2015 between 27,000 and 31,000 foreigners had traveled to Syria and Iraq, whereas up to 2014 there had been only 12,000.[48] By the end of 2015, the number of recruits from North America had remained relatively stable—apparently around 150 Americans traveled to Syria as private citizens to join military groups there since the beginning of the civil war in 2011, and some went to fight against rather than on behalf of ISIS. The number traveling from Western Europe had doubled from June 2014 to December 2015, from 2,500 to 5,000.

In their 2015 study, Patrick James and his colleagues used open-source data to identify 250 Americans who had left, attempted to leave, or expressed an interest in leaving the United States to join foreign conflicts since 1980.[49] The researchers found that these Americans expressed an interest in traveling or did travel to join more than thirty-five different militant groups: 56 were interested in affiliating with ISIS, 49 with al Qa'ida, 38 with al-Shabaab, and 28 with the Taliban. Of the 51 individuals in the foreign-fighter dataset who were eventually linked to terrorist plots in the United States, the majority expressed an interest in becoming foreign fighters but made no convincing attempts to do so. Instead they joined efforts to launch attacks in the United States. The reasons why these individuals gave up foreign travel to attack domestically varied. Some expressed frustration with financial or logistical obstacles to travel or were discouraged by law enforcement surveillance. Others were persuaded by messages from the foreign groups that they were seeking to assist. For example, ISIS had seemed to pivot from making pleas to join the Islamic State in the Middle East to emphasizing instead the importance of staging attacks in the West.

In December 2015 the *Washington Post* counted seventy-three individuals since January 2014 who had been charged with assisting the Islamic State, 22 of whom were convicted in U.S. courts of doing so, sometimes by intending to travel to Syria to fight.[50] This overall count of active rather than passive ISIS sympathizers is alarming, but closer scrutiny shows that only two of these individuals actually traveled to Syria or Iraq. Three seem to have gotten as far as Turkey, and at least seven were arrested attempting to board planes and two others had purchased tickets—but none of these were planning acts of violence at home. Of the total of seventy-three suspects charged, not necessarily convicted, only four had intended to or did travel abroad and also intended to attack at home, although none of them had advanced plans in place. Several simply explained that they wanted to die as martyrs in Syria.

As we explained in chapter 2, we cannot predict the future from past trends, but our data show that from 1993 through the summer of 2016 the threat to American security at home from returning foreign fighters was minimal. Europe has much more of a problem with returned foreign fighters, with greater numbers going and returning, with extremely lethal consequences, as the Paris and Brussels attacks in 2015 and 2016 demonstrate.[51] The *Washington Post* account confirms other academic assessments that individuals who want to travel abroad to fight do not necessarily want to return to carry out attacks at home. For example, Hegghammer argued that only a small minority of jihadis go to fight abroad and then through the experience acquire the motivation to attack at home.[52] Also, the mortality rate in the foreign country of such volunteers is high. We agree on the basis of our own empirical data that the distinction between radicalized individuals who want to attack domestically and those who want to fight abroad is important; the two phenomena should not be conflated.

Our records show that only three of the actual or would-be perpetrators on whom we have information in the FFP dataset, around 150 people, had actually fought or came close to fighting in a jihadist struggle abroad; they were responsible for a total of five plots in 2007, 2009, and 2015. In fact, this is a generous estimate, as the in-theater experiences of the individuals in question are hard to establish. All three returned foreign fighters were American citizens—again, a tiny minority of those who went or wanted to go abroad. It is worth reiterating that none of these foreign fighter plots reached an advanced stage of completion.

These individuals include, most recently, Abdirahman Sheik Mohamud, who was thought possibly to represent the first of a pattern of ISIS returnees in 2015, although his link to ISIS was unsubstantiated. Mohamud was of Somali origin, a naturalized American citizen who lived in Columbus, Ohio. We count him as a returned foreign fighter because he trained in Syria and was apparently instructed to return home to commit an attack rather than continue to fight there, where his brother had been killed. However, his specific group affiliation is unclear; he is charged with adherence to the al-Nusra Front, rather than to ISIS.[53]

We also include as a returned foreign fighter Daniel Boyd, an American citizen residing in North Carolina who at least claimed to have fought in Afghanistan sometime between 1989 and 1992. He organized a group plotting violence in the period from 2006 to 2009, including attacks on American military personnel, possibly at the Marine Corps base at Quantico, although the level of planning was rudimentary.[54] In the end Boyd cooperated with the government and testified against his co-conspirators.

The third returned foreign fighter was also an American citizen, Christopher Paul (born Paul Kenyatta Laws), who like Mohamud was from Columbus, Ohio. He was a convert to Islam. He admitted joining al Qa'ida in the early 1990s and fighting in Afghanistan and Bosnia before returning home with the intention of attacking here in 1999 and 2000.[55] Among the three returned foreign fighters, Paul probably posed the most serious threat. He had connections in Germany, possessed good bomb-making skills, and organized a group of followers in Ohio who trained in a local state park. Hegghammer and Nesser identified a total of sixty-nine jihadist plots in Europe, North America, and Australia combined between 2011 and mid-2015.[56] Almost half were linked to ISIS. Only sixteen of the plots involved the participation of a foreign fighter, and all but one of these occurred in Europe. Three plots involving foreign fighters resulted in attacks: the shootings by Mohammed Merah in France in 2012, the May 2014 attack on the Jewish Museum in Brussels, and the January 2015 Charlie Hebdo attack in Paris. Hegghammer and Nesser published their study before the devastating November 13, 2015, Paris attacks that killed 130 people, the deadliest attack in Europe since the March 2004 bombings in Madrid. ISIS publicly claimed credit for the attacks, which were coordinated by Abdelhamid Abaaoud, a Belgian citizen of Moroccan origin who was an experienced ISIS operative in Syria and who had even been featured in ISIS propaganda videos. At least three other members of the Paris team were also returned foreign fighters from Syria.[57] These attacks appeared in hindsight to be the beginning of a campaign, followed by the January 2016 attack on tourists in Istanbul and the March 2016 Brussels bombings. The United States responded to the Paris attacks with air strikes in Syria that killed several members of the ISIS external operations wing, the branch that organized attacks in Europe.

It is more likely that American domestic perpetrators have trained outside the country rather than that they have fought abroad, but the number is still only around 10 percent of those individuals we have information about. This category of citizens who have trained outside the country is important because it stands to reason that individuals seeking training are more likely to be doing so precisely in order to gain the skills and capabilities to attack at home, and that the training will make them more dangerous. As is often the case with motivations for terrorism, it is difficult to gain precise information on intentions, and some may seek training because they intend to stay abroad and fight there. It is sometimes difficult to distinguish between training and fighting, although we think it is important not to conflate the two.[58] If we omit the nineteen 9/11 hijackers and other accomplices in that complex plot, as well as the perpetrators who were returned foreign fighters, from 1993 through 2015 we identify fifteen perpetrators in the United States who trained abroad, out of the pool of around 150 perpetrators for whom information is available.

It is difficult to discern a pattern or trend in such small numbers, although most of these men had trained in Afghanistan or the tribal areas of Pakistan in al Qa'ida training camps. Bosnia was also a preferred training ground. One perpetrator trained in Saudi Arabia, another in Ethiopia, and Umar Farouk Abdulmutallab apparently trained in Yemen with AQAP. Only two instances of foreign training occurred before 9/11: Ramzi Yousef and Ahmad Ressam, both linked to al Qa'ida and trained in the use of explosives. We might also count Dhiren Barot, since he started reconnaissance and planning before 9/11 although his plot was discovered later. He was a committed al Qa'ida operative, not an amateur volunteer.

Some of these returned trainees may have traveled initially because they wanted to fight in the local conflict theater and were then persuaded to return home without fighting, but it is hard to be sure. Najibullah Zazi and his two accomplices, Adis Medunjanin and Zarein Ahmedzay, may fit this pattern. Zazi trained with al Qa'ida and planned attacks in New York in 2009. The important conclusion is that even if foreign fighters and those seeking training are combined, the numbers for the United States are still very small, under twenty people. The kind of useful training for aspiring terrorists is most likely to be in the use of explosives, but training is not a guarantee that they can build a device that will explode. Thus, al Qa'ida training for those in the Zazi-Medunjanin-Ahmedzay conspiracy and Faisal Shahzad's attempted Time Square car-bombing in 2010 did not ensure success. Note also that even though the shoe bomber, Richard Reid, and Abdulmutallab did not build their own bombs, their plots nonetheless failed owing to technical problems.

Why would jihadis prefer foreign fighting to domestic terrorism? Hegghammer concluded, "A majority of Western jihadis choose foreign fighting over domestic fighting, most likely because they have come to view the former as more legitimate after observing the distribution of views among religious authorities. The preference for foreign fighting among Western jihadis as a group has weakened over time, because foreign fighting has become more difficult and more ideologues encourage domestic fighting. Still, the preference remains strong."[59]

By 2015, however, Hegghammer suspected that attacking at home might be becoming more legitimate.[60] In addition, foreign fighting became more difficult as Western governments moved to block and punish travel attempts. As the resources available to ISIS in its caliphate were reduced by military pressure from its many enemies, the attractions of joining up as well as the ability of ISIS to organize foreign recruits might also have been diminished.

Although the issue of foreign fighters and especially ISIS recruitment efforts is serious and in many ways novel, the American foreign fighter phenomenon is hardly new. The study by Patrick James and his colleagues showed that Americans sought to associate themselves with foreign conflicts well before the advent of search engines and well beyond transnational jihadism.[61] The James study pointed out that Americans operated in well-organized volunteer brigades on the Republican side of the Spanish Civil War; American citizens joined British and Commonwealth forces many months in advance of an American declaration of war on the Axis Powers in 1941; and Americans with sympathy for Jewish nationalism flung themselves into the 1948 Arab-Israeli conflict. More recently, Americans have fought on both sides of the unrest in Ukraine, and possibly the number of Americans traveling to Iraq and Syria to join the Kurdish forces and Christian militias that are taking on ISIS was nearly the same as the number that have joined jihadist groups.[62]

Conclusions and Policy Implications

The terrorist threat to the United States from individuals and groups committed to jihadist causes is shifting and amorphous, showing the complexity that characterizes all aspects of terrorism. There are few clear patterns other than that most perpetrators behind U.S. plots are young men who are American citizens or residents, there are very few returned foreign fighters among them, and there also very few individuals who entered the country as refugees. Most are Muslims from diverse immigrant family backgrounds, although there is a significant proportion of converts to Islam. The majority are not formally associated with a known extremist organization. That said, individuals follow different pathways to the development of violent intentions and plans for action. Their backgrounds and experiences are heterogeneous, and it is difficult even for the FBI after investigation to predict who might become a terrorist.

Fortunately few of the plotters succeeded in their goal of killing Americans. In the period following 9/11 we count ten jihadist plots that resulted in ninety-three victim fatalities. None of these plots were the work of large-scale conspiracies or organized networks, and there was no question of any degree of community support. Only one person was responsible for each of eight plots, and two people carried out the other two, yielding a total of ten individuals who had the intention, capability, and opportunity to kill people. Three of the targets of the plots were military, four were ordinary civilians (nightclub patrons, a workplace party, a marathon crowd, and four random individuals shot in public places), and the last was an airline counter. All were shootings except for the Boston Marathon bombing.

In addition, context has to be taken into account in evaluating individual ideological commitment. When al Qa'ida was the leading representative of violent jihadist extremism and the centerpiece of media attention, more perpetrators identified with or were dispatched by that organization, and when ISIS came to dominate the field, after 2014, the trend shifted correspondingly. This brand change is not surprising. Similarly, communications via social media appear increasingly to play an integral role in arousing sympathy for violent jihadism, again quite predictably because all contemporary fads and trends, especially among young people, are shaped, if not driven, by social media.

Thus, policies developed to counter violent extremism or prevent radicalization need to be more specific and more flexible. Ostensibly directed at all ideological extremists, the policies are understood as targeting those who express violent jihadist sympathies that are loosely linked to terrorism. Even if restricted to jihadism, the policy applies the same treatment to a variety of activities. Such a one-size-fits-all approach cannot possibly produce useful results. Programs designed to halt the small flow of American foreign fighters to conflict zones are unlikely to halt violent attacks at home. In the end, by publicizing the popularity of, first, al Qa'ida and then ISIS, government and media may make it more likely that young men and a few young women will find the jihadist cause an attractive outlet or excuse for inclinations toward adventure, rebellion, or antisocial behavior.

Aspirations to achieve personal significance, express anger, or establish identity may be channeled into a path that is available and salient and provides meaning.

In addition, by emphasizing comprehensive prevention of terrorist attacks ("zero tolerance") American policies have pushed the interruption of plots further back in the sequence of development, leading to the apprehension of individuals whose commitment and abilities are questionable. Although this approach is understandable in a failure-averse policy environment, the government risks loss of credibility if the plots seem naive and unsophisticated and the would-be attackers inept and confused. Officials have also moved to criminalize diverse manifestations of what they label extremism and extremist views, not just actual plans to use violence against the United States. The Obama administration's Countering Violent Extremism (CVE) policy was couched in benign terms: its ostensible aim was to persuade those presumed to be susceptible to resist the temptation of ideological radicalization, counter the jihadist narrative, engage local communities in prevention and resilience, and build awareness of indicators of radicalization and recruitment. In practice, however, preventive counterterrorism policy has been characterized by large numbers of arrests for many different criminal offenses, most based on charges of some form of "material support" of terrorism. The brunt of operational policy is punitive. For example, on December 25, 2015, the *Washington Post* reported that according to the Justice Department sixty people had been charged with terrorism-related offenses so far that year, with the majority under the age of twenty-five.[63] Sentences are generally severe.[64]

The focus of official CVE efforts is on Muslim communities in Boston, Los Angeles, and the Twin Cities. However, our information on place of residence of perpetrators who plotted violent attacks at home shows that none of the individuals on whom we have data resided in the Twin Cities, four resided in Boston and Cambridge, and six were located in Los Angeles. This last set is anomalous in including four individuals who were radicalized in Folsom Prison, where they came under the influence of a charismatic convert to Islam. The conspirators had no known outside links but established their own organization, the Jamiyyat ul-Islam Is-Saheeh (JIS), or Authentic Assembly of Islam. The CVE measures introduced in 2015 were unlikely to have altered their behavior and their city of residence appears to be irrelevant.

An additional difficulty is that U.S. counterterrorism policy has not integrated domestic CVE efforts with foreign policy initiatives that would diminish the appeal of jihadist organizations and ideologies. Many of the individuals in our dataset explained their motive as opposition to the American use of military force against Muslims in civil conflicts abroad. If there is a consistent theme it is an emotional one of punishment or revenge. Military responses to terrorism, such as drone strikes against leaders or retaking ISIS territories in Iraq and Syria, have not diminished the appeal. Ideologues' reputations remain strong after the men's death. Americans leaving to fight or train abroad would not be a concern if there were not civil wars pitting Muslims against each other and against non-Muslims. Fighting in Somalia or Syria, or Bosnia and Afghanistan before that, responds to a call to arms to defend a religious, ethnic, or national community against its perceived enemies, foreign and domestic. More young men went to Syria after 2011 because travel through Turkey was logistically feasible, fighting against the immense brutality of the Assad regime was easy to justify, after 2014 ISIS had territory to defend, and the promise of a reborn caliphate that would build support for Islam worldwide was compelling. In many ways, American policy is trying to discredit the jihadist narrative and degrade ISIS messaging through social media without addressing the content of the communications to be countered.

CHAPTER 4

Pinning Down an Elusive Adversary

What Is a Terrorist Organization?

Our analysis of failed and foiled plots in the last chapter stressed the importance of arriving at a comprehensive and realistic view of the jihadist threat to Americans at home. Because so many plans are blocked at an early stage, it can be difficult to judge the seriousness of the danger. The perpetrators are also diverse, although the majority are U.S. citizens or residents. In this chapter we examine the more general problem of specifying the precise organizational nature of the actors responsible for terrorism, an issue for both academic researchers and government policymakers and analysts. We describe and explain the organizational variety, complexity, and fluidity that lie behind a constantly shifting terrorist threat.

These difficulties in pinning down a definition of the enemy have important policy implications because in order to respond effectively to terrorist attacks policymakers must link attacks to individuals or entities against which the government can direct a well-designed and consistent response. Identifying perpetrators is essential to understanding the causes of terrorism and establishing policy priorities. Who should be the subject of counterterrorism policy, whether the target of military force abroad or the object of softer efforts to counter extremism at home? How can specific adversaries be identified in order to diminish their capability and influence their strategic calculus and behavior, assuming that there is a strategy behind terrorism?

Discussions of counterterrorism often refer to the terrorist's lack of a street address, but the problem goes well beyond inability to physically locate shadowy enemies and identify their material assets. Without knowledge of terrorist decisionmaking structures, leadership, and cohesiveness as well as other organizational dimensions, governments will struggle to anticipate how terrorists will react to counterterrorism measures. For example, if the adversary has no leader, "decapitation" strikes cannot be effective.

Academic research on defining terrorist actors has been less than systematic.[1] Although there are many qualitative and quantitative studies of the actors using terrorism, the precise concept of what constitutes a terrorist group or terrorist organization is still disputed. Most definitions are inconsistent, incompatible, or not made explicit at all, even though how a terrorist group is defined has important implications for research findings, especially those based on quantitative measures. Government labeling of a group as a terrorist organization also has important political, economic, and social ramifications. In the late 1990s, during the Balkan wars, Robert Gelbard, the Clinton administration's special envoy to the Balkans, famously called the Kosovo Liberation Army (KLA) a terrorist group and was subsequently accused of giving Serbia the green light to crush popular resistance in Kosovo, thus sparking NATO intervention. (When American leaders decided that it was prudent to negotiate with the KLA, they called it an insurgency.) Putting a group on the State Department's official list of foreign terrorist organizations (FTOs) results in serious financial and other penalties that constrain their activities. It is illegal for any person in the United States to knowingly provide material support to an FTO through financial contributions or any other services. Representatives and members of FTOs may not be permitted entry into the United States and if they are not citizens, may be removed from the United States. Financial institutions are ordered to take possession of funds controlled by FTOs.[2]

It could be said that a terrorist group is any nonstate political organization that uses terrorism, but researchers still need to figure out what an organization is, and this question is hard to answer and the answers are often contentious.[3] It is not easy to link organizational characteristics to terrorist behavior and to threat levels and then to the appropriate counterterrorism response.

Our principal argument in this chapter is that from both a policy and research standpoint the concept of a terrorist organization is an abstraction around which there is a great deal of variation, even leaving aside the political and pejorative connotations of labeling a group a terrorist organization. First, the degree of organizational complexity of the entities that carry out terrorist attacks differs significantly. On one end of the spectrum are individuals who are not members of any known political movement and who have no recognized or formal links to a specific group. They do not appear to have received help in planning or carrying out a specific attack. Many of the threats analyzed in the preceding chapter came from "homegrown" extremists or "self-radicalized" individuals. On the other end of the spectrum of complexity are highly organized groups that persist over time, have a more or less well-defined chain of command, and exhibit stable leadership along with hierarchical organizational structures. They have names such as al Qa'ida or ISIS under which they issue claims of responsibility and offer explicit justifications for violence. In principle, researchers could trace how such groups' collective decisions are made. In between these two extremes are unconnected or only loosely connected groups as well as shadowy networks that sometimes can be identified only generically in very general ideological terms, such as "violent jihadists." All these disparate entities are typically in a state of evolutionary flux within and among themselves; change is constant and stability rare. Yet understanding the dynamics of different group trajectories is essential for sound policymaking.[4]

Second, the organizational capacity of different actors as displayed in attack patterns over time is highly uneven. Some groups are able and willing to attack frequently over many years; others attack only sporadically or over a short period of time. A surprisingly large number of groups identified in the Global Terrorism Database (GTD) are linked to a single attack only. A handful of groups have continuous operations over decades, but many stage all of their attacks in less than a year. It is typical to think of terrorism as a type of political violence that occurs in sustained campaigns with clearly observable beginnings and endings, but such a distinctive path is not always evident. At the very least many acts do not fit neatly into this model—they are more inconsistent and unpredictable or follow a pattern that cannot easily be discerned.

Third, there is the question of group cohesion and the reality of splits, splinters, and factions. What appears to be a relatively stable entity can quickly disintegrate or spin off new groups. The splinters may form new organizations with independent strategies or merge into other existing groups.

This process is related to a fourth additional source of uncertainty, which is the state of relationships among groups. It is unusual for a government to confront a monolithic adversary. Instead, counterterrorism strategy, whether domestic or international, usually has to take into account multiple groups of different types who compete, cooperate, and merge in kaleidoscopic fashion. Splits are not the only cause for the multiplicity of groups; new groups can enter the scene. For example, a hitherto peaceful political party might spin off a violent offshoot.

Finally, influencing the development of all of these processes within and between organizations is the growing transnational importance of electronic media. Ease and ubiquity of communication provide contemporary terrorist actors with broad new options for connectivity. In many ways social media can impose unity of effort and purpose over a broad array of actor types. Social media can link the individual to the organization in virtual space. Even actions that are individually planned and executed may still form part of a larger campaign that shares goals and methods.

We conclude the chapter with observations on policy implications of the analysis of dynamics within and between groups. Responses are complicated by the fluid, multifaceted, and adaptive character of the adversary.

How Is a Terrorist Group Defined?

For many people, the first thing that comes to mind when they hear the term "terrorist group" is the extremely active organizations that have become household words around the globe: violent jihadist groups such as al Qa'ida, ISIS, the Pakistani Taliban, al-Shabaab, and Boko Haram, and nonjihadist groups such as the FARC (Fuerzas Armadas Revolucionarias de Colombia, or Revolutionary Armed Forces of Colombia) and Hezbollah in Lebanon. Many other groups that have not been active in recent years—the Provisional IRA, the Italian Red Brigades, the German Red Army Faction, the Shining Path of Peru, Black September, the Popular Front for the Liberation of Palestine, the Liberation Tigers of Tamil Eelam—were nonetheless deadly, well-known, and seemingly long-lasting in the past. But these impressions of enduring and formidable structures can be misleading. They suggest a degree of concreteness and indeed simplicity that is often greatly at odds with a confusing reality. The organizational disaggregation of the threat that we analyzed with regard to U.S. plots is a wider and more general phenomenon.

Lone Actors

In recent years individuals using terrorist methods have been variously referred to by researchers and policymakers as lone wolves, lone attackers, bottom-up solo terrorists, lone offenders, or simply loners.[5] A typical view is that attacks by such isolated individuals are growing in number and are extremely difficult to predict and prevent. These different labels obscure important operational distinctions, some of which were hinted at in chapter 3. For example, the criminologist Brent Smith and his colleagues distinguish true loners from affiliated loners.[6] According to their research, true loners had no help planning or engaging in precursor activities with organized groups or movements prior to the attack, had no assistance committing the attack, and claim no ideological affiliation with a group or a movement. A possible example is the case of Paul Ciancia. On November 1, 2013, Ciancia opened fire on Transportation Security Administration agents in a terminal at Los Angeles International Airport, killing one TSA agent and wounding two others as well as five civilians. Although Ciancia claimed responsibility, saying that he wanted to kill and to instill fear in TSA officers, he had no apparent help in planning or committing the attack and did not identify with a specific group or movement. On November 2, 2013, federal prosecutors charged Ciancia with murder of a federal officer and committing violence at an international airport. Prosecutors subsequently sought the death penalty. He was awaiting trial as this book went to press. This true loner's actions had a major impact on airport security.

Affiliated loners likewise receive no apparent help in planning for or committing a terrorist attack, but they consider themselves to be part of a broader extremist political movement. The mass shooting at Fort Hood, Texas, on November 5, 2009, by Nidal Malik Hasan, the U.S. Army major and psychiatrist, may be classified as the work of an affiliated loner. Hasan had no known help in preparing for or executing the attack. However, he claimed some loyalty to a somewhat vague version of jihadist ideology and had asked Anwar al-Awlaki, the leader of al Qa'ida in the Arabian Peninsula (AQAP), for religious advice via e-mail correspondence. Another example of an affiliated loner is Arid Uka, who carried out an attack that killed two U.S. servicemen at the Frankfurt airport in March 2011. Uka had no known personal contacts with or assistance from anyone else but claimed that through his participation in several Islamist forums he came to the belief that his Muslim fellows were in global war with the United States.

Smith and his colleagues also identify lone conspirators. Like true loners and affiliated loners, lone conspirators act on their own when carrying out attacks. However, the lone conspirators consider themselves to be part of a broader extremist movement and also receive help in planning attacks. Timothy McVeigh is an example. McVeigh, a Gulf War veteran, became increasingly obsessed with the power and reach of the federal government and hoped to inspire a revolt against it. He acted alone when he launched the devastating attack on the Alfred P. Murrah Federal Building in downtown Oklahoma City on April 19, 1995. The bombing killed 168 people, injured more than 650 others, and destroyed or damaged 324 buildings within a sixteen-block radius. McVeigh was eventually convicted, sentenced to death, and executed.

But while McVeigh delivered the bomb alone, he considered himself to be part of a general far right extremist movement that was especially upset by the federal government's handling of the stand-off with Randy Weaver at Ruby Ridge in 1992 and the 1993 stand-off between the FBI and members of the Branch Davidian religious cult in Waco, Texas. McVeigh was aided by several others, especially Terry Nichols, whom he met in 1988 at Fort Benning during basic training for the U.S. Army. McVeigh and Nichols purchased or stole the materials they needed to manufacture the bomb, which they stored in rented sheds. Nichols was eventually sentenced to life without parole for his role in the attack. Michael Fortier, McVeigh's Army roommate, assisted McVeigh in scouting the Murrah Federal Building, and his wife, Lori, helped McVeigh laminate a fake driver's license, which was later used to rent the Ryder truck that delivered the bomb. Michael Fortier agreed to testify against McVeigh and Nichols in exchange for a reduced sentence and immunity for his wife and was convicted and sentenced to twelve years in prison.

The Tsarnaev brothers, who carried out the Boston Marathon bombings, represent another variation in the general category of lone actors. They might be classified as affiliated loners—they apparently considered themselves a part of the radical Chechen separatist movement—but they received no known help from anyone in planning or conducting the Boston bombings. Indeed, the Boston bombing case represents a further complexity in lone offender classifications: while it resembles other cases in which offenders operated without direct participation in an organized group, there were two brothers rather than a single lone actor.[7] The psychological and social dynamics in such cases are surely different, as they presumably were in the more recent case of the married couple in San Bernardino, California, who killed fourteen people and seriously injured twenty-two in a shooting spree on December 2, 2015. All of these designations presuppose that we have sufficient information on attacks to accurately make these types of classification decisions.

These examples raise an important question: Should we simply exclude lone individuals from our organizational framework? Our view is that when lone actors do not see themselves as acting alone but in the framework of a collectivity, we are justified in explaining them in organizational terms. These individuals believe that they are acting in the name of a larger identity and for a shared cause. They have a sense of group solidarity and purpose, even if they are not formally members of an organization. Their behavior may be situated in a broader discourse or narrative—whether violent jihadist, as in the case of the Fort Hood shooter, Major Hasan, or anti-Muslim and antimulticulturalist "patriotic resistance," as in the case of Anders Breivik, who killed seventy-seven Norwegians, mostly teenagers, in 2011, first by bombing government buildings and then staging a mass shooting at a youth camp. In addition, their actions may be their response to deliberate appeals by an established organization to protect the interests of a community. The actions of such individuals are not spontaneously generated from a sense of individual grievance but steered by a group and its ideology, even if the adoption of that set of beliefs is opportunistic or driven by personal frustrations.

Again, the Boston Marathon bombers are a case in point. The two brothers apparently took it on themselves to act in the name of what they believed to be a persecuted Muslim community. However, had it not been for the organized expression of these views through al Qa'ida and its propaganda branches, it is difficult to imagine the Tsarnaev brothers choosing the path that they did—constructing bombs to kill random civilians, fellow Americans in the case of Dzhokhar Tsarnaev (a factor that counted against him in the prosecution's demand for the death penalty).

We need to understand at least three elements of the process whereby violence results from possible individual self-radicalization: the source or author of the messages; the communications themselves—the content and means of transmission; and the susceptibility of the recipients. References to self-radicalization of violent extremists or homegrown or self-generated terrorism are common, but these terms may confuse the issue of responsibility. The individuals did volunteer, but they were often answering an appeal. It is hard to say that they were not recruited in light of the fact that al Qa'ida and ISIS have called specifically for inspirational violence at home by individual followers. The call to arms represents a deliberate strategy from the top of the organization, which with such long-distance, unidirectional contact gives up control of operatives in return for high levels of activity on the ground and greater global reach. In part the strategy is an adaptation to U.S. government countermeasures since 9/11 that have made it increasingly difficult for foreign-based organizations to act directly in the United States. Presumably organizations such as AQAP or ISIS will continue to try to strike from outside, as the 2009 Christmas bombing plot showed.

Levels of Organizational Complexity in Groups

Even if the discussion moves beyond lone actors to focus on groups, there are still major conceptual and methodological challenges. These problems are illustrated by a sometimes acrimonious debate among experts about whether terrorists coalesce in largely transitory pick-up groups without any real leadership, consistent direction, or permanence ("bunches of guys" or "leaderless resistance") or are organized in conspiracies with authoritative leaders who maintain the loyalty of followers and possess and communicate a strategic sense of purpose.[8] These arguments are related to another contentious academic discussion over "old" versus "new" terrorism, with some experts claiming that trying to inflict mass casualties, entertaining apocalyptic ambitions, and forming decentralized organizations are characteristics completely new and unprecedented in the world of terrorism, whereas others argue for historical continuity and the value of comparisons across time.[9] Some proponents of the "new" terrorism argument claim that the organization of terrorism has changed forever to "flat," decentralized organizations, while the other side stresses the importance of leadership, hierarchy, and direction.

These debates are further influenced by the assimilation of theories that treat the terrorist group as an informal social network rather than a top-down organization.[10] From this perspective the social network and internal group dynamics come first, engagement in terrorist activity second. Trust among the members of an operational cell is established by prior affiliative ties among friends and family as much as by commitment to an ideological cause. Another implication of the social network argument is that it is through such informal connections that small independent groups stay in touch with each other. Social networks can produce in-group cohesion as well as cross-group connectivity.

The messy reality is likely somewhere in the middle of these opposing views. Speaking in general terms, the next step up in structure from individuals is the small group or cell that is formed largely on the basis of social networks, which may be local or transnational, if it involves different nationalities and places of residence, a mix that is more common in Europe than the United States. There may not be extensive role differentiation within such friendship and kinship groups, but there is informal leadership, communication within the group, and some division of responsibility. The Norwegian researcher Petter Nesser has argued that small groups are not necessarily leaderless at all. Even in cells of four people, someone plays the role of leader.[11] Such small cells can also exhibit impressive staying power across generations of militants.

As time has passed since 9/11, a key question in dispute among terrorism experts has become whether such groups, however small and transitory, have organizational links to al Qa'ida or ISIS or are autonomous players acting in their own name or with the diffuse (or confused) intent of furthering violent jihad. That is, are such small groups more like an organization or more like a haphazard conglomeration of self-directed individuals? It has proved difficult to tell which is which, certainly in a timely way.

This issue is important if there is any chance that a small, informal group has links to larger, more organized, and more dangerous groups such as al Qa'ida, its regional associates such as AQAP or Lashkar-e-Taiba, and ISIS and its respective allies that are correlated with more destructive terrorism. If perpetrators have gained experience fighting or training abroad their attacks at home might be more lethal. This is one reason for intense concern about the engagement of foreign fighters in the Syrian conflict. Will they return to their home countries with enhanced skills and determination because of their organizational links to seasoned fighters? As we noted in chapter 3, research findings are mixed, but the multiple and deadly attacks in November 2015 in Paris and in March 2016 in Brussels by ISIS-organized cells exhibited a disturbing professionalism.

The debate about the extent to which small cells operate independently or are more directly linked to a centralized organization has implications for public concerns about terrorism. The threat of terrorism is frightening if we assume that there is central direction of a worldwide network capable of a sustained series of coordinated campaigns, but it is also frightening if we assume that violent jihadism as an ideology can metastasize effectively through free-lancers who are radicalized via the Internet without direct contact with each other or an organization.

The extent to which groups are independent versus closely connected to a parent organization may also change over time. The German terrorism expert Guido Steinberg has argued that in the immediate aftermath of the overwhelming security reaction to the 9/11 attacks, would-be violent jihadists in Germany formed independent local cells in order to evade detection.[12] However, they quickly discovered that although there was an advantage to being under the radar (for example, there were no communications with the center that could be traced by government intelligence agencies), the disadvantage was lack of access to training and transfer of operational skills. As a consequence, the process began to reverse itself as local cells themselves reached out to the center for assistance rather than being recruited by the center. Thus centralization gave way to decentralization, only to be reversed.

Certainly groups like the original al Qa'ida and ISIS as it operated in Syria and Iraq are at the most tightly organized end of the organizational complexity spectrum. There are many historical precedents for hierarchical organizations with differentiated roles and functions as well as impressive operational continuity, and these are the ones usually portrayed as stereotypical terrorist organizations. On the nationalist side there is the pre-1998 Provisional Irish Republican Army, which had an Army Council and a public relations and political party wing, Sinn Fein. On the left revolutionary side the FARC in Colombia exhibits unity of command and effort. The original al Qa'ida as founded in the 1980s through the 1990s was highly structured, with an impressive organizational chart and well-established decisionmaking processes. What mainly differentiated it from other disciplined groups was its transnational ambition. In this respect, historically, the anarchist movement of the late nineteenth and early twentieth centuries is the closest precedent, but one might also think of the relevance of the communist revolutionary movement (despite its ultimate direction by a state rather than a nonstate actor). Anarchist violence was more centrally directed and coordinated than is commonly thought, and as we mentioned in chapter 1 it originated the concepts of "inspirational" terrorism and "propaganda by the deed." However, it was by no means as structured as the original al Qa'ida.

After the fall of the Taliban and the relocation of al Qa'ida to Pakistan, it became harder for the group to maintain control from the center, and the organization began to transition to a decentralized operation more likely to inspire or delegate than to plan attacks. It also relied increasingly on its affiliates and subsidiaries to act in its name. This transformation represented organizational adaptation to a new and more dangerous security environment. It is noteworthy that the only attack claimed by the core al Qa'ida organization and included in the GTD after 2008 was the kidnapping in Lahore, Pakistan, of Warren Weinstein, a seventy-year-old American employed as a contractor by J. E. Austin Associates, on August 13, 2011. In December 2011, al Qa'ida leader Ayman al-Zawahiri released an audio recording claiming responsibility for the kidnapping and stating that Weinstein would be released if a number of demands were met, including the release of prisoners and an end to bombing in Pakistan, Afghanistan, Yemen, Somalia, and Gaza. In 2015 Weinstein was unintentionally killed in an American drone strike. Although al Qa'ida has claimed no attacks since 2008, its affiliates such as al-Nusra, AQAP, and AQIM (al Qa'ida in the Islamic Maghreb) took up the banner.

Al Qa'ida's evolution shows how difficult it is for any tightly structured organization to maintain security and control under pressure. Key problems for al Qa'ida's organizational maintenance were communication blockages and delays and the absence of a secure sanctuary for efficient direction from headquarters. Bin Laden himself was eventually isolated and alone in a compound in Abbottabad, communicating exclusively through courier although still involved in collective decisions. It became difficult to ascertain whether local groups claiming to act in the name of al Qa'ida were linked directly to the leadership in Pakistan (at first under bin Laden and, after his death in 2010, Ayman al-Zawahiri) or were opportunistic adopters of the al Qa'ida brand. (We will take up attribution problems in the next chapter.)

These complications emerged as early as 2003, when Zarqawi in Iraq assumed the al Qa'ida mantle but was so determinedly independent and ruthless that Zawahiri tried to rein him in. His tactics were alienating even the most committed Sunni Islamist supporters in Iraq. By 2014, Zawahiri had explicitly disavowed ISIS in favor of al-Nusra, and he also maintained good relations with some of the other non-ISIS violent Islamist groups in Syria. In the summer of 2016 al-Nusra in turn broke from al Qa'ida and assumed the new name of Jabhat Fath al-Sham.

Groups such as Lashkar-e-Taiba (LeT) in Pakistan, AQIM in Algeria and West Africa, and AQAP in Yemen probably follow a local and national agenda more than an al Qa'ida internationalist program. By signing on to al Qa'ida they risk incurring the wrath of the United States and its fleet of remotely piloted aircraft as well as special operations forces. Yet despite the apparently unfavorable balance between costs and benefits, the brand is still valuable to them for reasons that are poorly understood but surely have much to do with its ideological appeal to potential followers. These prospective recruits come not only from the general population but also from militants in rival Islamist groups who could be enticed to defect, thus affecting group cohesion in ways that we will discuss in a following section.

Violent nonstate actors can be formed and organized in myriad ways. Many models coexist, from loose pick-up groups to tightly organized conspiracies, along with other forms and hybrids. One type can evolve into another, and quickly. Moreover, there are also umbrella and franchise operations.[13] In other words, real-world cases fit into many different organizational frameworks, and academic researchers and government analysts may never have sufficient information to take even an approximate measure to make clear categorization possible. The policy implications of this limitation is that despite their best intelligence efforts, governments combatting terrorism must be resigned to operating under conditions of high uncertainty.

Since the reality involves shades of gray—there are complicated and multiple varieties of organizational categories—the problem is to figure out the why, where, when, and how of these dynamics. Certainly some organizational imperatives are forced on all violent extremist groups by their circumstances, such as intense concern for secrecy and security, and underground conspiracies face many of the same routine challenges as any other organization.[14] They need to recruit members and supporters, maintain their members' loyalty, pay at least some of them, organize activities, raise money, communicate, and gain public visibility without endangering security. Some, like ISIS, need to govern and conduct major military operations as well as transnational terrorist activities. These needs and constraints impose some uniform features on all of them.

However, actors also have different missions and adapt differently to their environments. We pointed out how the original al Qa'ida adapted to new pressures and new opportunities. It is important to recognize that constraints and opportunities vary according to specific context, such as how tolerated a group may be by local authorities and the extent of popular support. Some groups have much more organizational flexibility than others, despite all being equally violent opponents of the state. For example, underground groups may function as the armed wings of recognized political parties with representation in legislative assemblies. They may operate in failed or failing states or ungoverned spaces within established states. A case exhibiting both characteristics is al-Shabaab in Somalia, which emerged as an independent entity in 2006. It was previously the military wing of the Islamic Courts Union. Somalia is a classic failed state and safe haven, as well as an attraction for aspiring American foreign fighters. Another environmental condition is the number of groups in a given oppositional constellation. Some groups have many competitors operating in the same space for the same audience, while others dominate a struggle or are part of a broad coalition.

Of course researchers often do not know the level of organization of terrorist perpetrators, at least not in the short run. An instructive case is the ambiguous status of the group responsible for the Madrid train station bombings in 2004, which killed 191 people. Experts still disagree as to whether the perpetrators were free-lancers or representatives of al Qa'ida. The GTD lists the Abu Hafs al-Masri Brigades as the suspected perpetrator and notes that the group is associated with al Qa'ida and that it claimed responsibility for the attacks as retribution for Spain's cooperation with the United States in the Iraq War. But the GTD then concludes that the Abu Hafs al-Masri Brigades' claim of responsibility may not be valid.[15] The group is named after Abu Hafs, an Egyptian who was a member of Ayman al-Zawahiri's al-Jihad al-Islami (Islamic Jihad). Abu Hafs became a relative of Osama bin Laden after his daughter married bin Laden's son. Abu Hafs was killed by U.S. airstrikes in Afghanistan in late 2001. But what organization is behind the name? The Brigades' existence is known only through communiqués sent to the press, and some of the claims were patently false. It is not listed by the United States as a Foreign Terrorist Organization or proscribed by any other government. Most of the members of the Madrid group died in an explosion of their own making. On the other hand, taking into account court proceedings and subsequent intelligence discoveries, the Spanish terrorism expert Fernando Reinares argues that the bombings were the direct work of al Qa'ida.[16] A local social network existed, but al Qa'ida's leadership approved its operations. Some of the members of the network were also members of North African groups formally affiliated with al Qa'ida, showing how overlapping memberships can obscure the boundaries between organizations and how social networks can be part of a top-down process.

The 2005 London subway and bus bombings are another example of both belated discovery of the apparent facts and mixed organizational responsibility.[17] Two members of the four-person cell of suicide bombers who committed the July 7 attacks, including the leader, were directly recruited by al Qa'ida. But they were also part of a group of friends who frequented the same gym and went on outdoor excursions together in Beeston, North Yorkshire, where they grew up. The leader was a popular figure in the community who worked with disadvantaged youths.

Another thorny complication for governments trying to prevent or contain terrorism is that the terrorists can be part of or allied with larger collectives such as political parties or social movements that are legitimate, legal, and public. In Pakistan, for example, some of the Islamic political parties that contest elections and occupy governmental positions not only espouse the same goals as violent extremists but endorse or cooperate with them. Their militant connections include both Afghan and Pakistani Taliban organizations as well as the post-2008 incarnation of Lashkar-e-Taiba.[18] Extremist undergrounds recruit members from their mosques and madrassas. In Lebanon's nonjihadist universe, Hezbollah grew into a prominent if not indispensable member of governing coalitions, and its social service networks gained it widespread popular support that led to electoral success. It is also an ally of Iran and a major military force that has been critical to keeping Assad in power in Syria. Hamas is another case of a democratically elected organization governing territorial space in the Gaza Strip but that also practices terrorism against Israel. A related question with regard to both Hezbollah and Hamas is the extent to which they should be defined as nonstate actors. Banning such organizations, or in the case of external players, adding them to lists of designated terrorist organizations, can impose high political costs. Moreover, if the U.S. grand strategic foreign policy goal is to sustain democracy in the Middle East, its implementation faces complications when democratically elected political parties espouse violence.

FIGURE 4-1. Total Number of Attacks Attributed to
2,337 Terrorist Groups, 1970–2015

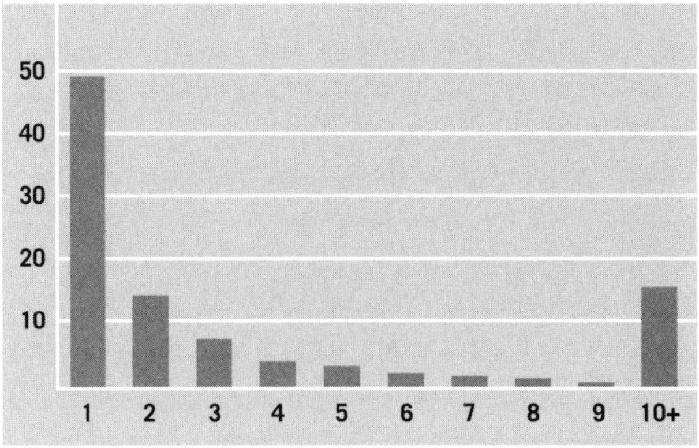

Source: Authors' compilation, based on Global Terrorism Database.

Sporadic and Short-Term Attackers

We also observe substantial variation in the attack patterns of terrorist perpetrators.[19] Terrorism does not necessarily come in waves or sustained campaigns neatly tied to specific actors. Even among those groups that are able to create an organizational structure, a fairly large number of groups do not attack repeatedly over time or attack more than once but over a very short period. We could characterize such groups as having sporadic attack patterns.

We can illustrate the scope of this phenomenon by doing a simple analysis of the Global Terrorism Database. In figure 4-1 we show the total number of attacks attributed to the 2,337 distinct terrorist organizations identified in the GTD from 1970 to 2015. Perhaps most remarkably, nearly half (49 percent) of all terrorist organizations recorded as active since 1970—1,147 organizations—have committed only one known attack. Another 14 percent have only two known attacks. Only 16 percent of all the organizations included in the GTD can be connected with ten or more attacks.

An important implication of this distribution is that the majority of even the organized groups that plan and execute terrorist attacks end up staging very few attacks. For example, a short-lived Greek organization called the Arsonists for Social Cohesion staged three coordinated attacks—on a Ferrari dealership, a Fiat dealership, and the

FIGURE 4-2. Percentage of Terrorist Groups
with Various Life Spans, 1970–2015

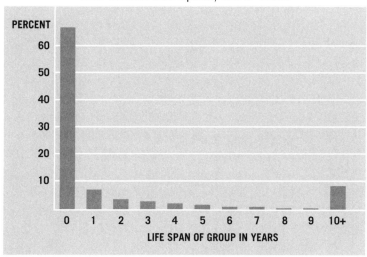

Source: Authors' compilation, based on Global Terrorism Database.

Italian Embassy, all in Athens and all on July 27, 1999. Despite property damage, no one was killed. Similarly, a group called Sons of the Gestapo staged only one known attack: the derailment of an Amtrak train in the United States near the city of Hyder, Arizona, on October 9, 1995. The incident took the life of one person and injured nearly eighty. The perpetrators were never heard from again. When perpetrators attack only once or twice it is obviously impossible for researchers or policymakers to study their past behavior to fashion effective future policies.

Not only do most terrorist perpetrator groups attack infrequently, in terms of actually carrying out the violent politically motivated acts that we call terrorism, most have very short life spans. In figure 4-2 we show the average life expectancy for the unique terrorist groups identified in the GTD since 1970. If we consider the life of a violent organization to be the amount of time between its first and last attack, we can see that a sizable majority of organizations—nearly 70 percent—last on average for less than a year. Another 7 percent on average last for a year. A small minority of groups—less than 10 percent—last for ten years or more. This means that for a high proportion of all known organizations using terrorism in the modern era, researchers have less than a year to study their structure, tactics, and strategies. From a policy standpoint, it means that for the majority of terrorist perpetrators we have very little time to adjust our strategies. Moreover, we are not particularly adept at predicting which terrorist organizations will quickly dissipate and which will continue to stage deadly attacks for years.

Organizational Cohesion: Splits, Splinters, and Factions

Even groups that manage to develop a fairly high degree of organization and maintain a public identity are not likely to be perfectly unified internally. Terrorist actors, like gangs and criminal organizations in general, show great variability in terms of the internal cohesiveness and density of their organizational structure. Groups frequently experience internal strife, competition, ideological disagreement, and splits. Sometimes factions within organizations conduct specialized operations and develop separate identities after these operations are completed. In other cases multiple groups form coalitions and operate together under new names. Some factions defect to rival groups in the same social movement sector. Name changes further confuse the landscape.

Why are some organizations more cohesive and resistant to fragmentation than others? What divides groups internally? Differences over strategy matter, and excessive violence against civilians can be divisive, as seen in the case of al Qa'ida's criticisms of Zarqawi's actions in Iraq between 2004 and 2006. If the parent organization moves to compromise, such as negotiating with the government in a formal peace process, spoiler factions may break away from the main body to continue violence. This occurred in the wake of Pakistan's attempts to negotiate with the Pakistani Taliban, the TTP (Tehrik-e-Taliban Pakistan).[20] Terrorism, especially when it involves high-casualty attacks on civilians, is an attractive tactic for spoilers, as exemplified by the Real IRA and Continuity IRA factions after the 1998 Good Friday Accords between most of Northern Ireland's political parties as well as the British and Irish governments. Similar patterns were observed by extremist Palestinian groups in the 1990s following the Oslo Accord between the government of Israel and the

Palestine Liberation Organization (PLO). Alternatively, groups may splinter along preexisting political, economic, or social fault lines.[21] In our earlier discussion of social networks we pointed out that groups based on common and strong informal ties are likely to be more cohesive than others.

As an illustration of the daunting complexities of internal organizational evolution, consider the Algeria-based al Qa'ida in the Islamic Maghreb (AQIM), which was established in 2006 as a formal sworn ally of al Qa'ida.[22] AQIM was previously known as the Salafist Group for Preaching and Combat (GSPC is the French acronym). The GSPC had been formed in 1998 when several leaders of the Armed Islamic Group (GIA is the French acronym) broke away from the parent group because the GIA had moved to conducting indiscriminate attacks on civilians. At the time Algeria was in the throes of an extremely bloody civil war that pitted violent Islamists against the government— it has been estimated that the war caused 200,000 civilian deaths. In 2012 AQIM moved outside Algeria to form an alliance with Tuareg rebels and local West African Islamist groups to fight the government of Mali, a challenge that provoked French intervention on behalf of the government in 2013. At the same time AQIM itself began to split when a faction under the leadership of Mokhtar Belmokhtar broke away. His new group, the al-Mulathamun Battalion ("Those Who Sign in Blood"), carried out the attack on the Amenas natural gas facility in Algeria in 2013 that killed forty people. Shortly after, Belmokhtar's faction became part of a new grouping, al Mourabitoun, by merging with another group, the Tuareg-affiliated Movement for Oneness and Jihad in West Africa, or Mujao. In November 2015, a week after the Paris assaults, al Mourabitoun claimed responsibility for an attack on a luxury hotel frequented by foreigners in Bamako, Mali's capital, which killed nineteen people. Not long after that, there were reports that Belmokhtar might mend fences with AQIM, both sides in the quarrel possibly reacting to the growing influence of ISIS.[23]

Another example of an organization prone to confused factional infighting that often leads to escalation is the Pakistani Taliban, or TTP (Tehrik-e-Taliban Pakistan). This is a group whose transformations are complex to the point of incomprehensibility, and what follows is only a sketch. Formed of numerous militant groups in

2007, the TTP has some close ties to al Qa'ida and has also coordinated attacks with the Afghan Taliban. The TTP has posed a threat not only to Pakistan's security, because it wants to overthrow the government and establish an Islamic State, but also to the United States, having directed the 2010 Times Square bombing attempt. As we discussed in chapter 3, Faisal Shahzad was a U.S. citizen of Pakistani origin who tried to explode a car bomb in New York's Times Square. Fortunately, the explosive device malfunctioned, although Shahzad had received training in bomb-making in Pakistan. The TTP was also responsible for the suicide bombing attack on the CIA outpost in Khost, Afghanistan, which killed seven people in 2009. In 2012 the TTP became infamous for shooting the schoolgirl Malala Yousafzai.

A fractious coalition to begin with, the TTP's most serious splits came in 2014. First a faction broke away in opposition to the TTP's negotiations with the Pakistan government. Then, after the group's leader Hakimullah Mehsud was killed in a U.S drone strike, the faction that he led, which dominated the TTP, broke away from the new leadership.[24] The Mehsud faction also claimed that the rest of the TTP was too violent, undisciplined, and prone to "un-Islamic" activities. Another source of the dispute may have been financial: how to distribute funds gained from extortion in the port city of Karachi. In August 2014, another major faction defected, in part because its commanders, too, rejected the new TTP leadership. This faction, Jamaat-ul-Ahrar, had close ties to al Qa'ida's leader, Zawahiri, who in September 2014 established al Qa'ida in the Indian Subcontinent to unite different militant groups. Jamaat-ul-Ahrar then seemingly rejoined the main TTP the next year. In December 2014, to retaliate for a Pakistani military offensive, the TTP attacked the Army Public School in Peshawar and killed 132 students. In March 2016, Jamaat-ul-Ahrar was responsible for a suicide bombing in a park in Lahore, aimed at Christians celebrating Easter, an assault that killed over seventy people. It is unclear whether the main TTP was complicit. In August 2016 both ISIS and Jamaat-ul-Ahrar claimed responsibility for a suicide bombing at a hospital in Quetta, which also killed over seventy people. Most of the victims were lawyers who had gathered to mourn the death of the leader of the Baluchistan Bar Association, who had been assassinated earlier in the day. Just a few days earlier the U.S. government had listed Jamaat-ul-Ahrar as a Specially Designated Terrorist group.

Interactions among Organizations

Our analysis has made it clear that the expansive jihadist wave of attacks that has emerged since the late 1990s is by no means unitary, a conclusion supported by the dramatic post-2014 split between al Qa'ida and its former partner, al Qa'ida in Iraq, which reemerged as the Islamic State.[25] The jihadist universe is a loose and swirling mix of diverse groups representing both local and transnational interests. Even before the al Qa'ida–ISIS power struggle it resembled a constellation of different organizational types more than a centralized actor with a single strategic purpose. This means that in order to understand the contemporary organization of terrorism we need to explain not only organizations but relationships among them. We have already pointed out that new organizations can be formed as a result of internal dissension when factions splinter off to become independent groups. They typically compete with their parent groups for the same constituencies and resources.

In asymmetrical conflicts such as those between state actors and terrorists, groups offering violent opposition are not monolithic nor shaped solely by ideology or individual interests. Consequently, researchers and policymakers must be attentive to the interactions among the groups. The relationships among organizations help determine their behavior and structure their responses to government actions. Conflict outcomes will depend not only on the identities, aspirations, and relative strengths of separate actors but on relationships among multiple challenging organizations, including both cooperation and competition. In addition, context and timing matter; militant groups position and realign themselves in terms of strategic expectations about the course of the conflict they are engaged in as well as considerations of future advantage. Each organization wants to win the struggle against the adversary, whether it is a local government or an international alliance, but it also wants to come out ahead of its like-minded rivals for power. Some groups also have dedicated enemies, such as

Sunni Islamist groups versus Shia militias in Iraq or Islamist groups versus the Free Syrian Army in Syria.

There can be monopolies of violent opposition to the state, but periods of monopolistic consolidation seem to be most likely to occur in the middle points of conflicts, not at the beginning or the end. They are thus transitory; two examples of this are the Provisional IRA in Northern Ireland and the Liberation Tigers of Tamil Eelam in Sri Lanka. If there are monopolies, their effects may be paradoxical. Their control of resources can make them formidable opponents but it may also mean that the government has a single, unified adversary to negotiate with in striking a compromise and negotiating an end to violence. Alternatively, cooperation or monopoly by one group over others may produce heightened levels of violence due to an opponent's acquisition of resources or control. Thus, under some circumstances cooperation among opponents or the monopoly of one group can make it easier for the government to find a credible negotiating partner that can commit to a bargain. Under other conditions, a unified opposition can force a government to make painful concessions. Governments often choose to encourage fragmentation, for example by decapitating the organization through removing its leaders or fomenting internal distrust through the use of informers or deception.[26]

More commonly the landscape features both cooperation and conflict among largely self-directed organizations.[27] The shifting and opportunistic character of many such relationships is well demonstrated by the 2016 split between al-Nusra and al Qai'da, an apparently amicable divorce symbolized by al-Nusra renaming itself Jabhad Fath al-Sham. Statements by the group indicated that the once valuable al Qai'da brand had simply become too costly in the context of civil war and intervention in Syria, since military strikes against al-Nusra could be excused as strikes against al Qa'ida.[28] The link with al Qa'ida was also said to impede al Nusra's ability to unify the Islamist opposition to Assad. A spokesman explained benignly that all such interorganizational affiliations are temporary and pragmatic, and that in a new context al-Nusra simply needed more freedom and independence to appeal to a more diverse audience. At the same time, the new Jabhad Fath al-Sham continued to share al Qa'ida's hostility toward ISIS.

This break appeared to be strategic, but some coalitions are merely tactical, as independent groups join for a specific operation and then return to old routines. Other cooperative arrangements, such as the relationships between the Afghan Taliban, the Pakistani Taliban, and al Qa'ida, are more durable and appear to be based on ideological cohesion and like-mindedness. Some alliances appear to be relatively egalitarian, with evenly matched participants, whereas others feature a dominant organization that attracts smaller groups into its orbit in something like a bandwagon effect. The Islamic Front in Syria, for example, had a few large "anchor groups" such as Ahrar al-Sham and several smaller and more localized groups about which little was known. The former was considered a more moderate Islamist group than the al-Nusra Front or ISIS, although it cooperated on the battlefield with al-Nusra and seemingly had cordial relationships with al Qa'ida leaders. Relationship types may be localized; groups that are antagonistic at the national level may cooperate at the local level, and vice versa.

Academic researchers are seeking to understand the conditions under which fragmentation occurs as well as its consequences. In particular, not only why is there rivalry, but when does competition lead to violent rivalry among ideologically similar groups? In February 2014, ISIS killed the commanders of two different groups in the Islamic Front.[29] What caused hostilities to develop between ISIS (before the declaration of the caliphate in June 2014) and groups in the Islamic Front umbrella organization in Syria? Such competition may produce escalated violence against the government and its supporters through processes such as outbidding in extremism. This phenomenon was first described in terms of ethnic conflicts, as rival groups competing for the support of the same constituency tried to outdo each other in escalating violence against the common enemy of the state. But outbidding is not restricted to ethnic conflicts.[30] Like-mindedness may be the result of ideological affiliation as well as shared ethnic identity. Outbidding is not an automatic result of multiparty conflicts, however, and research has not yet determined when competitive escalation is likely to occur. For example, the political scientists Michael Findley and Joseph Young used GTD data between 1970 and 2004 to examine the hypothesis that outbidding among rivals led to the escalation of suicide attacks. They found that an increase in the number of competing groups could not explain increases in rates of suicide bombings, and that there was even less empirical support for the general idea that outbidding led to increased levels of all forms of terrorism.[31]

These shifting relationships among groups complicate counter-terrorist strategy. First is the basic challenge of understanding what is going on. For example, analysts have tried to explain the nature of the paradoxical relationship between ISIS and former Iraqi Ba'athists. After Saddam Hussein's death in 2006, the Jaysh al-Tariqa al-Naqshbandia (JRTN) was founded as a largely nationalist organization composed of former military officers, in part to protect Iraqi Sufis from al Qa'ida in Iraq but primarily to oppose the American-led military coalition and the Shia-led Iraqi government. At the time the JRTN rejected sectarianism and the killing of fellow Iraqis. The incorporation of these experienced cadres was considered a major factor in ISIS's rapid expansion and territorial consolidation in Iraq since 2014. The explanation for this alliance is certainly not found in the nature of their organizations. The alliance is better explained by the domestic political behavior of the Iraqi state and the growing influence of Iran than by the specific political context at a particular point in time.

Another problem for policymakers is figuring out how to destroy or defeat one group, such as ISIS, without simultaneously helping another almost equally extreme group, such as al-Nusra, until 2016 the official al Qa'ida ally. An action against one group, such as leadership decapitation, has ricochet effects on other actors. Such coercion might be beneficial, say, in deterring groups that might have allied with the targeted group. But the intervention might also be harmful if, for example, the targeted organization disintegrates with the loss of its leader and its individual members migrate to other extremist groups. Such movement of members from one group to another characterized the relationship between the TTP and al Qa'ida in the Indian Subcontinent after 2014.

The Impact of the Internet

What unites the multifaceted violent jihadist movement in recent years is not language or national or ethnic identity but a shared aspiration to unite and defend Muslim lands against perceived foreign threats, overthrow apostate regimes, and replace them with states founded on a rigidly conservative interpretation of Islamic law. In the jihadist worldview, violence is both necessary and justified to achieve these transcendent aims. The transmission of this message has come increasingly to depend on the Internet, especially as other means of communication have been closed down and more and more potential adherents have gained access to the web.[32] Without the Internet effective coordination of jihadist strains around the world would be impossible.

The issue is of particular concern in the West, due to fear of radicalization of homegrown extremists by increasingly sophisticated propagandists. The forces of transnational ideological contagion are powerful, although practical experience still counts (hence the continued concern over individuals seeking to train or fight abroad). To understand what al Qa'ida or global jihadism is in today's world one must understand the role of Internet forums and websites and especially social media such as Facebook, Twitter, Kik, Instagram, and YouTube, among many others. There seems to be an endless proliferation of propaganda outlets.

Al Qa'ida's media sophistication is usually spoken of as a post-2001 development, but bin Laden was an astute manipulator of the contemporary media even before the 9/11 attacks. Television networks competed for access to the dramatic figure of bin Laden, bearded, patriarchal, dressed in white robes, and ensconced in labyrinthine caves in the rugged mountains of Afghanistan. His image or persona was carefully constructed to impress a watching audience. By 2001 he was already moving beyond the old terrorist world of pamphlets, printed magazines, and tape-recorded sermons on cassettes to a carefully cultivated image for television.

By 2008, media networks extending well beyond al Qa'ida linked jihadists worldwide. Media offices became essential branches of all organizations. They branded jihadist efforts through standardized logos that established the authenticity and credibility of their claims and became a major source of mainstream media reporting. Their message spread quickly far beyond conflict zones. The jihadist media network also connected the activities of disparate and far-flung armed groups, including in locations in Morocco, Algeria, Somalia, Iraq, Afghanistan, and Pakistan. Thus, the jihadist media network sustained a virtual organization and permitted implicit coordination of action without risky face-to-face contact.

English-language jihadist forums began to proliferate with the ascendance of Anwar al-Awlaki. In 2013 a study of such forums and of the use of Twitter (launched in March 2006) noted that forums remained more popular than Twitter, despite its growing importance and its real-time advantage, and that Arabic-language forums were still the most active, although the use of English was more prevalent on Twitter.[33] The process of virtual communication was becoming increasingly elaborate, detailed, and professional. In 2005 Abu Musab al-Suri had already publicly criticized the top-down approach to media via tightly controlled forums in Arabic. He called for generating more jihadist media in languages other than Arabic, including English, and for crafting communications that had more mass appeal. These forums, now increasingly interactive, were in effect the headquarters of the global jihadist movement. Now social media platforms are even more expansive—or democratic—in that users or consumers do not have to seek out the information or wait for edited transmission. It comes to them in real time through networks. Twitter can also take the place of websites if they are shut down by governments, which happens periodically. And modern communication techniques rely on smartphones, not computers.

Recruitment via social media also has a material effect on the capacities of the organizations behind terrorism. As we have noted, since 2014 ISIS has recruited thousands of foreign followers from the Middle East and from the West to join its ranks in Syria. The terrorism expert J. M. Berger claims that ISIS has now developed an online recruitment strategy that includes four distinct elements: (1) first contact; (2) create a micro-community; (3) shift to private communications; (4) encourage action.[34] There is little doubt that the Internet has greatly increased opportunities for establishing contact between potential recruits and active recruiters. In early 2015 Berger and Jonathon Morgan found 46,000 accounts that supported ISIS on Twitter alone.[35] The authors claim that once first contact is established, ISIS recruiters work quickly to secure the target's allegiance, tweeting as much as fifty to sixty times a day. Recruiters also start to suggest that targets isolate themselves from nonsupporters of ISIS. Once a trusting relationship has begun to develop, ISIS recruiters encourage targets to move communications to private channels. This generally shifts potential recruits to sites with strong encryption, including WhatsApp, Kik, Surespot, and Telegram. For the recruits who are brought along to this stage the final step is to promote some type of direct action. This could range from simply encouraging the recruit to be a more active social media advocate to promoting travel to territories controlled by ISIS to advocating terrorist attacks at home.

What effect has the increasing use of the Internet had on terrorist perpetrators and the threat they pose?[36] The answer is mixed. While the Internet has clearly made it easier to develop contacts and form micro-communities, the importance of direct action is still uncertain. The usefulness of foreign fighters in conflict theaters can be questionable. For example, when ISIS was still al Qa'ida in Iraq, it found foreign fighters to be so troublesome to integrate into the ranks that it cut off the flow. Although some recruits such as those from Central Asia and the Caucasus have military experience, many others do not. The battlefield utility of these green recruits is as suicide bombers. Thus, the influx of foreign recruits may lead to excessive reliance on this particular tactic, which could be good or bad for ISIS's strategy. The ISIS central leadership cannot control who comes—they may know very little in advance about new recruits because the message is spread so widely. Volunteers may be inept or mentally disturbed, or they may be spies. They may lack language skills and local knowledge. The newcomers need to prove their worth before they can be trusted.

On the other hand, foreigners lack local and particularistic allegiances—they are likely to be more ideological and thus more devoted to the central cause in a way that is untainted by local grievances, which makes it easier to direct them. Also, foreigners can bring linguistic skills that make them useful in communicating with non-Arabic-speaking audiences, thus reinforcing the outreach process that brought them to the conflict in the first place. They have a multiplying effect on the social media apparatus. ISIS leadership, local and global, may become increasingly dependent on this flow of recruits and thus find it hard to adjust if the supply is cut off or diminished. A further wrinkle is that foreign fighters may become disillusioned and return home—not to commit acts of spectacular terrorism but to expose ISIS's barbarity and the harsh reality of life under the caliphate, which then presumably tarnishes the ideological cause.[37]

These drawbacks would not apply to recruits motivated to take direct action in their own countries. The development of increasingly sophisticated encryption technology is a further plus for keeping recruits in their home countries: once recruits shift to private communications, it becomes increasingly difficult for law enforcement to track and counter their attacks.

Conclusions: Terrorism Is More than a Method

Perhaps the most obvious conclusion from this examination of the wide range of actors and organizations behind terrorism is that identifying them with any precision is an enormous challenge for researchers and policymakers. First, those who use terrorist methods are a diverse group, ranging from solo actors who do not seem to have been actively aided in preparing or carrying out their attacks, to informal cells based on social networks that show some degree of commitment to a movement or group and receive aid in planning and carrying out attacks, to structured, long-lasting organizations. All pose real threats, but it is unlikely that individuals or social networks would be so dangerous absent ideological and operational leadership to galvanize them. Second, following on the first conclusion, many of the terrorist attacks that threaten the world are launched either by groups that stage few attacks or maintain organizational coherence for a very short time, or both. Finally, even among organizations with a fair degree of coherence there is constant change: tactical and strategic evolution, splits, mergers, births, and deaths. The complexity can be bewildering.

We found that all of the terrorist activity of more than three-quarters of the organizations included in the GTD took place within the time frame of a year or less. We also found only twenty-eight organizations in the GTD that lasted for more than thirty years. Of more than 2,300 separate organizations identified in the GTD, about half were linked to only a single attack. In fact, groups that strike frequently and continuously over time are exceptional in the universe of terrorism: in the entire period from 1970 to 2015 the GTD includes only six terrorist organizations that survived for at least five years and that were responsible for more than 100 attacks per year (Boko Haram, al-Shabaab, the Farabundo Marti National Liberation Front, the Communist Party of India—Maoist, Tehrik-e-Taliban Pakistan, and the Shining Path). We should hasten to add that some of the specific details about the attack patterns of these groups may be inaccurate. Members of evolving groups continue to assume different names, and there may even be disagreement in the naming strategies of individuals in the same putative groups. Other organizations may claim attacks that they were not in fact responsible for or falsely attribute attacks to rivals. Extensive terror campaigns with more than 1,000 anonymous attacks in countries such as Iraq, Pakistan, Algeria, India, and Guatemala suggest that some organizations made the strategic choice to keep their identities hidden.

Certainly government analysts and decisionmakers have access to intelligence that academic researchers do not possess. Despite this unknown quantity of data that academic researchers cannot access but that may be available to government agencies, our studies convince us that U.S. counterterrorism policy still has to deal with high levels of uncertainty about the actors behind terrorism and that the elusiveness of our adversaries is only growing. Prevention of attacks on the territory of the United States is at the center of policy, but it is not possible to prevent all terrorism at home because specific threats are so unexpected and unpredictable.

The U.S. government faces acute paradoxes: for example, U.S. military pressure on ISIS may loosen its hold on the caliphate but simultaneously stimulate a strategic shift that would result in more attacks outside the active theater of conflict in Iraq and Syria. If ISIS is weakened, al Qa'ida and its allies are strengthened as a consequence, and they are no less virulent than the Islamic State. The United States is still targeting al Qa'ida in Pakistan through drone strikes. The effectiveness of targeted killings depends on knowing who is critical to an organization, and this awareness in turn depends on having a conceptual framework for understanding extremely fluid and complex organizational structures and forms. Individuals are linked to ideological narratives and to social networks that are connected to central organizations. The strategy of removing leaders also must rest on the premise either that leaders cannot be replaced or that they will be replaced by less talented or more moderate leaders. It is not clear, however, that organizational degradation has been the outcome of drone warfare, and there is evidence that drone attacks can have a radicalizing effect. In Iraq, the death of Zarqawi led to the rise of al Baghdadi, who apparently possesses much more credibility as a religious authority. Controlling or even restricting the use of social media by terrorists to mobilize followers is a formidable task. Western governments disagree as to whether they should punish or rehabilitate departing or returning foreign fighters.

The main argument made in this chapter is that from both a policy and a research standpoint the concept of a terrorist group is an abstraction that can obscure an enormous amount of structural, organizational, and logistical variation. This does not mean that the perpetrators of terrorism cannot be studied or that groups with varying levels of organizational coherence and complexity do not have beginnings and endings. In our view the organizational complexity of terrorism strongly supports three conclusions. First, we must accept the fact that terrorism as a type of political violence does not always occur in sustained campaigns with clearly observable beginnings and endings. Many acts are random and unpredictable or follow a pattern that cannot easily be discerned. We should be less doctrinaire in our policy recommendations, especially when the consequences of overreaction are high. Rather than arguing that certain outcomes are true for all terrorist perpetrators we may have to be satisfied with the conclusion that some outcomes may be true for some terrorist perpetrators under some conditions.

Second, not all terrorist perpetrators are equally capable of inflicting major damage, and therefore they do not all deserve equal attention. Indeed, policymakers are not interested in all groups equally. If nothing else, resource constraints impose priorities. A central goal is to devise strong counterterrorism policies for groups that threaten significant harm, ones that survive past the orchestration of one-off attacks. Separating the groups that are only transitory from those that pose a serious threat over a period of time is difficult but critical to effective counterterrorism policy. At the same time, the one-off attack by an individual without direct organizational connections can be extremely damaging, as the June 2016 mass shooting in Orlando, Florida, demonstrated. It caused the largest number of victim deaths, forty-nine, of any mass shooting in American history. In July in Nice, France, an individual with no apparent links to any organization used a commercial rental truck to mow down a crowd watching Bastille Day fireworks. He killed eighty-four people. The occasional exception to the rule of who poses the greatest threat can have enormous political and social impact.

Finally, we advocate taking a broad approach with regard to the methods used to study and understand the groups behind terrorist threats. While these techniques provide no panacea, the growing sophistication of geo-spatial mapping, advanced statistical analyses, and the availability of "big data" provide unparalleled new opportunities to identify conflict hot spots and rapid changes in characteristics associated with terrorism-related violence. But at the same time, establishing context for the data being collected and interpreted requires regional expertise and a deep understanding of languages, cultural settings, and the politics and history of particular conflicts. And even with improved methods we must accept the fact that terrorist adversaries are formed and organized in diverse ways, threats are often unexpected and unpredictable, and it is not possible to stop all attacks.

CHAPTER 5

Who Did It?

The Attribution Dilemma

A t the most elementary level, responding effectively to a terror-ist attack requires knowing who committed the act. Obtain-ing this knowledge is greatly complicated by the ambiguous, sometimes ephemeral nature of both attacks and their perpetrators. In this chap-ter we examine the problems associated with establishing responsi-bility for a terrorist attack after the fact. In a very large proportion of all terrorism cases, government authorities and the researchers who study these issues never know for sure who did what. We use the 156,722 terrorist attacks in the Global Terrorism Database (GTD) to examine the complexities of assigning responsibility for an attack to a specific organization or individual. The results may surprise many: For a majority of the attacks in the GTD, no specific group or individ-ual was ever unambiguously identified as the perpetrator. In fact for some regions, countries, and time periods few attacks can be linked to specific groups or individuals.

Why? As we saw in earlier chapters, attacks may be launched by loners, affiliated loners, or lone conspirators who are working more or less independently of any specific group. In other cases, media and official sources may provide general information on the attackers—for example, "Protestant extremists" or "Muslim militants"—but not sufficient evidence to assign responsibility to a named group. In still other cases there may be multiple or false claims: more than one group may claim the attack, or a group may claim responsibility when in reality it had no connection to the attack, or, in a false-flag scenario, the actual perpetrators may claim that another group was responsible. Assumptions or convictions about responsibility for an attack can also change over time—indeed controversy over attribution can persist years after the attack. In some cases we may simply never have enough information to reach a conclusion or to distinguish between competing accounts as to which one is true.

The fact that timely and accurate attribution is difficult has profound implications not only for the credibility of scholarly research but for policy responses to terrorist attacks. Attributing responsibility can be a delicate and potentially controversial political issue, especially if there is the possibility of state involvement in the attack. The pressure on policymakers to identify the guilty party and offer a swift response is likely to be considerable, especially following a major attack that claims lives. And of course, the consequences of incorrect attribution can be enormous.

The implications of identifying perpetrators of attacks are particularly grave for policies on deterrence and punishment, especially if governments face a threat of weapons of mass destruction and even more so nuclear terrorism—a threat long anticipated that fortunately has so far never been carried out. If we cannot establish responsibility, we obviously cannot threaten to punish or actually punish the perpetrators. Thus, while official U.S. policy is to use overwhelming force against states or nonstates responsible for the use of a nuclear device, what happens if we are unable to discover rapidly and conclusively who is responsible for an attack?

Assigning Responsibility for Attacks to Terrorist Organizations

One of the most daunting challenges in developing policies on terrorism is determining responsibility in a timely way. Although the GTD team at START (National Consortium for the Study of Terrorism and Responses to Terrorism) works entirely in the unclassified, open-source domain, its efforts to assemble a worldwide database on terrorism faces many of the same problems as policymakers and intelligence analysts face, even when they have access to classified information. Terrorism is a form of clandestine political violence committed mostly by shadowy nonstate actors, and information about it is inevitably contradictory, confusing, or entirely absent. But the consequences of getting an attribution wrong are considerably greater for policymakers than for academics. To provide a more complete understanding of the scope of this problem, in the next section we examine how the GTD research team attributes responsibility for terrorist attacks, how often these procedures identify a specific individual or group in the thousands of cases that we consider, and why the difficulties and limitations are so great.

Systematic Attempts to Attribute Responsibility for Attacks

The GTD allows four levels of attribution of terrorist attacks:

1. A specific group is assigned responsibility.
2. A "generic" group is assigned responsibility.
3. The attack is carried out by an individual with no clear group affiliation.
4. The attack cannot be associated with a specific group or individual or a generic group.

We classify the first level above as the "attributed" attacks and the next three levels as "unattributed" attacks. For the attributed attacks the GTD team records the name of the organization using a standardized list of terrorist group names that they have developed over the past decade, based in large part on names recorded from the print and electronic media. These perpetrator attributions are constructed from open-source media accounts and do not necessarily reflect either uncontested admissions by the groups or individuals responsible or legal findings of culpability. Because criminal justice systems adjudicate individuals rather than groups, the groups attributed with responsibility by the GTD team are not found guilty through a formal legal process.

Occasionally more than one group claims responsibility. For example, on November 20, 2015, two assailants opened fire on the Radisson Blu Hotel in Bamako, Mali. In addition to the two assailants, twenty people, including a U.S. citizen, were killed, two people were injured, and 170 people were taken hostage in the attack. The hostages, including six U.S. citizens, were rescued the same day. Al-Mua'qi'oon Biddam Brigade (those who sign with blood) and Movement for Oneness and Jihad in West Africa (MUJAO), two groups that reportedly merged into Al-Mourabitoun, claimed responsibility and stated that the attack was carried out in retaliation for alleged government aggression in North Mali and demanded the release of detainees being held in France. Additionally, al Qa'ida in the Islamic Maghreb (AQIM) and the Macina Liberation Front separately claimed responsibility for the incident. Because we had no further information on responsibility, we noted all four of these groups in the case description.

The second category above references cases where no specific organization is named but general or "generic" information on the attackers is recorded by the news media. About 23 percent of the unattributed attacks are classified as generics. From 1970 to 2015 the GTD includes a total of 951 generic perpetrator identifications (as opposed to 2,337 named groups). The single most frequent generic category in the GTD is "Maoist," which includes 1,141 attacks. Other major generic categories include "Palestinians," 1,124 attacks; "Sikh extremists," 714 attacks; "Huthi extremists," 554 attacks; "Algerian Islamic extremists," 373 attacks; "narco-terrorists," 368 attacks; "Protestant extremists," 333 attacks; and "Chechen rebels," 325 attacks.

The third category is an attack by an individual with no clear group affiliation. For all data after 1997, the GTD team designates perpetrators as "individual" when the media sources assign responsibility to an individual with no known connections to a specific terrorist group (before 1998 these cases were put in category four above). Since the GTD staff started collecting data on these individual perpetrators in 1998, it has only designated 545 attacks—less than 1 percent of the post-1997 unattributed cases—as perpetrated by individuals with no clear group affiliation. Frequently all that is known in these cases is that an unidentified individual was responsible. However, in some of these cases a specific individual has been identified as the perpetrator but no group can be labeled as responsible because the individual appears to have acted alone. A prominent example of this is the case of Major Nidal Malik Hasan, the Fort Hood shooter, who appears to have had his own ideological predispositions but lacked verifiable links to a specific organization. In this case we can be reasonably certain that the correct perpetrator has been identified, even though we cannot assign responsibility for the attack to a specific group. As discussed in earlier chapters these cases are variously referred to as lone-wolf or lone-attacker cases. The designation of responsible individuals, like responsible groups, is based on media reports, not formal adjudication. Some individual suspects are never apprehended by authorities and some die or are killed before they can be brought to trial. Although it has happened in relatively few cases, if a formal adjudication process results in a different outcome than the one we recorded in the GTD, we update the data to reflect the legal ruling.

As explained in the previous chapter, there are challenging conceptual problems in distinguishing terrorist organizations from individuals who use terrorism. The two most vexing of these in terms of assigning responsibility for an attack are identifying what constitutes membership in a group and determining the extent to which the actions of an individual are carried out on behalf of a specific group. When an attack is directly controlled by an established group that claims responsibility in the media, the outcome may be fairly straightforward: for example, when a group such as the Basque separatist ETA or the FARC in Colombia openly claims responsibility for an attack.[1] However, determining whether an attack was group- or individual-based is much more complex in attacks that do not appear to be instigated or controlled by a specific group. The difficulty of attribution is perhaps greatest in cases where the individual appears to have had no interaction with like-minded extremists of any sort.

An example of the difficulty of classifying an attack as genuinely "individual" is the recent case of Faisal Mohammad. On November 4, 2015, Mohammad attacked students with a hunting knife on the University of California Merced campus. Four students were injured and the assailant was shot and killed by police officers. Mohammad claimed responsibility in a note left at the scene and police initially characterized the stabbings as the misguided acts of a disgruntled student. However, investigators found an image of an ISIS flag in the attacker's backpack and upon further investigation, the FBI determined that Mohammad had visited websites for ISIS and other terrorist organizations. Investigators also found a two-page, handwritten plan detailing the perpetrator's intentions to take hostages and kill students and police officers. Although the FBI concluded that the attack was "inspired" by ISIS,[2] they found no evidence that Mohammad had direct ties to ISIS or any foreign terrorist organizations and ISIS never officially claimed responsibility for the attack. Accordingly, the GTD classified this attack as being carried out by an "individual."

Between cases like this, where a lone individual seems to be operating without any support from or contact with a known terrorist organization, there is a sliding scale of connectivity that includes individuals who may not have contact with a terrorist organization but may have contact with nonterrorists who share extremist ideologies. Even more complexity is added in cases involving more than one individual operating outside of a specific group. With multiple individuals it is possible that one may have had training from a specific group while other individuals involved in the attack did not. Different experiences of this sort were evident in the Boston Marathon bombing case.

Tamerlan Tsarnaev appears to have had more direct contact with extremist organizations than his younger brother, Dzhokhar. U.S. House Homeland Security Chairman Michael McCaul said he believed that Tamerlan received training during a January 2012 trip to Russia, where he visited the North Caucasus, an area of separatist movements, ethnic rivalries, and extremist Islamic ideology.[3] According to media reports, Tamerlan was seen by police in Makhachkla, the capital of Dagestan, where he visited a known Islamic militant in a Salafist mosque founded by an associate of Ayman al-Zawahiri.[4] Once in Dagestan, Tamerlan is said to have met on several occasions with Makhmud Mansur Nidal, a nineteen-year-old Dagestani-Palestinian man. Nidal was under close surveillance by Dagestan's antiextremism unit for six months as a suspected recruiter for Islamist insurgents, before the police killed him in May 2012.[5] When Tamerlan returned to the United States on July 17, 2012, the *Washington Post* reports, his life took on an "increasingly puritanical religious tone" and he expressed "Islamist certainty."[6]

Dzhokhar Tsarnaev appears to have had far less exposure to extremist ideology than his brother, either online or in person. According to an article in *The Economist,* he seems to have been much more concerned with sports and cheeseburgers than with religion, at least judging by his Twitter feed.[7]

Finally, there are cases where the GTD team has no information on perpetrators—no specific group, generic category, or individual name. The GTD analysts endeavor to update these cases when new information becomes available, but in the more than ten years since the GTD was created, this has happened infrequently. When a case cannot be linked to any group or individual we have no way of knowing the exact circumstances under which it was carried out. Thus, a bomb may detonate in a particular location and we never know for sure whether an organization, a small group of individuals, or a specific individual acting alone was responsible.

With all of these complexities in mind, in figure 5-1 we show the annual percentage of all attacks in the GTD that we were able to attribute to a known terrorist organization.[8] Overall, a smaller percentage of attacks are attributed (40.3 percent) than are unattributed to a specific group. The year with the smallest percentage of attributed attacks is 2013, when only 25 percent of the 11,990 attacks were attributed. Conversely, the year with the largest percentage of attributed attacks was 1974, when we were able to link 72 percent of 580 attacks to an identified terrorist organization. When we step back and look at overall patterns, we see that the percentage of attributed attacks has generally decreased from 1970 to the present. In the first two decades of the GTD, 1970 to 1989, 59.9 percent of all attacks were recorded as attributed. In the second portion of the database, 1990 to 2015, that figure fell to 33.5 percent. The lowest levels of attributed attacks occurred during the last ten years of the database and no doubt reflect in part the large number of incidents occurring in the context of ongoing war and the conflicts in Afghanistan, Iraq, and Syria—locations where assigning responsibility from open sources is notoriously difficult.

The Characteristics of Unattributed Terrorist Attacks

In the previous section we demonstrated the magnitude of the problem of allocating responsibility for terrorist attacks. In this section we examine the 93,485 unattributed cases from 1970 to 2015 in terms of their characteristics: Where do they occur and what types of targets are most common?

FIGURE 5-1. Attributed Attacks as Percentage
of All Attacks, 1970–2015

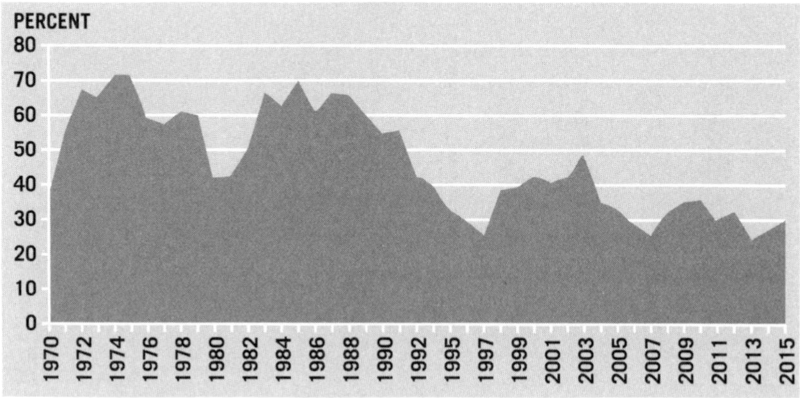

Source: Authors' compilation, based on Global Terrorism Database.

Attributed Attacks and Location (Region and Country)

Figure 5-2 shows the proportion of attributed attacks in terms of the region in which they occurred. For this exercise we have divided the world into twelve different regions (see appendix 5-1 for the countries included in each region). There is tremendous variation in the proportion of attributed attacks by region of the world. We find the largest percentage of attributed attacks in South America (67 percent), Western Europe (62 percent), and Central America and the Caribbean (59 percent) and the smallest percentage in Eastern Europe (5 percent) and Central Asia (6 percent). In other words, in the first set of regions it is easiest to identify group perpetrators and in the second set it is the most difficult.

The high level of attributed attacks in South and Central America and Western Europe may reflect the dominance of a handful of very prominent terrorist organizations in these regions. For example, over time, the most active terrorist organizations in South America were the Shining Path, the Revolutionary Armed Forces of Colombia (FARC), the National Liberation Army of Colombia (ELN), the Manuel Rodriguez Patriotic Front (FPMR) in Chile, and the Tupac Amaru Revolutionary Movement (MRTA) in Peru. These five organizations operating in South America accounted for nearly 10,000 terrorist attacks from 1970 to 2015—over half of all terrorist attacks in South America during this period. In situations where there is only one major

FIGURE 5-2. Attributed and Unattributed
Attacks by Region, 1970–2015

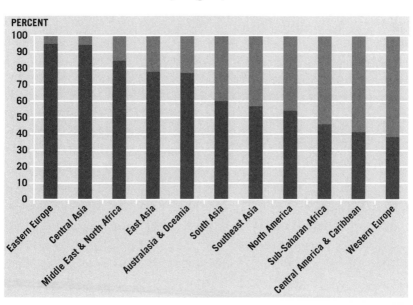

Source: Authors' compilation, based on Global Terrorism Database.

group responsible for most of the violence it is likely that both the media and policymakers are more likely to assume that any unclaimed attacks are in reality the work of the dominant group—whether or not this can be demonstrated to be true.

By contrast, Eastern Europe, Central Asia and the Middle East and North Africa are regions with a good deal of unattributed terrorist violence. A relevant example is the various attacks associated with Chechnya, where violence has all of the characteristics of terrorism but is often not linked to any specific terrorist organization.

In general, terrorist attacks in the four regions within the Western Hemisphere (South America, Western Europe, Central America and the Caribbean, and North America) were attributed to specific organizations nearly twice as frequently as attacks in regions within the Eastern Hemisphere. This contrast is especially great for Eastern Europe, Central Asia, and the Middle East and North Africa, where only 5 percent, 6 percent, and 15 percent of attacks, respectively, were attributed to specific groups. Several countries in these two regions

TABLE 5-1. Ten Countries with the Largest
Percentage of Unattributed Attacks, 1970–2015

COUNTRY	TOTAL UNATTRIBUTED AS PERCENTAGE OF TOTAL ATTACKS	TOTAL UNATTRIBUTED
Iraq	98%	18,333
Russia	95%	2,008
Yemen	94%	2,438
Thailand	92%	3,087
Pakistan	80%	10,241
Algeria	77%	2,101
India	60%	5,941
Afghanistan	42%	4,078
Philippines	36%	2,016
Colombia	34%	2,786

Source: Authors' compilation, based on Global Terrorism Database.

were part of the former Soviet Union, which also had very low attribution rates (3.8 percent, or three out of seventy-eight attacks). Certainly these low rates might be due in part to the extreme controls imposed on media investigating and reporting by the Soviet government. This practice might have continued in the newly independent states after the break-up of the Soviet Union, but the low rates also may reflect in part the problems faced by overwhelmed new governments.

In table 5-1 we consider the top ten countries in the database in terms of the total percentage of unattributed attacks. The country in the GTD with the single highest percentage of unattributed attacks is Iraq. Most of the unattributed attacks in Iraq are recent, following the U.S.-led invasion in March 2003. For example, from 2004 through 2015, 32 percent of all of the unattributed attacks recorded in the entire GTD took place in Iraq.

Afghanistan also finishes in the top ten countries with regard to the percentage of unattributed attacks. However, it is clear from table 5-1 that being at war is only part of the explanation for unattributed attacks in a given country: many countries that have not been at war in recent years nonetheless have large numbers of unattributed attacks. Russia, Yemen, and Thailand have percentages of unattributed attacks that are nearly as high as Iraq. Pakistan and India have unattributed percentages that are higher than Afghanistan. In terms of sheer numbers, Pakistan has 55 percent as many unattributed attacks as Iraq but about twice as many as India and Afghanistan. Filling in the bottom of the top ten list in terms of percentages are Colombia and the Philippines.

Unattributed Attacks and Targets

In table 5-2 we compare the percentage of attacks that are unattributed to those that are attributed in terms of different terrorist targets. We find that the targets of attacks least likely to be attributed to a specific group are abortion-related such as clinics, religious figures and institutions, and violent political parties. They are about twice as likely to be unattributed than attacks on targets such as public utilities, military installations and figures, and food and water supply. Perhaps the reason is the clarity and salience of the target or the legitimacy or lack thereof, in terms of the expectations of constituencies. Some attacks may be harder to justify to an audience or are more likely to call down the wrath of authorities.

Perhaps when perpetrators attack abortion clinics, particular types of religious institutions, or violent political parties they feel that the nature of their perceived grievances is clearly communicated by their target choices. In contrast, when attacking more anonymous types of targets such as utilities, food or water supply infrastructure, or telecommunications, it may be more important for perpetrators to announce their identity.

Unattributed Attacks and Weapons Used by Terrorists

Table 5-3 links attribution to the different weapons used by terrorists. What is perhaps most alarming about connections between attributions for attacks and weapons is the high proportion of cases involving chemical, biological, and radiological (CBR) weapons where we are unable to attribute responsibility. Radiological weapons are connected to unattributed sources 85 percent of the time, biological 74 percent, and chemical 69 percent. Of course, we hasten to add that taken to-

TABLE 5-2. Percentage of Unattributed Terrorist
Attacks Worldwide, by Target Type, 1970–2015

TYPE OF TARGET	TOTAL UNATTRIBUTED AS PERCENTAGE OF TOTAL ATTACKS	TOTAL UNATTRIBUTED
Abortion Related	90%	235
Religious Figures/Institutions	74%	2,877
Violent Political Party	71%	1,167
Terrorists/Non-State Militia	69%	1,750
Educational Institution	69%	2,704
NGO	67%	581
Private Citizens & Property	66%	23,707
Journalists & Media	64%	1,712
Government (General)	63%	12,179
Government (Diplomatic)	63%	2,105
Tourists	60%	252
Transportation	59%	3,793
Police	57%	12,130
Airports & Aircraft	54%	702
Business	53%	10,054
Military	50%	11,489
Food or Water Supply	49%	145
Telecommunication	45%	423
Maritime	45%	142
Utilities	37%	2,040

Source: Authors' compilation, based on Global Terrorism Database.

gether, these types of weapons are extremely rare—about one-tenth of 1 percent of all the cases in the database.

The finding that a strong majority of CBR weapons attacks cannot be linked to a specific terrorist organization may seem surprising in terms of prior arguments that the decision to claim responsibility for attacks is often strategic and that perpetrators of terrorism most often use it to signal the strength of their organizations.[9] We might

TABLE 5-3.Percentage of Unattributed Terrorist Attacks
Worldwide, by Weapon Type, 1970–2015

TYPE OF WEAPON	TOTAL UNATTRIBUTED AS PERCENTAGE OF TOTAL ATTACKS	TOTAL UNATTRIBUTED
Fake Weapons	85%	28
Radiological	85%	11
Vehicle	83%	86
Biological	74%	26
Chemical	69%	160
Melee	68%	2,056
Explosives/Bombs/Dynamite	65%	51,369
Incendiary	59%	5,767
Firearms	53%	27,418
Unknown	52%	6,460
Other	50%	46
Sabotage Equipment	47%	58

Source: Authors' compilation, based on Global Terrorism Database.

think that CBR attacks would be likely candidates for claiming responsibility to the extent that they might signal the operational capacity of the organization. However, when we take a more in-depth look at the 279 CBR attacks in the GTD we see that most are relatively inconsequential. Over 80 percent of the CBR attacks in the GTD resulted in no casualties. Many of the attacks involve mailing letters or packages laced with anthrax or cyanide, not the most lethal delivery method. The big exception thus far has been the 1995 Aum Shinrikyo case in Tokyo, where the group actively sought to make chemical weapons and then actually deployed them to deadly effect. Other groups like the LTTE have come across caches of chemical weapons such as chlorine gas and have opportunistically tried to use them. But in the case of the LTTE at least, they apparently found chemical weapons not very effective and abandoned efforts in this area.

While CBR weapons have high percentages of unattributed attacks, by far the largest absolute numbers of unattributed cases (more

TABLE 5-4. Percentage of Unattributed Terrorist
Attacks Worldwide, by Tactic, 1970–2015

TYPE OF ATTACK	TOTAL UNATTRIBUTED AS PERCENTAGE OF TOTAL ATTACKS	TOTAL UNATTRIBUTED
Unarmed Assault	69%	568
Hijacking	67%	373
Bombing, Explosion	65%	49,316
Assassination	61%	10,794
Facility, Infrastructure Attack	57%	5,038
Armed Assault	53%	19,745
Hostage taking (Kidnapping)	52%	4,706
Unknown	49%	2,708
Hostage taking (Barricade Incident)	28%	237

Source: Authors' compilation, based on Global Terrorism Database.

than 78,000) involve explosives and firearms. Attribution rates for firearms are 53 percent and for explosives 65 percent.

Unattributed Attacks and Terrorist Tactics

In table 5-4 we show which tactics are associated with attributed versus unattributed attacks. As with earlier comparisons, we see major differences across tactics. Unarmed assaults and hijackings are least likely to be attributed to a specific group. Hijackings often involve one or two individuals, often with weak or no ties to specific groups. Before 9/11 the last domestic U.S. hijacking was in 1991. Between 1984 and 2000 there were no hijackings with more than one perpetrator, and no casualties. There are a few more international hijackings in the GTD, but 9/11 is the first case ever of suicidal hijackers. The closest comparison may be the December 1994 hijacking of an Air France flight from Algiers by four members of the Armed Islamic Group of Algeria (GIA). After the murder of three passengers, a special operations unit of the French Army stormed the plane in Marseilles, killing all hijackers and freeing all passengers. There were reports that the hijackers planned to crash the plane into the Eiffel Tower, but the reports were never confirmed. Most of the rash of hijackings from the United States to Cuba in the 1970s were done by mentally disturbed individuals.

Assassinations are often accompanied by perpetrator plans to flee the scene of the crime and avoid being identified. By contrast, hostage-taking situations (both barricade and hostage taking) make escape and hence anonymity, much more difficult.

Generalizations about Unattributed Attacks among Terrorist Organizations

In more than half of the terrorist attacks in the GTD since 1970 we simply do not know which, if any, specific organization was responsible. We have already seen that the main reason is not that most terrorism is due to lone actors. A scant proportion of the cases where we have information (less than 1 percent) are committed by lone wolves without a clear group affiliation. In a much larger proportion of unattributed cases—about 17 percent—we have only generic information from the news media about the group responsible. We have also already seen that the number of unattributed attacks varies greatly by region. More than 80 percent of the attacks in Eastern Europe and Central Asia and the Middle East and North Africa could not be linked to a specific organization. By contrast, over 60 percent of attacks in South America and Western Europe were attributed to specific groups. War-torn Iraq had the largest total number of unattributed attacks, over 18,000. But several other countries combined (Pakistan, India, Afghanistan, Thailand, and Colombia) have over 26,000 unattributed attacks during the period covered by the data.

In many ways, the situation is just as complex when someone claims responsibility for an attack. It could be that for their own personal reason they are claiming responsibility for an attack that they did not actually carry out. It could also be that one group is falsely attributing responsibility to another group, again for its own complex reasons. In short, although researchers working from open sources do their best to attribute responsibility correctly based on the unclassified data available, we must be very realistic about the accuracy of these attributions.

Modeling Terrorist Responsibility

Determining responsibility for a specific terrorist attack has been approached traditionally through extensive investigation, using a range of forensic methods, including, where relevant, analysis of types of weapons and explosive and bomb components. In addition, event databases now contain information on thousands of terrorist attacks that have been attributed to specific organizations. Can we take the information about group responsibility in known cases and apply it to assess responsibility in unknown cases? Can such information provide another potential avenue for assigning responsibility in specific cases through statistical modeling?

There are some potential benefits of such an approach. At present, investigations of terrorist attacks are conducted much like other police investigations and rely heavily on the specialized knowledge of investigators regarding such things as the tactics commonly used by different terrorist organizations, their operational histories, weapons choices, and targeting strategies. But all of the individual decisions of investigators are susceptible to bias. In principle, statistical approaches based on examining patterns from known events could provide a mechanism not only for forecasting but also for offering a context for forecasts that have been made that provide researchers and policymakers with metrics about how accurate their estimates are. In other words, statistical tests can not only point to likely perpetrators but also establish parameters for how confident we can be in our predictions.

Statistical methods also make it relatively easy to determine which variables are most important in forecasting as well as the relative impact of important variables. Basically, statistical approaches hold out the promise of allowing researchers and analysts to formalize the identification process and make it easier to generalize into the future. Also, traditional investigations rely on the knowledge and skill of individual investigators: if we are fortunate enough to have highly skilled investigators on the scene with a great depth of specialized knowledge the outcome is likely to be far better than if less experienced individuals are the only ones available. By contrast, statistical programs do not require individuals with specialized knowledge of the scene.

For years social science methods have been used to establish the identity of legal actors.[10] For example, both criminal and mental health law have long relied on social science to assist in the identification of who should be confined to institutions such as a prison and how long should that confinement continue. The most common application in criminal law has been in developing predictive models for parole. In 1928, the sociologist Ernest Burgess and his colleagues developed the first "expectancy table" for predicting parole success.[11] They examined the records of 3,000 former inmates of Illinois prisons to find the variables that distinguished those who committed new crimes while on parole from those who did not. He found twenty-two such variables, and in 1933, the prediction instrument he devised was put into practice in the Illinois prison system.[12] Similar prediction instruments have been widely used in the United States and elsewhere ever since. Prediction methods have also been widely used in mental health law in the context of involuntary commitments to mental hospitals. The success of such prediction instruments has been repeatedly confirmed.[13]

Social science instruments have also been developed and deployed to identify potential aerial hijackers, illegal aliens, high-risk prison inmates, drug couriers, domestic violence risks, and rape victims.[14] Probably because of a general lack of suitable data, such predictive methods have only recently begun to appear in the area of attributing responsibility for terrorist attacks. For example, Joshua Hill, Daniel Mabrey, and John Miller apply forecasting methods to a dataset on terrorism in the Philippines from January 1, 2004, through June 30, 2008.[15] They divide possible terrorist organizations operating in the Philippines into four groups: the Moro National Liberation Front (MNLF), the New People's Army (NPA), the Abu Sayyaf Group (ASG), and all others. Analyzing 941 attacks where a group was assigned responsibility, the researchers extracted information on eighty-seven variables, including day of the week, month of the year, time of day, incident type, target type, and target nationality. They then used this information to determine whether they could statistically sort the groups into the correct categories.

The idea here is to use information from groups for which full information is available to make educated guesses about groups with incomplete information. To do this specific test, Hill, Mabrey, and Miller took a sample of cases where the perpetrating group was known and used the methods to see if they could accurately guess the unknown group's identity on the basis of their known background characteristics. The analysis worked best for the largest group, the

NPA, where the statistical analysis correctly classified 99 percent of the NPA attacks. The method also worked reasonably well for the second most active group, the ASG, correctly classifying 83 percent of the cases. However, the methods were far less successful in predicting attacks by the MNLF, where accuracy rates were only 28 percent; and the "all others" category, where accuracy rates were only 24 percent. In short, the methods used did much better at classifying the most active groups—which is certainly a logical outcome.

We should also note that the Hill, Mabrey, and Miller study was limited to a fairly specialized problem: classifying known attacks into four terrorist groups for a single country over a four-and-a-half-year period. The authors argue that this type of application is in fact a sensible approach because in most real-world cases, the analyst will know the country where an attack occurs and can identify the main potential groups responsible. This reasoning seems defensible for most terrorist groups; however, it might not be applicable to groups such as al Qa'ida and its affiliates, which have operated in many different countries over time. Moreover, the authors use the methodology to attribute attacks to terrorist groups in cases where the actual attacker is already known. In theory, similar methods could be used in cases where the attacker is not known. However, it is precisely in these cases where many of the eighty-seven predictor variables that form the basis for the analysis are likely to be missing.

In addition to these limitations, other constraints make it likely that these methods will never offer a reliable way to identify most attackers. First, it is hard to imagine that these forecasts will ever approach perfect accuracy. Of course there are important consequences when authorities are unable to attribute responsibility for a criminal action, but from the point of view of justice and due process there are also significant costs if responsibility is attributed incorrectly.

Second, the data that researchers and analysts have at their disposal in forecasting group responsibility are nearly always incomplete; the less complete the data, the less accurate the forecasting is likely to be. Moreover, the completeness of the data is frequently time-sensitive—more complete data often emerge after a lengthy investigation.

Third, statistical forecasting models work on the basis of having large enough samples to provide reasonably sound statistical inference. But as we have seen in earlier chapters, terrorist attacks are often carried out by organizations that attack either a single time or very infrequently. Forecasting methods are likely to be most useful for the relatively few groups that have attacked frequently.

Finally, some individuals may be uneasy about the whole rationale for doing such forecasting. These procedures work by taking a particular attack in, say, Spain and estimating the probability that a specific group, say, the ETA, carried it out. Let's say we run such an analysis and determine that there is a 70 percent probability that a specific unclaimed attack in Spain was carried out by the ETA. The ethical issue that such a forecast poses is that the true probability that ETA carried out the attack must be either 0 percent or 100 percent—after all, the group either did it or did not do it. So, imposing some probabilistic estimate other than 0 or 100 is incorrect on its face.

Developing statistical methods that analyze existing cases to provide analysts with information about the likely perpetrators in cases where they are unknown or uncertain is likely to become increasingly important in the future, and we can expect progress in terms of the sophistication and accuracy of prediction methods. At the same time, more sophisticated analytical methods will most likely never eliminate the very real attribution dilemma that policymakers confront. In fact, although statistical methods of attributing responsibility for attacks are not irrelevant and are becoming more useful over time, they are unlikely to ever provide perfect or even near-perfect attribution of responsibility.

Consequences of the Attribution Dilemma for Policymakers

Our review of worldwide terrorist incident data demonstrates the practical difficulties of attributing responsibility for attacks. These limitations pose problems for policymakers as well as researchers, but in the world of politicians the barriers to resolution are often political as much as factual—even though government analysts have access to classified information that researchers do not it is often difficult to obtain evidence, especially in the short run. Moreover, one comment we have heard repeatedly from colleagues who do work in classified environments is not to overestimate the amount of valid data that is available, even to those with security clearances. And, although researchers

seek comprehensive evidence to support theoretical explanations, political leaders may not always want to know who did it.

Whatever the reason—whether an absence of hard facts or absence
of political willingness to accuse likely perpetrators—difficulty in attributing responsibility for terrorist attacks is an obstacle to crafting
an effective response. Attribution needs to be both timely and credible,
but these two requirements are often incompatible. It takes time to
make a convincing case of responsibility, and even then the outcome
may never be conclusive. The domestic political costs of either mistakes
or inability to assign blame can be extremely high. A response that
comes years after an attack is not likely to be effective punishment,
and it may not be regarded as legitimate by domestic and international
audiences, especially if it involves the use of military force.

The example of the attack on Pan Am 103 over Lockerbie, Scotland, shows how hard it can be to bring closure even in an extremely
important case that involved two governments with expert intelligence agencies and that was drawn out over a long period of time—
more than twenty-five years. The midair explosion on the aircraft
over Scotland, which killed 279 passengers, occurred in December
1988, but the resolution was contentious for decades. By 1991 the
United States and Great Britain had indicted Libyan officials. Libya
handed over two suspects years later, in 1999, and a trial before a
special Scottish court sitting in the Netherlands opened in 2000. The
Libyan dictator, Muammar Qaddafi, was then engaged in a process
of political rehabilitation that also involved giving up Libya's nuclear
weapons program. In 2001 one of the accused was acquitted, but the
other was convicted. In another unexpected development the single
convicted perpetrator was released in 2009 owing to his deteriorating health. He died in Libya in 2012, after having received a hero's
welcome on his return, but the controversy did not die with him.

There are still questions about the extent of the involvement of
Qaddafi himself, perhaps operating through the proxy of the Abu
Nidal organization, a Palestinian group, and even about whether
responsibility actually lay not with Libya but with Iran via the Popular
Front for the Liberation of Palestine–General Command (PFLP-GC).[16]
Both Libya and Iran had reasons to seek revenge against the United
States—Libya to retaliate for the 1986 American air raid that killed
Qaddafi's adopted daughter, and Iran for the downing of a passenger

jet by the U.S.S. *Vincennes* in July 1988 during the Iran-Iraq war. The CIA went so far as to post a statement on its website explaining that during the trial of the Libyan officials a CIA officer had conclusively identified the timer for the bomb as Libyan and it was not the work of the PFLP-GC.[17]

To provide further context for the complications raised by what we are calling the attribution dilemma, we describe three sets of non-mutually exclusive attribution issues that can impede an effective government response and impose political costs: (1) mistaken attribution, at least in the short run; (2) lack of timeliness (identifying the perpetrators, but too late to respond); and (3) no resolution (never knowing who did it). We briefly discuss the implications of each.

Mistaken Attribution

Governments can make serious mistakes in attributing responsibility for terrorist attacks. The false impression may be fleeting, a judgment made in the heat of the moment before many of the facts are in, but an appropriate response is delayed and there may be considerable political embarrassment with long-term consequences. There are real risks to getting out front with the media and the public with a possibly wrong attribution when the situation is still fluid.

A prominent example of the perils of misattribution is the aftermath of the September 2012 attack on the U.S. State Department Temporary Mission Facility in Benghazi, Libya, which resulted in the death of Ambassador Christopher Stevens and three other Americans (the assault on the facility was followed by attacks on the nearby CIA annex). Susan Rice, the U.S. ambassador to the United Nations, appeared on five Sunday morning news talk shows the following week, and on one of them she remarked:

> Our current best assessment, based on the information that we have at present, is that, in fact, what this began as, it was a spontaneous—not a premeditated—response to what had transpired in Cairo. In Cairo, a few hours earlier, there was a violent protest that was undertaken in reaction to this very offensive video that was disseminated. We believe that folks in Benghazi, a small number of people came to the embassy to—

or to the consulate, rather, to replicate the sort of challenge that was posed in Cairo. And then as that unfolded, it seems to have been hijacked, let us say, by some individual clusters of extremists who came with heavier weapons. . . . And it then evolved from there.[18]

Although she pointed out with appropriate caution that an FBI investigation was under way to discover the facts, and that the administration's assessment was based on limited evidence, still the takeaway headlines were that her official account contradicted that of Libyan officials, who said that the attacks were planned and deliberate. Her statements were based on talking points prepared by the White House with the assistance of the CIA and the State Department, and they were actually intended for Democratic congressional leaders. Nine months later the controversy still simmered, leading the Obama administration to feel compelled to release a lengthy e-mail chain in order to show that there had not been a deliberate effort to deceive Congress or the public (selections of the e-mails had already been leaked). The CIA and State Department struggled over how much to disclose while under severe time constraints that were due to pressure from Congress. Concerns centered on avoiding interference with the ongoing FBI investigation, responding to the charge that the State Department had not provided adequate security for the outpost, and deciding what information to give Congress that was not also being provided to news reporters. In the end, the final version of the talking points—the version used by Ambassador Rice—struck out a reference to CIA warnings about the dangers of the security environment in Libya and the presence in Benghazi of extremists linked to al Qa'ida.[19]

Circumstances at the time were indeed confusing. The attack occurred under conditions of high insecurity following rapid changes in the groups claiming authority in Libya after the overthrow of Qaddafi. The extremist actors involved were multiple, shifting, and fragmented. Their allegiances were uncertain, probably obscure even to themselves, although the United States relied on some local militias for protection. The situation was so volatile and dangerous that the official FBI investigation had to be conducted from a distance. On the basis of lengthy inquiries, Michael Morell, CIA deputy director at the time, concluded that there was no coordinated, well-thought-out plan to attack the compound but instead a mob, some of whom were Islamist extremists, looting and vandalizing with tragic results.[20]

Morell was perplexed that the administration did not declassify video footage that demonstrated the haphazard, albeit deadly, nature of the attacks. According to Morell's account, CIA intelligence analysts were simply mistaken in their initial judgment that the attacks started with a protest demonstration. During an internal review of the talking points to be sent to the White House—which then used them to develop its own talking points, which were what Ambassador Rice relied on—CIA officials also deleted an original phrase that referred to ties to al Qa'ida because they did not want to compromise the ongoing FBI criminal investigation with a premature attribution of responsibility. The FBI also explicitly asked that references to the participation of Islamist extremists be watered down so as not to impede the investigation. And the State Department requested the removal of a sentence linking the extremist group Ansar al-Sharia directly to the attacks because the evidence for the statement was classified.

Rice's comments immediately aroused the ire of Republican politicians, many of them determined to take partisan advantage of a slip, indignant that the Obama administration seemed to refuse to call terrorism by its name, or outraged that security for American diplomats was apparently so weak. Critics charged the administration with failing to take robust security precautions due to misdiagnosis of the threat or, worse, concealing a known danger in order to improve the president's chances for reelection. The controversy lingered through the elections and well into the 2016 presidential campaign.

However convincing the excuses for the error might be, and never mind that the administration admitted that the talking points were in error, and that Susan Rice did not participate in drafting them, the result was that the president's intention to appoint Susan Rice as secretary of state in his second-term administration was derailed. The general consensus was that after the scandal she could never be confirmed by the Senate for a cabinet position. After Republican Senators McCain, Graham, and Ayotte vowed to block her nomination because of the Benghazi controversy, she withdrew her name from consideration. Instead, in June 2013, the president appointed Rice national security adviser, a post that does not require confirmation.

Another politically damaging effect of the publicity surrounding the mistaken or misinterpreted attribution of the Benghazi attacks was the public disclosure of extensive and clandestine CIA operations in Libya—in fact, the existence of a large classified annex in Benghazi, something that U.S. decisionmakers would undoubtedly have preferred to keep secret.[21] CIA employees outnumbered State Department personnel, and two CIA intelligence contractors were among the four Americans killed, although they were at first listed as State Department employees.

An earlier and equally controversial case involved the Spanish government's reaction to the deadly Madrid train station bombings in March 2004, when 191 people were killed and nearly 2,000 injured as four trains were struck almost simultaneously. (The organizational amorphousness of this case was discussed in chapter 4.) The bombings occurred just days before a Spanish general election that the incumbent party appeared likely to win.

Although the multiple coordinated bombings of commuter trains headed into the central Atocha railway station were uncharacteristic of the Basque separatist group ETA, the government of Jose Maria Aznar of the Partido Popular immediately blamed ETA.[22] ETA typically was willing to take credit for their actions; yet ETA denied any involvement, and many knowledgeable observers were skeptical of the government's claims. But the government stuck to its story even as it became increasingly hard to justify. Aznar himself telephoned leading newspaper editors, ambassadors were instructed to tell foreign audiences that ETA was to blame, and Spain even insisted that the UN Security Council name ETA in its condemnation of the bombings.

The reality was that the perpetrators were members of an extended jihadist group either inspired by or organizationally linked to al Qa'ida. The question of whether al Qa'ida could be blamed for the bombings remained disputed for years. Shortly after the attacks someone who identified himself as an al Qa'ida spokesman claimed credit for them, but claims are not always to be believed. The CIA's conclusion, based on its own intelligence and the Spanish investigation, was that despite the fact that the attacks were well coordinated and simultaneous, no evidence linked the attacks to bin Laden.[23] Many members of the jihadist cell were first-generation Moroccan emigrants. Most of the perpetrators were cornered by the police in an apartment on the outskirts of Madrid and blew themselves up. Whoever was really responsible, al Qa'ida or its sympathizers, it was certainly not ETA.

Why did the government insist on ETA and insist for so long? Electoral concerns appear to have been paramount, not the quality and quantity of the evidence. The Aznar government may have feared that designating the bombers as Islamists would fuel more public opposition to Spain's support for the U.S. invasion of Iraq. The government had built a reputation of being tough on ETA, so heightened salience of the threat might remind voters of the government's hard-line position (although it seems reasonable that the opposite might also be true—such a terrible strike would show that the government's policy was not working). The opposition Socialist Party was vulnerable on this count, having been associated indirectly with an effort to orchestrate a truce between ETA and the government. But the Aznar administration's misstep remains a puzzle.

Whatever the motive, the consequences of the government's mistake were massive. The conservative Partido Popular, although in the lead in early days, lost decisively to the opposition Socialists. The bombings themselves probably contributed to greater turnout than usual, and many voters felt that they had been manipulated. There were protests in Madrid against a cover-up protecting the real perpetrators. Although some analysts interpreted the election results as a capitulation to al Qa'ida's demands that Spain get out of Iraq, and thus as a success story for terrorist coercion of democracies, this interpretation does not seem to be supported by evidence.[24]

Lack of Timeliness

It can take a very long time after a terrorist attack for even the best intelligence services to figure out who did it—as we noted above, timeliness and credibility of attribution are a combination that can be impossible to achieve. Getting an answer can take many years or may never come at all. The perpetrators may aim to deceive rather than publicize their role, and as clandestine political actors they are skilled at concealing their tracks. The world of conspiratorial violence is murky and group survival depends on secrecy. Most attacks against U.S. citizens and interests take place outside the country, under the formal jurisdiction of foreign governments who may not be fully cooperative in investigating the attacks or may lack the capability to assist. At home, policymakers and analysts may fail to reach a consensus, disagreeing despite access to the same intelligence assessments. Thus bringing terrorists to justice may be delayed for so long that retribution is no longer feasible or politically possible or as satisfying to the families of the victims.

A prominent example of this dilemma is the bombing of Khobar Towers, a U.S. Air Force housing complex, in Khobar, Saudi Arabia, in 1996. The attack killed nineteen American military personnel, with hundreds left wounded, and President Bill Clinton immediately promised swift justice. No stone would be left unturned, he said. The trail led to Iran and Hezbollah, but Saudi Arabia was reluctant to cooperate with the FBI investigation and would not allow the suspects to be interviewed. Finally, at FBI Director Louis Freeh's request, George H. W. Bush, the former president, personally asked Crown Prince Abdullah to intervene. American policymakers were also divided among themselves. Some insisted that bin Laden was responsible. The 9/11 Commission hinted at this, and more recently, in 2007, William Perry, a former U.S. secretary of defense, publicly claimed that he believed that al Qa'ida was responsible for the attack.[25] By the time charges of Iranian complicity seemed credible it was no longer politically advantageous to blame Iran because moderates appeared to be gaining traction in the domestic power struggle. Moreover, Saudi Arabia was not keen on supporting a public charge against Iran. President Clinton thus took a more subtle approach by writing a secret letter to the newly elected Iranian administration explaining that failure to resolve the case was a major impediment to improving U.S.-Iranian relations. Still Iran was not forthcoming. Eventually, under the second Bush administration, suspects were indicted in the United States, but they were not tried. In 2006 ten years after the bombing, a lawsuit against Iran filed by survivors of the victims was thrown out by the presiding judge for lack of evidence. Louis Freeh testified on behalf of the plaintiffs, to no avail.

Another prominent case with a long time frame is also instructive: the 2000 bombing of the U.S.S. *Cole* in Yemen, which killed seventeen

Navy personnel and inflicted massive damage on the ship. Efforts to establish a case were slow and frustrating—it took months before the United States was reasonably sure that al Qa'ida could be blamed. In the spring of 2001 there was still a dispute in the Bush administration over how clear the evidence was. According to the president's CIA briefer Michael Morell, the CIA assessment was that al Qa'ida leadership directed the plot, but it was impossible to "nail down responsibility with certainty."[26] As recently as August 2001 the *New York Times* reported that the FBI investigation had "ground to a halt" and that the government's efforts to link the U.S.S. *Cole* bombing to bin Laden had been frustrated.[27] Indictments of individuals and a definitive charge that al Qa'ida was responsible were finally handed down by the Department of Justice in May 2003.[28]

Why had it taken so long? The Yemeni authorities were even more uncooperative than the Saudis had been in the Khobar Towers case, and the FBI investigation was short and unpleasant on all sides. FBI agents felt themselves to be in personal danger from Yemeni security forces.

Disputes between the FBI and the State Department also hampered investigations. Ambassador Barbara Bodine objected to the methods employed by the FBI and even denied John O'Neill, the head agent, reentry into the country when he went home for Thanksgiving. (Tragically, on 9/11 O'Neill was killed in the World Trade Center.) Contentious issues apparently included the conduct of property searches and interviews. Critics thought the FBI sent too many agents (over a hundred) with too few cross-cultural skills and too many weapons.

The aftermath was scarcely satisfactory. Over the years Yemen allowed detainees to escape, some more than once, or simply released them from prison. After 2002 several of the suspected perpetrators were killed in unilateral drone strikes, most recently in May 2012. Two others were held in U.S. custody at Guantanamo until they were transferred to Senegal in 2016.

Since 2004 the families of the seventeen sailors who were killed have been pursuing legal action in U.S. courts to collect financial damages against Sudan, which is accused of helping al Qa'ida finance the attack and permitting an al Qa'ida operative to ship the explosives to Yemen. In 2012 and again in 2015 U.S. federal judges found the government of Sudan liable and awarded over $300 million in damages. In 2015 a district court judge in Washington, D.C., found both Sudan and Iran responsible for the bombing and awarded $75 million in civil damages. The judge ruled that Iran had directly conspired with al Qa'ida to establish a Yemen branch.[29]

An unresolved question related to the frustrating effort to ascertain responsibility for the U.S.S. *Cole* bombing is whether a more thorough and efficient investigation would have revealed the outlines of the 9/11 plot. One of the chief conspirators in the *Cole* plot was present at the January 2000 meeting in Malaysia that included two of the 9/11 hijackers.[30]

No Resolution

There are cases where agreed-upon attribution of responsibility never occurs. One such instance of failure to establish attribution despite persistent efforts over many years involves the 1985 bombing of the El Descanso restaurant outside Madrid, not far from the American-leased air base at Torrejon, near the airport. The case did not officially involve American authorities. The restaurant, known as the House of Ribs, was popular with U.S. military personnel, but none were killed, although several were wounded. Nevertheless, it is probable that American soldiers were the real targets and that most of the actual victims, eighteen killed and over eighty injured, all Spanish, were unlucky bystanders. The attack also occurred before passage of the Omnibus Diplomatic Security and Antiterrorism Act of 1986, which expanded American jurisdiction over terrorist attacks against American citizens abroad.

There were multiple claims of responsibility as well as multiple accusations. At the outset, ETA, Hezbollah, and the Popular Front for the Liberation of Palestine–General Command were named as possible instigators. In Spain, the first court trial closed without result in 1987, and the second opened in 2005 following the discovery of somewhat dubious new evidence implicating Abu Musab al-Suri, a well-known jihadist ideologue. In 2005 the United States captured al-Suri in Pakistan and turned him over to his country of origin, Syria, but he was apparently released in December 2011. It is unlikely that he was involved, and it is possible that the Spanish government knew that the PFLP-GC was responsible but avoided accusing the group publicly due to a desire to improve relationships with the Algerian government, which was supporting the PFLP-GC at the time.

The bottom line is that official attributions of responsibility are sometimes wrong, sometimes governments eventually identify the perpetrators but take so long that a response is impossible or ineffective, and sometimes resolution is never reached at all.

Radiological or Nuclear Weapons

The consequences of the attribution problem are especially acute with regard to the potential terrorist threat from radiological or nuclear weapons. The United States considers nuclear terrorism by nonstate actors, whether acting alone or with the assistance of hostile states, to be a major national security threat.[31] If there should be an act of terrorism using nuclear materials, whether an actual nuclear bomb or a radiological dispersal device (a "dirty bomb"), how likely is it that the U.S. government would know who did it? A credible claim of responsibility would make attribution easier, but in the absence of a claim it could be extremely difficult to establish authorship and thus to punish. If attribution is problematic, then a policy of deterrence through threats of retaliation is unlikely to be effective. Yet deterrence is the cornerstone of current American policy.

For example, expert forensic investigations might reveal the physical source of materials, but the investigators would still not know how the materials were acquired. Were they stolen or purchased? Was a state officially complicit? At what level of the government bureaucracy— leaders at the top or lower officials? Civilian leadership or military establishment? Conditions in Pakistan are particularly disturbing, as some violent jihadist groups have enjoyed the support of the Inter-Services Intelligence (ISI), the premier military-operated intelligence service of Pakistan. Indeed, bin Laden resided peacefully in Pakistani territory for years. How convincing would proof of responsibility have to be before the United States would punish an ally?

The likelihood of effective attribution is a subject about which academic specialists relying on GTD data come to different conclusions. On the one hand, Keir Lieber and Daryl Press argue that states are unlikely to provide nuclear materials to terrorists because attribution will be near certain and thus the move would be far too risky.[32] In general, in their view, a nonstate actor would have about a 60 percent chance of anonymity. There is a statistical correlation between the number of fatalities and the likelihood of attribution. Thus, as the number of fatalities increases, so does the rate of attribution. If an attack kills more than 100 people the attackers are identified 73 percent of the time. In addition, the United States and its allies outperform other states in attribution capability. In the cases of attacks on the United States and its allies the attackers are identified 97 percent of the time.

Philip Baxter takes a different view. He questions whether nuclear forensics could provide an answer quickly enough.[33] He also argues that identifying the source of a nonconventional nuclear or radiological attack is more difficult and time-consuming than tracing a conventional attack—which, as we have seen, is not necessarily easy. GTD-recorded attacks involving CBR weapons are rare, and they are less likely than others to cause casualties, thus inferences based on their occurrence should be regarded with caution. Whereas to Lieber and Press the United States should advertise its impressive attribution capabilities because states can effectively be deterred (leaving aside the question of nonstates acting independently of states), to Baxter expectations of timely attribution should be more realistic.

Past experience tells us that the process of establishing responsibility could take many years and might never result in a conclusive attribution. Yet political pressure to find out who was responsible would be intense, even overwhelming. One implication is that preventive security measures become even more critical. Another is that the U.S. government should be prepared to resist calls for a hasty response. Think of the consequences of a severe retaliation that later turned out to be based on a misattribution of responsibility.

The Attribution Dilemma

Attributing responsibility for a terrorist attack correctly and rapidly is challenging. In over half of the 156,722 cases in the Global Terrorism Database we are unable to make even a strong guess about which organization or individual was responsible. The proportion of unattributed attacks varies greatly over time, across regions and countries, by targets, and by weapons. Statistical methods based on taking characteristics of known perpetrators and attributing responsibility for attacks is getting more sophisticated but is unlikely ever to be accurate enough to form the basis for sound policy. Mistaken attribution can have serious and long-lasting consequences. The lack of timely attribution can carry major political costs. And cases where there is never a resolution are especially unsatisfying to both the public and policymakers. Although the world has experienced very few acts of radiological terrorism and no nuclear terrorist attacks to date, the current U.S. reliance on deterrence against nuclear and radiological attacks through threats of retaliation is problematic, because it is often the case that governments cannot say with certainty who is responsible. Attribution difficulties may make reliance on methods such as targeted assassination more attractive to policymakers, because the standards of evidence are not publicly revealed. If the executive branch makes the decision about who is responsible, there is no need for a lengthy and restrictive investigation preparatory to a trial.

Of course not all terrorist attacks are equally significant in terms of the need for attribution. A one-off attack causing minor economic damage may not be a high priority for determining attribution, whereas a major high-casualty attack is much more important. Nonetheless, unattributed terrorist attacks have claimed the lives of thousands. In the six years since 2010 alone, the GTD records 76,239 fatalities in unattributed attacks. At the most basic level, responding effectively to a terrorist attack requires knowledge of who committed the act, and that conclusion must be reached rapidly. Unfortunately, in too many cases such certainty simply does not exist.

Appendix 5-1: Countries in Each Region of the Global Terrorism Database, 1970–2015

REGION	COUNTRIES
Australasia and Oceania	Australia, Fiji, French Polynesia, New Caledonia, New Hebrides, New Zealand, Papua New Guinea, Solomon Islands, Vanuatu, Wallis and Futuna

(continued)

REGION	COUNTRIES
Central America and Caribbean	Antigua and Barbuda, Bahamas, Barbados, Belize, Cayman Islands, Costa Rica, Cuba, Dominica, Dominican Republic, El Salvador, Grenada, Guadeloupe, Guatemala, Haiti, Honduras, Jamaica, Martinique, Nicaragua, Panama, St. Kitts and Nevis, St. Lucia, Trinidad and Tobago
Central Asia	Armenia, Azerbaijan, Georgia, Kazakhstan, Kyrgyzstan, Tajikistan, Turkmenistan, Uzbekistan
East Asia	China, Hong Kong, Japan, Macau, North Korea, South Korea, Taiwan
Eastern Europe	Albania, Belarus, Bosnia-Herzegovina, Bulgaria, Croatia, Czech Republic, Czechoslovakia, East Germany (GDR), Estonia, Hungary, Kosovo, Latvia, Lithuania, Macedonia, Moldova, Montenegro, Poland, Romania, Russia, Serbia, Serbia-Montenegro, Slovak Republic, Slovenia, Soviet Union, Ukraine, Yugoslavia
Middle East and North Africa	Algeria, Bahrain, Egypt, Iran, Iraq, Israel, Jordan, Kuwait, Lebanon, Libya, Morocco, North Yemen, Qatar, Saudi Arabia, South Yemen, Syria, Tunisia, Turkey, United Arab Emirates, West Bank and Gaza Strip, Western Sahara, Yemen
North America	Canada, Mexico, United States
South America	Argentina, Bolivia, Brazil, Chile, Colombia, Ecuador, Falkland Islands, French Guiana, Guyana, Paraguay, Peru, Suriname, Uruguay, Venezuela
South Asia	Afghanistan, Bangladesh, Bhutan, India, Maldives, Mauritius, Nepal, Pakistan, Sri Lanka
Southeast Asia	Brunei, Cambodia, East Timor, Indonesia, Laos, Malaysia, Myanmar, Philippines, Singapore, South Vietnam, Thailand, Vietnam

(continued)

REGION	COUNTRIES
Sub-Saharan Africa	Angola, Benin, Botswana, Burkina Faso, Burundi, Cameroon, Central African Republic, Chad, Comoros, Democratic Republic of the Congo, Djibouti, Equatorial Guinea, Eritrea, Ethiopia, Gabon, Gambia, Ghana, Guinea, Guinea-Bissau, Ivory Coast, Kenya, Lesotho, Liberia, Madagascar, Malawi, Mali, Mauritania, Mozambique, Namibia, Niger, Nigeria, People's Republic of the Congo, Republic of the Congo, Rhodesia, Rwanda, Senegal, Seychelles, Sierra Leone, Somalia, South Africa, South Sudan, Sudan, Swaziland, Tanzania, Togo, Uganda, Zaire, Zambia, Zimbabwe
Western Europe	Andorra, Austria, Belgium, Cyprus, Denmark, Finland, France, Germany, Gibraltar, Greece, Iceland, Ireland, Italy, Luxembourg, Malta, Netherlands, Norway, Portugal, Spain, Sweden, Switzerland, United Kingdom, Vatican City, West Germany (FRG)

Note: Over time some countries have disappeared (e.g., the Federal Republic of Germany, [West Germany], the Soviet Union, Yugoslavia, and Czechoslovakia) while others have been created (Eritrea, Germany, South Sudan). To capture these changes the GTD attaches terrorist attacks to the officially recognized political entity over time. For example, a 1989 attack in Bonn would be attached to the Federal Republic of Germany (or West Germany). An identical attack in 1991 would be recorded as taking place in Germany. For a complete listing of political changes in the boundaries of countries over time and how they are conceptualized in the GTD, see http://www.start.umd.edu/gtd/downloads/Codebook.pdf, pp. 18–19.

CHAPTER 6

Counterterrorism Results

Can Effectiveness be Evaluated?

Why is it so hard to assess the effectiveness of counterterrorism measures? Evaluation is a challenge for academic researchers as well as policymakers. While it is difficult to get an accurate grasp of the terrorist threat, it is even harder to get an analytical grip on counterterrorism. Substantial progress has been made in gathering data on terrorist attacks and the organizations and individuals conducting them, but there is far less reliable and comprehensive information on government policy and its implementation. And certainly there is nothing close to a worldwide database on counterterrorism measures similar to the databases that now track worldwide terrorist attacks and actors. Admittedly, since the problem of terrorism is so complex, it would be unrealistic to expect counterterrorism to be less complex.

Why be concerned with evaluating the effectiveness of measures against terrorism? Limitations of time and space preclude a detailed appraisal of the costs, financial and otherwise, of counterterrorism, but without being able to judge how effective policies are against terrorism it is impossible to balance overall costs and benefits. Counterterrorism goes far beyond military and other security sector activities. The financial costs of counterterrorism are spread across diverse government programs, some of which are highly classified, such as the National

Intelligence Program. The budget trail is further obscured by distinguishing costs that are strictly for counterterrorism from those that are related to more general government functions. For example, the Department of Homeland Security deals directly with counterterrorism but also has broad responsibilities for areas as diverse as relief from natural disasters and customs enforcement. The FBI tracks crime as well as terrorism. Even so, according to data collected by the Stockholm International Peace Research Institute, the United States spends far more on counterterrorism than other countries.[1] However, this estimate is also complicated by the fact that it is difficult to disentangle counterterrorism spending from general military spending. The security experts Gordon Adams and Cindy Williams estimate that the United States spends at least $100 billion a year on counterterrorism efforts.[2] Their finding substantiates John Mueller and Mark Stewart's conclusion that from 2001 to 2011 the United States spent more than $1 trillion on domestic counterterrorism measures. This figure excludes overseas expenditures such as the wars in Iraq and Afghanistan.[3] In 2013 President Obama said that the U.S. government had spent over a trillion dollars on these wars.[4]

The massive financial costs of counterterrorism alone are ample justification for analyzing the effectiveness of measures. If we add to monetary costs other less tangible but serious consequences such as effects on civil liberties and privacy, citizens' trust in government, or international legitimacy and reputation, the need is even more compelling. How can governments show that policies are working in order to justify the costs? For example, according to the economists Sendil Mullainathan and Richard H. Thaler, the Transportation Security Administration (TSA) spent $7.55 billion on airport security in 2015, but this figure does not include the cost of passengers' time spent in interminable security lines or the inconvenience of missing flights.[5] Without having this information about cost, sensible trade-offs are impossible. If only budgets are measured, the TSA has an incentive to promote the appearance of safety rather than genuine safety. There have been no catastrophic attacks on U.S. aviation since 9/11, but is airport security actually the reason?

A similar story can be told about efforts to counter the radicalization of individuals so that they do not become violent. In early 2016 the Department of Homeland Security announced the establishment of an interagency Countering Violent Extremism Task Force with the aim of coordinating myriad counter-radicalization efforts at all levels of government and bringing order to a disconnected mix of programs and sponsors. The San Bernardino attacks were a major impetus for the move, which was in part an effort to improve outreach to U.S. Muslim communities. The *Washington Post,* noting the absence of evidence of prospective effectiveness, commented, "One of the biggest problems the administration has faced is determining whether any of it is working." In the story an anonymous official was quoted as saying, "That is the billion-dollar question. We don't have great, perfect data on why people become radicalized or why people change their mind. . . . You can't prove a negative—'How many young guys did you prevent going to Syria today?' "[6]

In this chapter we break the problem down into several components. First, one of the background difficulties in judging effectiveness is figuring out just what counterterrorism is, what it consists of. For academic and policy worlds, the scope of counterterrorism seems almost impossibly broad. Second, it is not easy to know the government's overall goal, the desired end state. In other words, how should effectiveness be defined? Is the major objective of the U.S. government to prevent all terrorist attacks, just those that threaten human life, just those that could be catastrophic, just those that harm Americans, or just those that undermine the security of the U.S. homeland? Since political and academic consensus on what the end state—what the long-term goal—should be is lacking, it is hard to decide which strategies are best suited to achieving this goal. In dealing with any complex problem government always seeks demonstrable measures of progress, yet given these constraints, it is not surprising that measuring counterterrorism effectiveness is hard. The search for metrics to evaluate success or merely reasonable progress toward specified goals has been inconclusive. What should be counted and how concrete can or should such measures be? Relying on number of attacks, lethality of attacks, or even more cerebral measures such as levels of public fear or concern as metrics has proved problematic. We discuss the mixed record of attempts to measure the effectiveness of deterrence and of decapitation, both cornerstones of U.S. policy. Last, we evaluate the prospects for developing methods and data for rigorous statistical analysis of counterterrorism measures.

The Scope of Counterterrorism

What is counterterrorism? The complexities of conceptualizing exactly what the content of counterterrorism is, or should be, impede efforts to determine its effectiveness. Ambiguity is in part a consequence of the wide scope and variety of government activities commonly defined as counterterrorism, a "counterterrorism is what you make of it" approach that also confuses matters by conflating goals, strategies, and implementation measures. This inclusiveness prompts the question of whether it is possible to evaluate effectiveness measure by measure or comprehensively—and in the latter case, how to integrate different activities conceptually, never mind at the level of actual bureaucratic practice.

Academic analysis has tended to be all-encompassing. For example, in a useful cross-national survey the political scientists Robert Art and Louise Richardson include political, legislative-judicial, and security domains in a variety of contexts.[7] Political measures range from negotiations and amnesties in civil conflicts to economic sanctions against state supporters of foreign terrorist organizations. Legal responses extend to all aspects of arrest, prosecution, and incarceration as well as legislation aimed at stopping material support for terrorist causes or authorizing emergency powers provisions. Legislative and judicial measures can also involve counter-radicalization policies. Security measures include both intelligence and military operations, thus curfews and search operations, military air strikes and tribunals, and targeted assassinations.

The criminologists Cynthia Lum, Lesley Kennedy, and Alison Sherley conducted what is perhaps the most extensive review of the literature on counterterrorism measures to date, although their survey is over ten years old.[8] They located over 20,000 articles on terrorism written in English, published between 1971 and 2003, that reference "political, social, legal, law enforcement, economic, preventative, reactive, or after-care responses."[9] They helpfully categorize the field in terms of counterterrorism as prevention, detection, management, or response. The list of actions included under each of these categories is expansive, crossing domestic and foreign policy arenas, from foreign aid and economic sanctions to scanning shipping containers to threat-level warning systems at home.

Laura Dugan and Erica Chenoweth criticize prior statistical evaluations of counterterrorism measures as too narrow: they spotlight repressive measures taken by governments but ignore conciliatory actions or attempts to reward violent political organizations for engaging in peaceful behavior such as opening schools or providing health services for their communities.[10] They measure Israeli government responses to terrorism from 1987 to 2004, from accommodation and full concessions to deadly repression.

The mission space for counterterrorism identified by the U.S. security establishment is, if anything, broader still. A 2014 report by the chairman of the Joint Chiefs of Staff defines counterterrorism (CT) as "activities and operations . . . taken to neutralize terrorists, their organizations, and networks in order to render them incapable of using violence to instill fear and coerce governments or societies to achieve their goals" and outlines three types of activities.[11] "Advise and assist activities . . . [include] all US military efforts to improve other nations' ability to provide security for its citizens, govern, provide services, prevent terrorists from using the nation's territory as a safe haven, and promote long-term regional stability."[12] Overseas CT activities are "offense, defense, and stability operations; counterinsurgency operations; peace operations; and counterdrug operations." Defense support of civil authorities includes "support to prepare, prevent, protect, respond, and recover from domestic incidents including terrorist attacks, major disasters both natural and man-made, and domestic special events." This is a daunting list of military responsibilities.

If we link nonmilitary efforts to counter violent extremism to security-oriented counterterrorism, the scope of what could be considered counterterrorism increases even more. Especially since 2015 and the White House Summit on Countering Violent Extremism held over three days in February, CVE, the "soft" side of counterterrorism, has been emphasized. Outside U.S. borders the State Department, USAID, and other agencies aim to mobilize civil society, prevent the alienation and marginalization of youth, and reduce political, social, and economic grievances, as well as prevent the emergence of failed states, all in conjunction with local partners.[13] Measures to combat extremism stress countering the narrative, or diminishing the ideological appeal of violent jihadism, in order to shrink the space and tolerance of extremist propaganda and discredit the online presence of jihadist voices.

They include initiatives such as the Strong Cities Network to connect urban officials;[14] community development programs such as youth conferences and soccer leagues; and combatting prison radicalization, including the rehabilitation and social reintegration of prisoners.

In short, the scope of measures that researchers and policymakers must evaluate in order to assess the effectiveness of counterterrorism may be so unbounded and elastic that almost any activity pursued by a government might qualify. Our list of examples of counterterrorism measures could have been much longer. Our point is not to take issue with these extremely broad conceptualizations of what constitutes counterterrorism—indeed, an expansive view of counterterrorism seems inevitable. Rather, we emphasize that the breadth of the definition of counterterrorism and the incredible range of actions that are typically included make it extremely challenging to establish priorities, integrate activities, and then to analyze outcomes.

Conceptualizing Ends and Means of Counterterrorism Activities

What is the long-term goal or desired end state? What objectives is the U.S. government actually trying to achieve when its agencies design counterterrorism policies and practices? How do these goals fit into broader sets of national interests? Then, what strategies can be designed to achieve these goals? Are means suited to ends? These questions elicit highly controversial responses.

The 2004 and 2008 presidential campaigns revealed deep divisions in the American political establishment. In an interview with the *New York Times,* the Democratic nominee, John Kerry, offered the judgment that the purpose of counterterrorism policy should be "to get back to the place we were, where terrorists are not the focus of our lives, but they're a nuisance." He compared terrorism to crime: "As a former law-enforcement person, I know we're never going to end prostitution. We're never going to end illegal gambling. But we're going to reduce it, organized crime, to a level where it isn't on the rise. It isn't threatening people's lives every day, and fundamentally, it's something that you continue to fight, but it's not threatening the fabric of your life."[15]

President Bush responded that the fight against terrorism was not "primarily a law enforcement and intelligence-gathering operation" but a "threat that demands the full use of American power." He continued, "Our goal is not to reduce terror to some acceptable level of nuisance. Our goal is to defeat terror by staying on the offensive, destroying terrorists, and spreading freedom and liberty around the world."[16] Vice President Cheney also entered the fray, saying that comparing terrorism to prostitution or gambling was "naïve and dangerous."[17] Rudolph Giuliani weighed in: "The idea that you can have an acceptable level of terrorism is frightening."[18] The Bush campaign released a campaign commercial to blast Kerry: "Terrorism, a nuisance? How can Kerry protect us when he doesn't understand the threat?"[19]

As the 2008 presidential campaign gained momentum, ABC News noted that the language used in the Bush administration's National Defense Strategy of 2008 bore a remarkable resemblance to Kerry's earlier remarks: "Victory will include discrediting extremist ideology, creating fissures between and among extremist groups and reducing them to the level of nuisance groups that can be tracked and handled by law enforcement capabilities."[20] ABC News noted as well that Dick Cheney had criticized Kerry for promising to fight a more sensitive war on terror that would reach out to other nations to bring them to the U.S. side.[21] Cheney had retorted that not one of America's wars had been won by being sensitive and that "a sensitive war will not destroy the evil men who killed 3,000 Americans and who seek the chemical, nuclear and biological weapons to kill hundreds of thousands more. The men who killed Daniel Pearl and Paul Johnson will not be impressed by sensitivity."[22] Yet the 2008 National Defense Strategy concluded that countering the ideological messages of terrorist groups "will require sensitive, sophisticated and integrated interagency and international efforts."[23] At the same time official rhetoric continued to refer to "winning the long war against violent extremists," "eliminating the ability of extremists to strike globally," and "victory" through their "defeat."[24]

Since 9/11, the White House and individual government agencies such as the Joint Chiefs of Staff and the Department of Homeland Security have issued a series of official strategy statements explaining national policy goals; these reveal significant shifts in emphasis and tone but at the same time there are commonalities across adminis-trations.[25] One important point of consensus that is strong and con-sistent is the goal of keeping "weapons of mass destruction" out of the hands of terrorists. Preventing nuclear terrorism in particular has been a high priority objective for decades. This objective is not in dispute. Others were and are.

President Bush initially proposed an extremely broad approach, promising the defeat of terrorism around the world and vowing to draw on all of the resources at his disposal, from intelligence to law enforcement to the military, to do so.[26] In his initial post-9/11 state-ment President Bush made no distinction between "the terrorists who committed these acts and those who harbor them." Nine days later, in an address to a joint session of Congress, he provided more details, narrowing the focus slightly to terrorist organizations with a "global reach," but still promising to punish not only terrorists but those who provide them a safe haven.[27] Despite Bush's broad brush, the clear target of the evolving policy was al Qa'ida and its affiliates and, more generally, organizations whose main areas of terrorist operations were in other countries. In the original 9/11 speech the president empha-sized the role of the law enforcement community in finding and bring-ing to justice those responsible, but nine days after 9/11, the president characterized the response more purely in military terms, stating: "Our war on terror begins with al Qa'ida, but it does not end there. It will not end until every terrorist group of global reach has been found, stopped and defeated."[28]

In the early days of the first George W. Bush administration, the goal of the global war on terrorism was "a world in which terrorism does not define the daily lives of Americans and their friends." The intent was to eliminate terrorism as a threat to the American way of life. The national interest was defined in a dual sense: opposing ter-rorism and preventing irresponsible states from acquiring weapons of mass destruction. This aim was defined not just as a matter of na-tional survival and self-defense but as a moral necessity in dealing with evil. The summary mantra of Bush administration policy was the "four D's": Defeat, Deny (state support), Diminish (by addressing "root causes"), and Defend (the homeland and Americans abroad). Strategy statements stressed preemption as "anticipatory self-defense" and bluntly advocated unilateral action. The Bush administration warned that the United States would seek international support but would act alone if American interests and "unique" responsibilities required.

The unilateralist approach was renewed in 2006, but its edges were distinctly softened. The second round of strategic statements no longer dwelled on going it alone but referred to "international standards" and strengthening coalitions and partnerships. For example, the Department of Defense's National Military Strategic Plan of February 2006 stressed the importance of the global coalition against terrorism and an international U.S.-led effort. In fact, allies and partners were said to be vital to combatting terrorism. The March 2006 strategy statement from the White House contained an entire chapter devoted to the subject of strengthening alliances and preventing attacks not just against the United States but against American "friends." It affirmed that the United States would take the fight to the enemy, but added the qualification that the fight would be conducted with the support of friends and allies.

At the same time, the Bush administration's statement of goals departed even more sharply from a realist view of international politics, which stresses the primacy of interest and power, to one of changing regimes from authoritarianism to democracy. Spreading *effective* democracy around the world was now named as the goal, based on the assumption that the spread of democracy would "bring an end to the scourge of terrorism." The stated intent became the defeat of violent extremism of all sorts and the creation of an international environment inhospitable to extremism. Thus, advancing democracy was considered both an end and a means. The term "violent extremism" had actually been introduced during the Bush administration in the summer of 2005 under the acronym SAVE (Struggle Against Violent Extremism), although the Bush administration treated it as one aspect of the global war on terrorism rather than a centerpiece of policy.[29] The 2006 strategy statements acknowledged the phenomenon of "homegrown" terrorism within democracies that was not always operationally connected to the leadership of al Qa'ida, although very likely inspired by its example. The U.S. government attributed this threat to "some ethnic or religious groups . . . unable or unwilling to grasp the benefits of freedom." Only three "D's" were now mentioned, including defeat, deny, and defend, as listed in 2002, but omitting the requirement of "diminishing" by addressing "root causes."

At the same time, the 2006 National Military Strategic Plan referred not just to defending the American homeland and attacking terrorists abroad but also to strengthening Muslim moderates who could resist violent extremism. It called for using all elements of American power in this effort, going well beyond the employment of military force. In a list of responses to terrorism, attacking the enemy is low on the list, after countering ideologies, promoting moderate alternatives, and strengthening the capacity of other governments to resist it. In fact, ideology was described as the enemy's strategic center of gravity.

The president's letter to fellow Americans that accompanied the March 2006 National Security Strategy contended that the strategy was idealistic about goals while being realistic about means. The ultimate goal of American policy was to end tyranny in the world. The goal of countering terrorism would only be achieved "when Americans and other civilized people around the world can lead their lives free from terrorist attacks."[30]

Soon after his election, President Obama outlined his approach to national goals for combatting terrorism in a speech at Cairo University in Egypt.[31] He expressed the intent of seeking a new beginning to relations between the United States and Muslims around the world and took great pains to distinguish the largely peaceful history of Islam from those who used Islam to further violent goals. Obama argued, "Islam is not part of the problem in combating violent extremism . . . [but rather] is an important part of promoting peace." He described "the world that we seek—a world where extremists no longer threaten our people, and American troops have come home; a world where Israelis and Palestinians are each secure in a state of their own, and nuclear energy is used for peaceful purposes; a world where governments serve their citizens, and the rights of all God's children are respected." He pledged that the United States would not impose a system of government on another country but would support human rights, religious freedom, and economic development. His speech was widely cited in the news media as evidence of profound differences between the Bush and Obama administrations.[32]

The National Strategy for Combating Terrorism (NSCT) proposed by the Obama administration in 2011 called for the establishment of concrete, realistic goals; consequently it narrowed the objective of counterterrorism strategy from bringing an end to terrorism around the world to the specific defeat of al Qa'ida. Now the "four D's" of the Bush administration became "disrupt, degrade, dismantle, and defeat" al Qa'ida. The president explained, "We aim for a world in which al-Qa'ida is openly and widely rejected by all audiences," where it does not shape perceptions, inspire violence, or serve as a recruiting tool. The 2011 NSCT stressed multilateralism and creating a "culture of resilience" at home while replacing al Qa'ida's ideological appeal abroad with a positive vision of the U.S. role in the world. It also referred to the aim of eliminating safe havens for al Qa'ida, echoing the Bush administration, as well as breaking the links between the al Qa'ida core and its affiliates and associates in the periphery. It is also noteworthy that this statement contained the explicit admission that the United States could not stop every attack, hence the need for resilience. Eliminating all terrorist attacks is now recognized as an unrealistic goal.

The Obama administration signaled a shift to a more domestic focus in a report released two months later by the White House titled "Empowering Local Partners to Prevent Violent Extremism in the United States."[33] The shift in aim was to prevention and resilience primarily at home, shaping individual attitudes to resist the ideological and emotional attractions of appeals to violence rather than crushing the actors behind it. Obama's CVE policy stressed a community-based approach that promised to increase federal support to local communities, improve relations between police and citizens in threatened communities, and counter the narratives of violent extremists on the Internet and on social media sites. This approach departed from the conception of prevention as advance detection of terrorist organizations and activities characteristic of the Bush administration.

In a 2013 speech, President Obama continued the restrained approach of the 2011 NSCT: "Neither I, nor any President, can promise the total defeat of terror. We will never erase the evil that lies in the hearts of some human beings, nor stamp out every danger to our open society. But what we can do—what we must do—is dismantle networks that pose a direct danger to us, and make it less likely for new groups to gain a foothold, all the while maintaining the freedoms and ideals that we defend."[34] He described a return to a world where the threat of terrorism was more like that preceding the 2001 attacks, in which terrorism was a real and present danger but not cataclysmic; there would be no return to a "boundless global war on terror."

The Obama administration's change in emphasis was also evident in the National Security Strategy released by the White House in February 2015.[35] The administration decisively moved away from countering terrorism through large-scale ground wars in Iraq and Afghanistan and shifted even more toward preventing the growth of violent extremism and radicalization at home. Overall terrorist threats abroad were said to have diminished and the remaining threats were seen as widely dispersed from South Asia through the Middle East and into Africa. The aim of counterterrorism was to degrade and "ultimately" defeat ISIL, although "our efforts to work with other countries to counter the ideology and root causes of violent extremism will be more important than our capacity to remove terrorists from the battlefield." An important objective was to coordinate collective action to remove ISIL safe havens, arrest their advances, and degrade their capabilities in both Iraq and Syria: "We will prioritize collective action to meet the persistent threat posed by terrorism today, especially from al-Qa'ida, ISIL, and their affiliates. In addition to acting decisively to defeat direct threats, we will focus on building the capacity of others to prevent the causes and consequences of conflict to include countering extreme and dangerous ideologies. Keeping nuclear materials from terrorists and preventing the proliferation of nuclear weapons remains a high priority."[36]

Measuring Progress

Because the scope and the goals of counterterrorism are expansive and often contentious, it is hardly surprising that observing and measuring progress toward the goals described by the Bush and Obama administrations is difficult. In October 2003, Secretary of Defense Donald Rumsfeld asked his field commanders and key staff, "Are we winning or losing the Global War on Terror?" He complained that the government lacked a long-term plan for winning and a set of "metrics" by which to judge success. He asked, "Are we capturing, killing or deterring and dissuading more terrorists every day than the madrassas and the radical clerics are recruiting, training and deploying against us?"[37] Three years later, Congressman Lee Hamilton, the former vice-chair of the influential 9/11 Commission, stated, "No one knows if we are winning or losing the war on terrorism."[38] That this critical question remains unanswered has not escaped the notice of the news media; as the *Washington Post* observed somewhat acerbically in 2013, "Counterterrorism may be the most significant area of government policy where we still have no idea what the hell we're doing."[39]

The historian William Martel reminds us that compared to evaluating the success of counterterrorism measures, victory and defeat in traditional warfare are much easier to specify as goals and to assess.[40] In a traditional contest between two standing armies, victory is usually determined by such metrics as how much territory is controlled, how much infrastructure is destroyed, and how many casualties are suffered. Declaring a "war" against terrorism may have given the mistaken impression that we can determine victory this easily. However, in the case of terrorism measuring such results as the number of perpetrators, the territory controlled, and even the infrastructure destroyed and the casualties inflicted is more difficult, and even positive scores on these measures may not predict victory in the long run. Success in counterterrorism may mean ascertaining what people do *not* do— they do not adopt radical ideas or attempt to travel to conflict zones to volunteer to fight for ISIS—as much as what they do. But, as is well known, there is no way to prove a negative—what people did not do or what did not occur. Some indicators can be observed and measured with relative precision while others are estimates or judgments that cannot be quantified. It is by no means certain that the most easily observed measures are also the most meaningful. Obstacles to comprehensive data collection are high.

The academic literature refers to a wide variety of measures, with minimal agreement on what they should be or what counts most. Perhaps the most obvious metric of effectiveness is the total number of terrorist attacks following a counterterrorism initiative, and this metric is widely cited, for example, in the study of counterterrorism in Israel by Dugan and Chenoweth. In addition to total attacks, Cynthia

Lum and her colleagues[41] suggested as metrics the number of groups who engaged in the use of terrorism or the frequency of activities engaged in by terrorist organizations. These measures can be applied at a general level (all terrorist attacks) or to more specific types of terrorism-related behavior (suicide bombings, chemical attacks, or aerial hijackings). Daniel Byman started with a list of five "measures of success": in addition to reduced number of attacks, reduced freedom of terrorists to operate (achieved via the elimination of safe havens), increased domestic support for counterterrorism, accurate understanding of the adversary's leadership and command structure (to focus the counterterrorism strategy adopted), and disruption of terrorist recruitment.[42] There could also be evidence-based appraisals of the willingness of the public to work with law enforcement agencies to respond to terrorism, to report suspicious terrorism-related behavior to the police, or simply to be familiar with government counterterrorism strategies. These could provide different metrics that could be judged relevant for measuring counterterrorism effectiveness.

Five years later Byman amended and shortened his list of metrics and added a cost estimate: (1) low levels of death from international terrorism, numbering less than a hundred each year; (2) overall reduction in the level of fear, so Americans go about their lives with little concern about terrorism, which "requires not only a low number of deaths in absolute terms, but also a particularly low level of deaths on U.S. soil"; and (3) counterterrorism accomplished "at an acceptable cost in dollars, lives and other policy priorities."[43]

The general effect of reducing public fears coincides perfectly with the aims of both the Bush and Obama administrations. Presumably a reduction in public fear could be measured by public opinion polls. However, Byman's causal connection between low levels of deaths on U.S. soil and a consequent reduction of public fear is not easy to substantiate. Numbers of deaths at the hands of terrorists in the United States are low on average, and no subsequent attacks have reached anywhere near the terrible casualty level of 9/11. Yet a Pew Research Center poll conducted in December 2015 found, "Since the start of this year, the share of Americans who say the government is doing well in reducing the threat of terrorism has fallen by 26 percentage points—from 72 percent to 46 percent—and now stands at its lowest point in the post-9/11 era."[44] The November 2015 mass-casualty attacks in Paris had a significant effect on American attitudes, despite being outside the United States.

Alex Schmid and Rashmi Singh developed a more complex and far-reaching set of eight disparate measures to gauge the success of U.S. efforts specifically against al Qa'ida, which corresponds more closely with the Obama administration's narrowed focus: (1) number of terrorist groups affiliating with or disassociating from al Qa'ida; (2) size and recruiting rate of al Qa'ida and related groups; (3) number of al Qa'ida–related attacks; (4) number of casualties among U.S. civilians and security force members from al Qa'ida and its affiliates; (5) losses of al Qa'ida and al Qa'ida–related terrorist jihadists (casualties, arrests, exit from struggle) and balance of losses, stock, and new recruits; (6) collateral damage (civilians wounded and killed); (7) number of countries and territories in which al Qa'ida and related terrorist groups are operating; (8) sophistication of al Qa'ida and al Qa'ida–related attacks.[45] Integrating these metrics into an evaluative framework would be the next obvious task. Some of Schmid and Singh's assumptions need to be updated to incorporate the rise of ISIS. In hindsight it seems clear that one reason for the spread of al Qa'ida outside of its core areas was the organizational weakness of the center and that al Qa'ida's loss of control was one reason for the emergence of ISIS. Thus, destroying a particular organization did not prevent the rise of successors.

Government efforts to identify progress seem to be at least as variable and open-ended as those provided by researchers. They are also likely to be biased toward demonstrating success and to be limited to short-term effects that may look like successes but that later developments disqualify. For example, President Bush in a statement made on September 28, 2005, "Fighting a Global War on Terror," emphasized four core elements of America's strategy for victory in the war on terror: (1) fighting the enemy abroad; (2) denying terrorists state support and sanctuary; (3) denying them access to weapons of mass destruction; (4) spreading democracy.[46] He then pointed to the killing or capture of more than two-thirds of al Qa'ida's top leadership and the seizure of over $200 million in terrorist financing as examples of progress. Other accomplishments cited included (1) removal of brutal regimes in Afghanistan and Iraq that harbored terrorists; (2) moving forward in the "march" of democracy worldwide, especially

Lebanon; (3) shutting down a major WMD black market network originating in Pakistan and Libya's rejoining the community of nations after renouncing nuclear weapons; (4) capturing a number of key terrorists in Pakistan and Iraq, as well as capturing and killing hundreds of insurgents in Iraq. Disruption of al Qa'ida terrorist plots and efforts to infiltrate the United States were subsequently cited as an additional indication of success by the president in his discussion of the war on terror at the National Endowment for Democracy on October 6, 2005.[47] Thus government statements of success can appear self-promoting, sometimes listing ostensible accomplishments that turn out to be anything but. For example, removing the regimes in Afghanistan and Iraq did not remove safe havens for terrorists, and democracy actually did not spread very successfully.

In a Congressional Research Service report, Raphael Perl was also expansive, arguing that effectiveness should be measured in terms of both capabilities and intentions. He included changes in group infrastructure (leadership weakness, lower recruitment and support base, limited target list) and in tactical and strategic goals (less radical and less focused on causing widespread damage).[48] Perl suggested that other measures of counterterrorism effectiveness could include (1) number of governments that do not embrace "appeasement" policies; (2) number of defectors from the terrorist ranks; (3) terrorists' levels of Internet activity; (4) the extent of media coverage terrorists receive.[49] Perl continued even more broadly to add that analysts should also evaluate "structural and environmental factors" that he puts as questions that would be extremely difficult to answer empirically:

Is the dependence on certain factors that terrorists or anti-terrorists can exploit as vulnerabilities increasing or decreasing? How seamlessly do terrorist organizations and networks interact? How seamlessly do new government anti-terrorist organizational structures and networks interact? Is the international operating environment becoming more or less inviting or restrictive for terrorists or for those combating them? Is it easier or harder today for terrorists to inflict the damage they seek to do?[50]

Measures of effectiveness are equally wide-ranging for policymakers outside the United States. Thus, Nadav Morag, a former senior director for foreign policy at Israel's National Security Council, outlined these key indicators of Israeli success in its counterterrorism campaigns: minimizing casualties, both Israeli victims of terrorism and among innocent bystanders in antiterrorist operations, reducing the economic impact of terrorism, maintaining Israeli social cohesion as well as domestic and international support for the Israeli government, and gauging changes in domestic and international support for the Palestinian Authority.[51] Based on these parameters, Morag concluded that the Israeli campaign against terror from 2000 to 2005 was largely successful.

While not taking issue with any of these efforts, we are struck by how broad, general, and difficult to measure and assess many of the proposed indicators of progress are. They include some concrete metrics that are easy to count and others that are intangible outcomes that are almost impossible to tally. Even when metrics are numbers, they can be confusing and even misleading. For example, it is not always easy to decode the meaning of the government's performance metrics even when they are made public. The number one strategic goal of the FBI is preventing terrorism; the aim is to disrupt and prevent terrorism, thwarting those intending to conduct attacks, and stopping terrorism of any kind at any stage. In Fiscal Year 2015, the bureau claimed to have exceeded its target goal of 125 "disruptions" to reach a total of 440, but the "disruptions" are not defined.[52]

The Effectiveness of Deterrence: An Example

In general, most of the metrics for assessing counterterrorism assume that implementation of one or more counterterrorism measures will result in a reduction in one or more of the negative results of terrorism such as attacks, casualties, geographic and organizational expansion, foreign fighters, or public fear. These ideas align generally with rational choice or deterrence models. The belief that credible threats of punishment or harm will deter violent or criminal behavior is as old as criminal law itself and is a key attribute of theories of military strategy. It has broad appeal to both policymakers and the public. Deterrence models generally assume that human beings and states are rational, self-interested actors seeking to minimize cost while maximizing gain.[53] The implication is that terrorist behavior can be altered by the threat and imposition of punishment that makes the projected act of terrorism not worth the anticipated cost.

Especially since 9/11, deterrence models have been popular for understanding terrorist violence, because many terrorist attacks are carefully planned and include at least some consideration for risks and rewards. Indeed, deterrence-based thinking has long dominated counterterrorist policies in most countries. Whether deterrence is an effective approach is nevertheless hotly debated. The amorphousness of the actors behind terrorism makes accurate and timely attribution and hence threats of punishment problematic. Moreover, it is not clear that democratic countries can issue credible threats of harm to what radical jihadist groups value—even if we could be certain what those values were. For example, a threat to destroy ISIS headquarters in Syria and Iraq is well within the reach of American military capabilities, but it would involve such massive civilian casualties that it is hard to imagine that the United States would issue such a threat, let alone carry it out.[54]

Research on conditions that promote escalating violence in response to counterterrorist interventions—so-called "backlash" models—is less common and more theoretically scattered than research on deterrence models. Nevertheless, there is strong support for backlash models: the argument that the imposition of punishment on a particular individual or group may increase future levels of violence. Commentators have argued that a major part of ISIL's strategy in the Middle East has been to goad the United States and other Western countries to retaliate, kill innocents, and thereby demonstrate the extent of the West's hatred of Muslims.[55] Researchers have long argued that terrorists rely on the response of governments to mobilize the sympathies of would-be supporters and that they deliberately intend to provoke overreaction.[56] The extent to which government-based counterterrorist strategies outrage their targets and energize a base of potential supporters may increase the likelihood of more terrorist strikes. Researchers have referred to this phenomenon as "jujitsu politics," because, as in the martial art of jujitsu, it is based on the principle of turning the opponent's own force against itself.[57] The psychologist Clark McCauley points out that because of this backlash principle, the counterterrorism measures taken in response to terrorism can be more dangerous than terrorism itself because they lead to intensified commitment on the part of the terrorists and thus are counterproductive.[58]

The fields of both psychology and criminology provide support for backlash models. Much psychological literature suggests that threats from out-groups generally increase the cohesion of in-groups as well as the pressure on in-group deviants to conform and support in-group leaders.[59] In criminology, researchers have long argued that punishment leads to identity changes in individuals as well as to social changes in society that result in criminal offenders' increasing their deviant behavior after their arrest, prosecution, and punishment. The criminologist Edwin Lemert famously referred to this concept as "secondary deviance"—crime that occurs in response to reactions to earlier crimes punished.[60] The psychologist Tom Tyler argues that punishment is more likely to be accepted when the punishment is perceived to be procedurally fair.[61] It is important to note that the perceived legitimacy of government actions is likely to be far more salient to the many potential supporters of terrorism than to the handful of individuals already actively involved in terrorism; this committed group may change little, regardless of government response. In other words, a backlash model predicts that government responses to terrorist violence may not only embolden those who already participate in terrorist attacks but also may encourage others to join terrorist organizations, support those organizations, or look the other way when they witness the activities of supporters.

Empirical research that directly tests which specific counterterrorist policies escalate or de-escalate attacks, fatalities, or fear of terrorism is limited. But in general, far more academic studies examine the deterrent effects of coercive policies than analyze backlash effects or gauge the impact of conciliatory policies.

Evaluating Decapitation

Another example of the problems described here is the tricky and disputed evaluation of the outcomes of the practice of "decapitation"— basically an assassination or targeted killing where a government seeks to reduce the striking capacity of a terrorist organization by eliminating some or all of its key leadership, under the assumption that the supply of leadership talent in a given organization is bound to be limited. In recent years it has been one of the most commonly studied counterterrorism tactics, probably because despite government secrecy assassination represents a relatively concrete behavior that is easier than most tactics to quantify.[62] Since 2008, this general interest has spread specifically to the use of drone strikes, where the targeted killings are accomplished through remotely piloted unmanned aircraft.[63] President Obama in his NDU speech in May 2013 predicted the effectiveness of drone strikes as counterterrorism measures: "Targeted action against terrorists, effective partnerships, diplomatic engagement and assistance—through such a comprehensive strategy we can significantly reduce the chances of large-scale attacks on the homeland and mitigate threats to Americans overseas."

On balance, much recent research, both case studies and a large number of quantitative studies, concludes that targeted killings or the removal of leaders by other means can reduce the ability of terrorist organizations to mount further strikes.[64] Thus, in a study of Pakistan from 2007 to 2011 Patrick Johnston and Anoop Sarbahi found that drone strikes were significantly associated with decreases in the incidence and lethality of terrorist attacks and reduction in the selective targeting of tribal elders.[65] Tribal elders are frequently seen by terrorist groups as conspiring with the enemy or disrupting group strategies.

However, other researchers stress that the effectiveness of the tactic depends a great deal on the specific context in which it is used. For example, several studies suggest that assassinations are more likely to reduce further strikes by organizations that are highly centralized than those that are less so.[66] Findings on the effectiveness of drone strikes are similar: the weight of the research suggests that drone strikes can reduce the subsequent ability of adversaries to attack but their impact depends on the specific context in which they are deployed and the specific characteristics of the adversary. Audrey Cronin concluded that decapitation might help to defeat groups that are "hierarchically structured, characterized by a cult of personality, and less than ten years old."[67] Jenna Jordan argued that the tactic of decapitation was unlikely to diminish al Qa'ida's capabilities; it was more likely to be counterproductive.[68] She focused on organizational resilience, analyzed in terms of bureaucratization and communal support. Groups that have complex, well-developed structures and attract deep popular support will be difficult to undermine by targeting their leaders. Interestingly, her measure of organizational degradation is reduction in frequency and lethality of attacks, an association that is disputed, since a powerful successful organization might not need to act as aggressively as a weak or failing one. Even prolonged campaigns of terrorism do not necessarily require large resources. In addition, she concluded that separatist and religious groups are more likely than more narrowly ideological groups to have extensive popular support.

Eric Van Um and Daniela Pisoiu argued that the conflicting interpretations of the success of drone attacks and other decapitation strategies has much to do with differing definitions of success.[69] The authors pointed out that those who consider the use of drones to have been successful usually refer to metrics such as the number of subsequent terrorist attacks carried out by the organizations targeted. By contrast, critics of drone strikes and targeted killings argue that decapitation is unsuccessful when judged against such metrics as the number of civilian casualties ("collateral damage"), or the amount of propaganda generated by the organizations being targeted.

Methods of Measurement: Empirical Tests of Counterterrorism Measures

Another problem in measuring counterterrorism effectiveness is how to use data to analyze outcomes. Given the complexities of conceptualizing and measuring counterterrorism measures, the conclusion is hardly surprising that analyzing effectiveness using statistical methods is extremely challenging. This no doubt explains why the vast majority of research on counterterrorism strategies has been based on expert opinion or qualitative case studies. Nearly thirty years ago Alex Schmid and Albert Jongman identified over 6,000 published works on terrorism from the social sciences and concluded that much of the research is "impressionistic, superficial [and offers] . . . far reaching generalizations on the basis of episodic evidence."[70] More recently, the psychologist Andrew Silke concluded that only 3 percent of articles in terrorism journals used sophisticated quantitative analysis compared to 86 percent in forensic psychology and 60 percent in criminology.[71] And the ambitious review by Lum and her colleagues found that of over 20,000 studies on terrorism only about 1.5 percent even remotely discussed the idea that a systematic evaluation had been conducted of counterterrorism strategies.[72] When the authors concentrated just on peer-reviewed journal articles they found that only 3 percent were based on some form of empirical analysis. Only seven of the studies contained what the authors considered to be moderately rigorous evaluations of counterterrorism programs. The review by Lum and her colleagues is now ten years old and research on counterterrorism continues to grow increasingly sophisticated. Nonetheless, the fact remains that the overwhelming majority of published work on counterterrorism is based on little more than educated guesses by the authors.

For the few, mostly recent, studies that have attempted more sophisticated quantitative analysis of the effectiveness of counterterrorism strategies, perhaps the most common method is interrupted time series analysis. Fundamentally, this technique is based on assessing whether some form of intervention (such as harsher prison sentences, peace accords) has a measurable impact on a specific metric related to counterterrorism (number of attacks or fatalities). Because policies are generally implemented at a specific point in time, interrupted time series analysis provides some control over rival explanations. It has been applied to a wide variety of counterterrorism measures, including extended prison sentences, passage of antiterrorism laws, assassinations, curfews, deportations, home demolitions, violent repression and military retaliation, and indiscriminate repression.

The logic of interrupted time series analysis is to identify a measure expected to be changed by a particular type of counterterrorism intervention, usually the number or lethality of future attacks, and then assess whether there is statistical evidence that this measure did indeed significantly change following the intervention. A useful feature of this method is that it can easily be used to measure either deterrence effects, where attacks decline following the intervention, or backlash effects, where attacks instead increase. The test is intuitive in that if an intervention is effective, we would expect it to have a measurable impact following its implementation. The fact that an intervention happened at a specific time increases the chances that a corresponding increase or decrease in terrorism is real. But at the same time, it is always possible that the result is not due to the specific intervention being measured but rather is produced by some other event that happened at the same time or close in time. Thus, in this uncontrolled experimental environment we can never be certain that a specific intervention caused a particular outcome.

The interrupted time series strategy is illustrated in a study by one of the authors and his colleagues on the effectiveness of efforts to reduce terrorist violence by the Provisional Irish Republican Army (PIRA) and its associates in Northern Ireland.[73] LaFree and his colleagues identified six highly visible British interventions aimed at reducing terrorist violence by the PIRA in Northern Ireland and tested their impact on subsequent attacks from 1969 to 1992. Taken together, three of the six interventions produced backlash effects; they were followed by an increased risk of future attacks.

The first intervention that produced a backlash effect was the criminalization-Ulsterization policies implemented on March 26, 1976. The aim of the criminalization policy was to treat paramilitary prisoners convicted of political-violence-related offenses as ordinary criminals and the Ulsterization strategy was aimed at relying on local police authorities to respond to terrorism rather than relying on outside police and military forces. The two policies shared the underlying perspective that treating convicted terrorists as ordinary criminals using local resources would undercut their claims for special status as political prisoners. In response to the criminalization-Ulsterization policies, imprisoned PIRA republicans first mounted "blanket protests" in which prisoners refused to wear prison uniforms, wrapping themselves instead in blankets, and "dirty" protests, in which prisoners smeared excreta on their cell walls. Next, they began a hunger strike. Kieran McEvoy succinctly describes the impact of the hunger strike on British efforts to criminalize the protesters: "Prisoners who were willing to starve themselves to death were clearly able to expropriate power, denigrate legitimacy, and politically contest the position of an intransigent British government."[74]

A second strategy resulting in a backlash was called "internment" and it was implemented on August 9, 1971. Internment was a prison crackdown in which over 2,100 suspected PIRA-related offenders were imprisoned. These imprisonments were immediately followed by protests that many had been erroneously arrested and imprisoned.[75] Additionally, the policy of internment without trial represented a serious departure from widespread norms of rule by law, deeply ingrained in Western liberal democracies—which may well have generated sympathy for the offenders.

And finally, a third strategy that produced backlash was the Gibraltar incident, a controversial military operation in which three members of the PIRA were shot dead by the British Special Air Service (SAS) in Gibraltar on March 6, 1988. The loss of life suffered by the PIRA in the Gibraltar assassinations at the hands of the British military was easily construed by activists as brutal overreaction. This event made it relatively simple for PIRA supporters to portray those murdered as martyrs.[76] The Gibraltar assassinations were still associated with significant increases in terrorist attacks thirty-six months after they occurred.

Two of the interventions, the Loughgall incident and the Falls Curfew, had no significant effect on the number of future terrorist attacks. The Loughgall incident took place on May 8, 1987, in the village of Loughgall, Northern Ireland, when an eight-man unit of the PIRA was ambushed and killed by a 36-man unit of the British Army's Special Air Service (SAS). A civilian was also killed by the SAS after unwittingly driving into the ambush zone. Although the results failed to show any long-term change in the risk of new terrorist attacks after the Loughgall assassinations, nonetheless there was no evidence that this strategy reduced further attacks.

The main stated purpose of the Falls Curfew—a military action to surround and search a district of Belfast, The Falls, that was staunchly Irish nationalist—was to disarm potentially dangerous activists.[77] However, the results supported the conclusion that any strategic benefits obtained by the curfew were overshadowed by the unprovoked ransacking of private homes and the killing of civilians. Given the controversial nature of the searches that took place under the Falls Curfew and of the use of CR gas, its failure to reduce terrorist attacks is hardly surprising.

Among the six interventions examined, Operation Motorman provides the strongest evidence that it had an effective deterrent effect. Operation Motorman began in the early hours of July 21, 1972, and involved a large military operation carried out by the British Army to retake "no-go areas" (areas controlled by residents, usually Irish republican paramilitaries) that had been established in Belfast, Derry, and other large towns. M. L. R. Smith and Peter Neumann concluded that Motorman "shattered the IRA's military bargaining strategy" and propelled "the republican movement down a path that would eventually lead it to question the value of its armed struggle."[78] The results of the analysis by LaFree and his colleagues of Operation Motorman suggest that it still had a strongly negative association with terrorist attacks thirty-six months after its implementation began. It is tempting to speculate that the reason why Operation Motorman was more effective in reducing future terrorist strikes than the other interventions is that it succeeded in raising the perception that acts of rebellion and violence would be met with an immediate response. Despite the fact that Motorman was a massive operation—involving thirty-eight army battalions, twenty-seven infantry battalions, and two armored battalions—it was not a particularly violent operation. It met with little resistance, and only two people lost their lives during the operation. But it greatly increased the British military presence in Northern Ireland and, thus, the certainty that republican strikes would have important consequences.

This study of terrorism in Northern Ireland demonstrates the utility of interrupted time series analysis for identifying counterterrorism measures that are associated with declines in terrorism, increases in terrorism, and no changes. It also provides an example of the weaknesses of interrupted time series analysis. First, although the authors did a thorough literature review to develop a set of high-profile countermeasures to examine, other policies implemented by the British during this period could arguably also qualify as counterterrorism measures and so any cause-effect relationship is unclear. Second, although the analysis included several control variables (crimes reported, number killed), in a nonexperimental design there is no way to know for sure that the analysis controls for all possible threats to the validity of the results. Third, the timing of the interventions sometimes restricts the ability of researchers to analyze impacts. This is demonstrated most obviously in the Northern Ireland case by the fact that criminalization and Ulsterization started at the same time and so there is no way to measure their separate impact with an interrupted time series design. Timing of the other events is less of a problem in measuring the other interventions, but even when interventions are separated in time their effects may still be blended in unknown ways. For example, the Falls Curfew took place the year before Operation Motorman began, but there is still no way to tell with absolute certainty that the effects of the earlier intervention strategy did not "bleed" into the subsequent strategy. Finally, studies like these are only case studies and do not allow us to conclude that similar counterterrorist strategies will have similar effects in other regions of the world, on different groups or individuals, or even in this region of the world during different time periods. In fact, policymakers often err by over-relying on useful earlier events for predicting later outcomes.

Another quantitative strategy for assessing the impact of counterterrorism measures on outcomes is to perform the kind of meta-analysis of existing individual studies undertaken by researchers Cynthia Lum and her colleagues. So far this strategy for assessing counterterrorist interventions has been rare, and the study by Lum and her colleagues illustrates why. The gold standard for these types of evaluations is a randomized controlled experiment, but for obvious reasons most types of counterterrorist strategies cannot be practically or ethically assessed with experimental methods. Instead Lum and her colleagues were guided by a team of criminologists, led by Larry Sherman, who devised a five-point Scientific Methods Scale (SMS) to score the methodological quality of evaluation research.[79] They ranked the highest-quality evaluation method—the randomized controlled experiment—5 and simple correlational studies 1 or 2. Lum's team used the middle SMS score of 3 as a general guide to exclude studies that were not at least moderately rigorous. Using these criteria, Lum and her colleagues identified only seven prior quantitative analyses of counterterrorism strategies that scored at least a 3 on the SMS scale. All seven studies shared the following features: (1) evaluated two or more units of analysis, comparing some with and without the counterterrorism intervention; (2) made some attempt to provide for controls within a statistical analysis; and (3) conducted an interrupted time series or intervention analysis to indicate some temporal ordering of effects.

An analysis of the seven studies led the authors to conclude: (1) the use of metal detectors in airports reduces hijackings; however, there may also be a substitution or displacement effect of airport security on other types of terrorism such as assassinations, bombings, hostage taking, death and wounded events; (2) fortifying embassies and efforts to protect diplomats do not appear effective in reducing terrorist attacks on these targets; (3) increasing the severity of punishment for terrorist hijackers does not appear to have a statistically discernible effect on reducing skyjacking incidents, although very little research is conducted in this area; (4) UN resolutions have not been shown to reduce terrorism; and (5) retaliatory attacks such as the U.S. attack on Libya in 1986 or attacks by Israel on the PLO have significantly increased the number of terrorist attacks in the short run, particularly against the United States, the United Kingdom, and Israel. Obviously this type of approach has merit, even though conclusions were limited by the fact that only seven studies met even the relaxed criteria for inclusion.

Another type of quantitative research on the effectiveness of counterterrorism strategies examines the natural variation between intervention levels and terrorist attacks and other metrics. These are called ecological studies, because they measure outcomes for entire populations (for example, residents of Northern Ireland in the 1980s). This method measures interventions continuously rather than by a single shift in a discrete value before and after its implementation. In principle, continuous measures are superior to interrupted time series methods because they portray a more nuanced assessment of authorities' level of effort. However, ecological studies require continuous information on all of the countermeasures undertaken by governments, and as we have already seen, such data are rarely available.

The study by Dugan and Chenoweth mentioned earlier is one of the few ecological studies of counterterrorism measures to date.[80] The authors examine the effects of repressive (punishing) and conciliatory (rewarding) actions on terrorist behavior using a dataset that identified events by Israeli state actors toward Palestinian targets on a wide range of counterterrorism tactics and policies from 1987 to 2004. Their results show that repressive actions were either unrelated to terror attacks or were related to subsequent increases in terror attacks, whereas conciliatory actions were generally associated with decreases in attacks.

Despite this method's promise, the data requirements make it difficult to apply. Thus, it is impossible to generalize Dugan and Chenoweth's results to other countries, other time periods, or even to Israel at different time periods. Moreover, even in the specific analysis undertaken there is disagreement among researchers about whether the Israeli case during this time period demonstrates the superiority of conciliatory actions. In a reanalysis of the Dugan-Chenoweth data using a statistical technique called vector autoregression, Vladimir Bejan and William Parkin reach different conclusions: their analysis indicates that an increase in repressive actions led to a reduction in terrorist attacks, and that an increase in conciliatory actions had no effect on terrorism.[81] Such innovative research is increasing our ability to model the effects of counterterrorism policies, yet at this point in time the results of even sophisticated analysis are at best limited to a specific time period and location and variation in the methods used may produce dramatically differing results.

Conclusions

Conceptualizing and measuring the effectiveness of policies and practices aimed at countering terrorism are tasks that are if anything even more difficult than conceptualizing and measuring terrorism itself. Analyzing only the benefits of counterterrorism measures, much less their costs, is dauntingly complex. Not only do analysts face all the legal, ethical, and political complexities of identifying terrorism but they also deal with an extremely broad set of policy options, a wide variety of metrics for measuring effectiveness, and a situation where it is difficult if not impossible to obtain reliable information. Researchers are operating in a situation where experimental data are difficult to obtain and generalization is dangerous. In sum, it is hard to construct a strategy on the basis of open-ended goals and extremely complex measures of progress toward meeting them. It is no surprise, then, that governments, especially the U.S. government, have difficulty convincing the public that counterterrorism policies are effective.

We should be clear that this is not an argument for abandoning efforts to develop conceptual strategies, collect reliable data, and analyze findings. What our review suggests is that all concerned be more forthcoming about what Donald Rumsfeld famously referred to as "the unknown unknowns" in efforts to measure the success of counterterrorism policies.[82] This suggests managing expectations about the quality of the information that is usually available and the ability to make strong predictions based on this information.

Research and policy on counterterrorism could certainly be improved by providing clear and systematic measures of counterterrorist policies implemented and their effectiveness. A half century ago David Easton provided a framework for political decisionmaking that distinguished between output effectiveness, outcome effectiveness, and impact effectiveness.[83] Output effectiveness refers to the implementation of regulations, policies, and legislation. Outcome effectiveness concerns the impact that these laws and regulations have on prohibited behavior. Impact effectiveness refers to how well the long-term goals of CT are met, especially reducing or stopping the behavior. Output effectiveness can be judged by whether a particular instrument of policy—say, the Patriot Act—was actually drafted and passed. Outcome effectiveness would be evaluated in terms of whether the contents of the legislation did what it was supposed to do—did it promote the sharing of intelligence across agencies? Impact effectiveness would be measured in terms of subsequent terrorist attacks or organizational strength of the actor behind the attacks. So, did a particular law or regulation get passed (output effectiveness), did it succeed in doing what it was intended to do (outcome effectiveness), and did the change built into the law or regulation actually succeed in reducing future terrorist behavior (impact effectiveness)? With regard to a specific type of counterterrorism, such as decapitation, researchers and policymakers should beware of confusing short-term success at assassinating a suspected terrorist with reducing the number of future terrorist attacks over the long run.

CHAPTER 7

Moving Forward

In this book we singled out some of the features of terrorism that make it such an intractable subject for research and policy. We have by no means covered all of the possible complications, because the problem is complex and the impediments to objective understanding are extensive. Many scholars and experts have presented critical appraisals of the counterterrorism policy record and the state of academic research. Our aim has been to combine analysis of both research and policy difficulties to inform the public debate over what counterterrorism policy should and could be. Our purpose is to present a balanced appraisal, avoiding the extremes of insisting on the one hand that there is no threat whatsoever and that all counterterrorism measures are a waste of time and money or on the other hand that terrorism is such a fundamental threat to American national security that it justifies any cost. We also think that research in what is now known as terrorism studies has made significant progress, although many questions remain.

In these conclusions, we look forward rather than restricting ourselves to pointing out the errors or missed opportunities of the past. What are the implications of the dilemmas we discuss for the study of terrorism and future counterterrorism measures, especially for American policy? What lessons can be learned from experience in the fifteen years since 9/11? We hope that researchers and policymakers have reached a higher level of maturity in explaining and dealing with terrorism, gaining a perspective through distance in time that will encourage more realism in expectations about the nature and scope of the threat as well as about what can be done about it. This hope may seem like wishful thinking in light of the polarized and simplistic qualities of many debates about terrorism in the public arena, but we are confident in presenting a case for the exercise of good judgment and policy-relevant research.

Overall we stress three principles: be prepared for change, disruption, and surprise in the terrorism threat universe, resist the temptation to magnify the image of the destructive power of terrorism as well as the vulnerability of its targets, and accept limits to the American government's ability to manage the threat from jihadist violence. Even superpowers cannot completely control their environments. Terrorist threats are constantly evolving, never static. Understanding of the threat must be realistic in the sense of being based on accurate judgments of the actual extent of terrorist capacity to harm national security interests. Governments, especially the American government, should avoid both overreacting and promising or threatening overreaction, which means entertaining modest expectations about what can be accomplished in an extremely complex and uncertain threat environment that requires constant adaptation and adjustment. Counterterrorism policy should be reasonable, practical, and balanced—in a word, sensible. There is no perfect solution. The main goal of the United States is to prevent attacks on American soil, especially highly destructive ones in terms of casualties. Although it is important to establish these priorities, no political leader can guarantee the public absolute security. If the goal is set as the complete absence of terrorist attacks, then policymakers become so anxious that a terrorist will slip through the preventive security net that they risk panic or overreaction. Fear of being blamed in the aftermath of an attack starts to take precedence over all other considerations.

In saying that for the United States the security of the country is the foremost national interest, we are not advocating indifference to the threat terrorism poses to others, especially allies, whether developed nations of the West or weak states in conflict zones whose populations suffer by far the most from local violence. Terrorism, both domestic and transnational, is destabilizing in many ways: it contributes to creating humanitarian disasters, undermining international order, and eroding normative standards of international legitimacy. Nor do we ignore the linkages between terrorism abroad and terrorism at home.

Counterterrorism Policy Paradoxes

Our analysis has revealed some underlying policy paradoxes. One paradox of counterterrorism is that policymakers have to set long-term overarching goals or risk being accused of not having a strategy. No politician wants to be called "reactive" rather than "proactive." But declarations of high-level objectives such as eliminating, eradicating, destroying, defeating, degrading, or even containing violent jihadist actors and actions are by their very nature vague or overly ambitious. At a minimum, such goals lack clarity, and if taken expansively they posit ends that are unattainable. In the aftermath of regime change or attempted change in Afghanistan, Iraq, Syria, Libya, and Yemen, the United States abandoned the idea of attempting to spread democracy around the world, overthrowing authoritarian regimes and tyrants in the process, as the antidote to terrorism. The United States has not, however, been able to avoid intervening militarily in order to restore or establish security and stability, in part to defend weak and embattled allies in critical geopolitical locations and in part in an effort to reduce the terrorist threat to this country.

One of the aims of future American policy should be greater precision about the strategic goals of military action abroad and their relationship to security at home. If the contradictions behind the paradox cannot be resolved, policymakers must find a middle ground between the tactical and strategic. It may not be possible to have a sensible counterterrorism grand strategy other than to say that its objective is to minimize both the threat and its consequences, enhancing the nation's capacity to recover quickly from attacks. In this respect, there is a need for improved public education and communication about ends and means. Fulfilling this need requires greater transparency, a theme we return to frequently.

A related problem is that even if the ambitions of counterterrorism policy are restricted to the tactical level, and the idea of comprehensive grand strategy is abandoned, the effectiveness of even short-term measures is questioned and doubted. There is widespread skepticism about the metrics of drone strikes, bombs dropped, targets struck, arrests made and cases prosecuted, convictions secured, territory seized or regained, plots foiled, websites taken down, Facebook postings and Twitter accounts deleted, deradicalization programs instituted, and other indicators cited as signs of progress. Are these measures of success against terrorism or measures of the extent of the government's efforts? These metrics calculate what government has done, not necessarily the effect of its actions on adversaries' calculations and capabilities—indeed government measures may be taken before a specific adversary exists. Even if the measure is an outcome such as numbers of terrorist leaders killed by drone strikes, there is disagreement as to whether loss of leadership cripples organizations or undermines the ideology that motivates their followers. These metrics do not indicate whether, when one entity is disrupted, another will rise to take its place. What are the premises behind assuming that these steps will downgrade or minimize the terrorist threat? Assumptions about the relationship between government action and the impact on the threat need to be made explicit. The problem of lack of transparency becomes troubling here as well; for example, the criteria used to make decisions to launch drone strikes have been obscure, so the public does not know exactly what the strikes are expected to accomplish. The Obama administration, under which drone strikes inside and outside of conflict zones became a dominant policy instrument in the struggle against terrorism worldwide, has been slow to offer a thorough explanation of the grounds for its authority and the reasons for its selection of targets.

Another policy paradox is that military "victory" in conflicts abroad, crushing or containing the expansion of structured organizations with territory and resources, may contribute to a shift in direction, as adversaries move to attack targets outside the battlefield or transfer operations to a different location, for example, from Afghanistan to Pakistan, or from Libya to Tunisia. Even if operationally weakened at the base, these organizations can deploy networks of followers outside the conflict zone and exploit social media to inspire sympathizers to act against their enemies. In effect, military success in the field may deflect the adversary's attention onto the intervener's civilian population. Al Qa'ida and the self-proclaimed Islamic State, along with their respective affiliates and adherents, may be trying to use terrorism to coerce the United States, Turkey, France, or Belgium into withdrawing from commitments or simply to punish and exact revenge and retribution. ISIS claims to be prepared to accept short-term setbacks in the struggle to establish a caliphate in Syria and Iraq because their faith assures them that their goal will be achieved in a distant future. Certainly terrorism wins them advertising and publicity in the short term. And policymakers, politicians, and pundits play into their hands when they exaggerate the threat.

This is not to say that as academic researchers we consider military intervention by outside powers in civil conflicts to be the cause of terrorism. But the contradiction remains that intervention abroad has not translated into dampening the emotions that lead to terrorism. In fact, Western military engagement has reinforced the jihadist narrative that Muslims everywhere are targeted. It may have made ISIS more determined to inspire rather than direct terrorism. Nor has military action blocked jihadist organizations abroad from regrouping, regenerating, and expanding. In 2011 coalition forces were withdrawn from Iraq with the assumption that what was then the Islamic State of Iraq was "defeated," but deteriorating security in Iraq and the collapse of order in Syria created power vacuums as well as grievances that created new opportunities for ISIS. The original al Qa'ida organization was crushed in Afghanistan and Pakistan but its branches in Yemen and Syria continued the fight, and momentum shifted to the even more virulent ISIS rival—hardly an optimal outcome. The rivalry between the two competing jihadist strains makes the terrorist threat even harder to manage. It would be shortsighted to ignore the link between transnational terrorism and civil wars in Muslim-majority countries, and there is need for better understanding of the relationship between the global and the local and of the mobility and transnational ideological appeal of the adversary. Furthermore, it is not certain that an adversary such as ISIS or al Qa'ida depends on sanctuary abroad in order to strike the United States.

Clarification of the conception of what can and should be done is necessary for sound research and policy, as we have repeatedly emphasized, and it is a task that in part depends on how the problem is defined and explained. We have not so far engaged the long-standing debate about whether terrorism should be considered as crime or war. Terrorism is not exclusively or simply one or the other, and it is not even a hybrid, although it shares some of the traits of both. There are important downsides to defining terrorism in a binary sense as either crime or war, especially since the categories are usually intended to be prescriptive as much as diagnostic. We have touched on the many problems of treating counterterrorism as war. The ad hoc prosecution of the war relied on methods of interrogation that were unacceptable under the laws of armed combat and on the designation of captured terrorist suspects outside the United States as "unlawful combatants" subject neither to the laws of war nor to the rights of suspects in civil criminal processes. The United States still refers to "bringing terrorists to justice" (once a hallmark of policy) while also practicing targeted assassinations that have ambiguous legal status and that deliver summary "justice" even to accused American citizens. Civilian courts had handled terrorism cases quite competently and continued to do so even as military tribunals at Guantanamo faltered. Preventing attacks on U.S. soil relies on good police and intelligence work, and transnational police cooperation is indispensable to international security. Practices of community policing are central to the Obama administration's approach to countering violent extremism. But if terrorism is considered exclusively as crime, its political character goes unremarked. It is hard to account for the ideological appeal of the cause, which is the major source of its power. And military force may be the only response to entities such as ISIS that operate from a sanctuary outside of U.S. borders. A last thing to remember is that good intelligence determines the effectiveness of both approaches, and this means not just the collection of facts but the interpretation of that information.

Another key question is whether policy should be based on trying to deal over the very long run with the causes of terrorism, particularly "root causes"—causes with their roots in highly complex and context-dependent structural conditions such as demographic pressures, inequality, inadequate education, lack of employment and upward social mobility, failure to integrate minorities, poor social services, weak states, corruption, ungoverned spaces, or civil wars. The more these factors coincide in particular times and places (young populations and economic distress in the context of the collapse of authoritarian regimes, for example) the harder the job of solving the problem is, but research has not been able to assign a weight to each factor in the equation that leads to terrorism. Some factors have been ruled out, such as the idea that poverty in itself causes terrorism, and it is definitive that there is no single cause. The causal chain is ambiguous and indirect. The role of contingency is important. Campaigns of terrorism do not end in the way they begin, and it is forbiddingly difficult to formulate policy that resolves root causes—the payoff is uncertain and even if positive, far in the future. By the time the international community tries to address problems such as poor governance, corruption, and unequal distribution of wealth, the momentum of violence is usually well under way. Measures to address root causes are also costly in every respect, even though they contribute to much more in the way of favorable outcomes than confronting terrorism alone. That is, ameliorating underlying conditions that may be tied to violence, whether at home or abroad, has advantages in its own right, regardless of the effect on terrorism. Probably economic, political, and social reforms should not be framed as counterterrorism at all.

These limitations bring the discussion back to the question of whether counterterrorism policy should focus mainly on incremental prevention and push-back measures, addressing parts of the problem rather than terrorism in its entirety. The answers here are not much clearer. How can the U.S. government "counter" the violent jihadist narrative? Is there an American or Western story that is more emotionally resonant? If there is no alternative narrative, would it be feasible to focus narrowly on restricting the communication of the narrative (for example, limiting access to social media)? Can recruitment or financing be blocked? Even when government bureaucracies know exactly what to do to prevent acts of terrorism, such as keeping would-be suicide bombers trained and armed in Yemen off airplanes flying to American airports, implementation has proved tricky. The coordination difficulties cited as a cause of intelligence agency inability to detect the 9/11 plot have not all been resolved by the establishment of new bureaucracies, and much work remains to be done even in an area where best practices are well known.

Terrorist Attacks Are Rare Events

By now we hope we have fully convinced our readers that compared with many other types of behavior that produce bad outcomes, terrorist attacks are extremely rare events. Despite the fact that there are a large and growing number of attacks worldwide, the total numbers are still relatively small. For example, as we have seen, the Global Terrorism Database reports about as many terrorist attacks worldwide as there were homicides in the United States alone in the same time period. And since 2010, total terrorist attacks on U.S. soil have hovered around ten per year. The number of attacks producing mass casualties is even smaller. So far, the 9/11 attacks remain the deadliest terrorist attacks in nearly fifty years. In a database that includes nearly 157,000 terrorist attacks from around the world and for four and one-half decades, only 7 attacks have claimed 500 or more lives.

In chapter 2 we argued that policymakers should be wary of quick and massive ad hoc reactions that cannot be rolled back easily and that will make it harder to adapt as the threat shifts, which it surely will. Institutional and legal structures adopted during periods of crisis limit subsequent flexibility, as do official framings of the threat as the equivalent of war. Crisis responses also pose other serious challenges stemming from unintended consequences, such as shrinking civil liberties and fueling public fears.[1] Policymakers should try to avoid seeing a black swan event as a predictor of more of the same, because the anticipation of repetition drives overreaction. Our analysis stresses the danger of inferring a trend from a single shocking case that was inherently unpredictable.

Resisting the temptation to see the unique as typical and being able to make that distinction and make it credibly are more easily said than done, both psychologically and politically. Early after 9/11, Cass Sunstein referred to "probability neglect," the tendency of people to react emotionally and exaggeratedly to low-probability risks because they are perceived as catastrophic and therefore likely, despite facts that indicate otherwise.[2] He also recognized that public fear is a real policy problem that governments cannot ignore even if they think the fear is unwarranted. Public opinion is demonstrably affected in many ways: in presidential approval ratings, measures of trust in government, ranking of threats to national security, and attitudes toward related issues such as immigration and open borders.

Publics are sensitive to attacks outside the country as well as at home; American opinion changed as a result of the Paris 2015 and Brussels 2016 attacks. It is also the case that sequencing matters, so that the coincidence in time of the Paris and Brussels terrorism with the San Bernardino attacks intensified the perception of threat.[3] Public responses are driven both by conventional media coverage—press, television, and radio—and also by ubiquitous and quick-reacting social media. Now audiences learn of attacks virtually instantaneously through Twitter and Facebook and other channels, completely unmediated conduits of information instantly available to attackers, defenders, and victims—anyone who possesses a smartphone. The communication overload as well as such communications' visual content makes it even harder for governments to frame the threat sensibly and reassure without alarming the public.

The immense 9/11 shock was understandable—the attack was a surprise, it was exceptionally destructive, and it was unprecedented. It was a strike by a foreign organization against the American homeland. Efforts to discover what could have prevented it, "what went wrong," were not conclusive or universally convincing. Had there been a follow-up attack, as top policymakers feared, despite lack of clear evidence, the damage would have been even more catastrophic, going well beyond material and human loss. Intelligence agencies did not know if a successor attack was being planned, and uncertainty encouraged reliance on worst-case-scenario analyses, seeing the attack as a precursor to more of the same. It might not have been possible to do otherwise at that time, but the lesson of that experience is that caution and restraint would be a better option in the future.

Thus it is not that the United States should do nothing if attacked, but that policymakers should think twice before reacting in ways that create even more disruption and disorder. National security decision-makers should avoid a repetition of the pendulum effect: a rapid swing to an opposite policy extreme. Prior to 9/11, terrorism was not regarded as a threat to national security or international order at the highest levels of government. Despite some official rhetoric, and the efforts of some individuals in the Clinton administration to draw attention to the threat of al Qa'ida, actual effort and budgets showed that attention was elsewhere. Then, the pendulum swung: over the space of a few short hours terrorism became the defining threat of the post–Cold War era. This disjuncture heightened the effect of surprise. Terrorist nonstate actors are indeed dangerous, but the danger is not the equivalent of mutual assured destruction.

There is also some indication that these issues are especially challenging for a popular democracy like the United States. In general public opinion polls show that concerns for another terrorist attack among the U.S. public soared after 9/11 and dropped somewhat in subsequent months. So far American concern about terrorism has never subsided to pre-9/11 levels. In fact, polling by the Pew Research Center in 2014 showed that the percentage of Americans who thought the likelihood of another major terrorist attack on the United States was actually greater today than at any time since 9/11.[4]

Several decades ago, the historian Samuel Walker referred to the legal system in the United States as "popular justice" and pointed out that the U.S. criminal justice system was unique in placing a very high degree of direct and indirect popular influence over its administration.[5] Unlike other countries or even other democracies, citizens in the United States apply the law directly as jurors; they directly elect many criminal justice officials, including sheriffs, prosecutors, and even judges; and in general, public opinion has a pervasive impact on critical criminal justice outcomes such as sentencing and imprisonment. Although this system has many strong democratic qualities it also has been implicated in exceedingly harsh criminal punishments, the highest per capita prison population in the world, and a country with a rate of executions exceeded only by a handful of authoritarian regimes.

There may be parallels to the impact of popular democracy on crime and counterterrorism policy. John Mueller and Mark Stewart conclude that public opinion is the "primary driver" of current U.S. policies on terrorism.[6] As we have noted in earlier chapters, when public fears are raised by a high-profile terrorist attack, even in a distant location, the demand for a strong response by policymakers may be nearly irresistible in the U.S. system. As the international relations expert Robert Jervis points out, policy in the United States "never strays too far and too long from what is desirable, or at least acceptable to the public."[7] In democracies, it is important for national leaders to frame the threat carefully and communicate its nature clearly, consistently, and reasonably.

Accounting for Failed and Foiled Plots

Policymakers and the public should thus be realistic about what the threat is, an admonition that sounds like the worst of tedious and oft-repeated policy bromides. But our empirical analysis of open-source data shows that Americans at home are rarely threatened by phenomena that nevertheless receive excessive media and government attention, such as returned foreign fighters or terrorists concealed among refugees or a rash of deadly "lone wolves." Most plots in the United States over the past two decades did not result in completed action, although there have been some close calls, such as the 2009 Christmas bombing attempt. This relatively benign outcome may be due to the post-9/11 FBI's efficiency at prevention, and the CIA and National Counterterrorism Center's prowess at detection, but it may also be because most would-be perpetrators in the United States are individuals who are not particularly skilled or clever and are easily taken in by informants who nurture their aspirations, provide emotional support, and acquire weapons for them. Their motivations are often indistinct and confused. In either case, or in both cases combined, it is essential to disaggregate and differentiate the threat, which means that in criminalizing and punishing behavior or in ranking its threat potential, plans to travel abroad, give money, or post favorable comments on Facebook and Twitter should not be equated with plots to use violence. Support for jihadist causes should not be condoned, but policy priorities should be clear. It is also important to recognize that a hundred plots in the United States over a period of almost twenty-five years is not a large number, and that many of the plots were sketchy at best. The roughly 220 plotters and perpetrators we identify hardly represent a trend toward mass mobilization or the formation of a grassroots social movement. Much more actual and planned violence is attributable to advocates of right-wing causes, and these activities are not treated as a national security threat.

Analyzing the murky world of plots, plans, preparations, and intentions, in addition to completed attacks, provides a more comprehensive and nuanced view of the nature and scope of the threat, particularly to the U.S. homeland, than a study only of successfully completed attacks can provide. Analyzing failed and foiled plots provides critical additional insights into actual risk. Overall, we see that the threat to the United States is episodic, sporadic, and inconsistent. There may be an inherent tension in reporting outcomes, in that the FBI and political leaders may want to maximize the deadly potential of all interrupted plots, to demonstrate that they are successfully protecting the public, whereas in reality the would-be perpetrators were simply inefficient. It is not clear what measures should or could have stopped the attackers who got through security barriers or evaded detection in the relatively few domestic cases between 1993 and 2016. Was it the content of policy, poor implementation of rules and regulations, or simply bad luck that allowed the attackers, as well as those who came very close, to get through? Major policy questions are raised by the fact that other than 9/11 the most lethal acts of violence in the United States involved guns rather than explosives. Whether tightening gun control measures would assist in countering terrorism is a subject of intense partisan debate, and there is no across-the-board answer that is broadly acceptable.

It is also important to point out the obvious: that the threat situation in Europe is much more critical. Distinguishing factors are, in combination, proximity to conflict theaters in the Middle East, ease of travel both to those hotspots and within the European Union's Schengen zone, and the presence of highly susceptible targets for jihadist recruiters among Muslim immigrant communities, particularly in major cities. Plots in Europe, in general, are more likely than those in the United States to be genuinely transnational and to involve large numbers of conspirators, as well as to have stronger operational connections to jihadist organizations outside the targeted country. The threat of returned foreign fighters is much more acute.

Identifying the Adversary

The differences that we have stressed in the identities of the perpetrators behind plots means that a one-size-fits-all approach to countering violent extremism or counterterrorism is not productive.

Identifying potential and even future terrorists is difficult. The actors are shadowy and often obscure. Our analysis makes it clear that there is tremendous diversity in terms of the organizations, networks, and individuals that actually carry out terrorist attacks. In fact, we argue that from both a policy and a research standpoint the idea of a "terrorist group" is a simplified abstraction that can conceal the reality of incredible variation. Levels of organizational complexity of the entities that carry out terrorist attacks differ substantially. On one extreme are individuals who are not a part of any known violent movement or cause, have no recognized links to a specific group, and receive no help from any organization in planning or carrying out an attack. At the other extreme are highly organized terrorist groups such as al Qa'ida that persist over time, have a well-defined chain of command, and are maintained by stable leadership and complex organizational structures. They are capable of long-term planning and sustained strategic direction. In between are loosely connected groups as well as shadowy networks that can be identified only generically in terms of overarching ideological affiliation such as "right-wing extremists" or "violent jihadists," if at all. These disparate entities are often in a state of evolutionary flux; change is constant and stability rare. Our arguments are based on academic research into the organizational dimensions of terrorism that has advanced our knowledge significantly while being far from comprehensive or infallible.

Even when we can attribute a terrorist attack to a specific group the organizational capacity and activity level of groups vary. Trajectories are different. Some groups are able and willing to attack frequently over many years; others attack only sporadically and over a short time period. About half of the more than 2,500 groups identified in the GTD are associated with a single attack only. Even for groups that manage to develop a high degree of organization and maintain this organizational structure over a period of time, ambiguity is still omnipresent.[8]

Sound policy must also take into account the interactive process: government action and indeed the reputation for action cause a reaction on the part of an adversary who thinks strategically. Government policies may contribute to radicalization, either by giving people a motive—reinforcing the belief that the United States and its Western allies are killing Muslims abroad and blocking jihadist aspirations—or in making individuals' choice of supporting ISIS or al Qa'ida into a dramatic act of resistance to oppression, elevating their status from criminal or disaffected loner to political or religious rebel. The political scientist Robert Powell noted in a 2007 game theoretic analysis that defending a country against a strategic adversary is an entirely different proposition than defending against vulnerability to natural disaster.[9] In this respect, however, it is also essential to note that terrorist adversaries also interact with each other, as rivals and as friends. Relationships among them matter to the outcomes of government policies. Thus American and allied efforts to assist "moderate" rebels in Syria and to combat ISIS alter the balance of power among all violent groups opposing the Syrian regime. Efforts to destroy ISIS may advantage al Qa'ida. Like-minded groups may compete with each other for influence through escalating violence against external targets. Smaller groups may jump on the bandwagon of entities that appear more powerful and likely to come out on the top of the power struggle. On the other hand, they may resist domination by larger groups and form counteralliances.

The reality of this fluidity and constant jockeying for position supports our warning against exaggerating the unity or power behind terrorism by inflating potential terrorists' significance and bolstering their myths. There is no unitary all-encompassing terrorist threat. Even apparently cohesive entities can split and splinter into factions, cooperate and merge with other groups, and indulge in vicious rivalries. These heterogeneous actors are constantly adapting to a changing environment, one defined substantially by pressure from opponents such as the United States and allies as well as local and regional governments. With such a shifting and disaggregated threat, it is impossible for the United States, even with its superior military power, to determine outcomes with any certainty. Every apparent status quo erodes quickly.

Attributing Responsibility

Partly as a consequence of the elusiveness and adaptability of the terrorist adversary, attribution is a pervasive obstacle to an effective response. Because the threat is amorphous, fragmented, and diffuse, establishing responsibility is not straightforward. In around 50 percent of all the cases in the GTD, the research team was never able to assign responsibility for an action to a specific group. For some years the percentage of unattributed attacks was over 70 percent. And in some regions of the world—Russia, Central Asia, Eastern Europe—over 80 percent of attacks are unattributed. Attributing responsibility for attacks from open sources is especially complex in war-torn countries such as Iraq and Afghanistan, but it is also challenging in countries not actively engaged in war such as India and Pakistan. It is hard to link attacks or plots to specific actors to be apprehended and punished, even if there is an effective way of imposing sanctions. Deception and concealment are, after all, at the heart of terrorism. Even if the actors responsible for terrorism can be identified and located, the process can take many years. Attribution that is not certain and timely is not useful in explaining and justifying the response. Matters are also complicated by the fact that policymakers hardly welcome the opportunity to admit to the public that they do not know and will probably never know who did it. So the question is twofold: Can governments improve their capabilities, and if not, how can they nonetheless move forward in a world where perfect attribution is impossible? If attribution is improved, is prevention also improved? Are terrorists dissuaded if they know they will not remain anonymous? When, for that matter, do they wish to claim credit? These are questions for further research.

Even if intelligence agencies can improve their abilities, it is prudent to avoid relying for deterrence exclusively on threats to punish terrorism. In the nuclear security arena, this means stressing prevention and nuclear security, not declaratory threats. Deterrence depends on attribution, but threats of retaliation, as well as forceful responses themselves, may just be provocative. And attribution is difficult to prove but cannot easily be assumed.

It is important, then, that both researchers and policymakers who focus on terrorism be transparent about what they do not know, the limitations of knowledge. The economist Charles Manski argues that sound policy analysis requires not only objective data but also an accurate account of the assumptions underlying policy recommendations based on data.[10] Often the assumptions that are implicit in an empirical analysis or a set of conclusions arrived at by a researcher either are not well understood or are not well articulated. In many cases assumptions are overly strong, unrealistic, or even heroic. Manski defines "incredible certitude" as policy conclusions that rest "on critical unsupported assumptions or leaps of logic."[11] In other words, conclusions derived from models using assumptions that are unrealistic cannot be the basis for sound policy. Another way to phrase this issue is to note that the absence of evidence is not evidence of absence. Simply because policymakers lack evidence that something exists, such as a concrete plot or a link between an individual and an organization, does not mean that they have evidence that it does not exist. And yet almost always, when policymakers and analysts make threat assessments, they end up basing their recommendations on data that are at least partially incomplete. In short, a necessary condition for credible empirical conclusions requires transparency on the part of researchers and policymakers as to what assumptions they are making in evaluating available data and reaching conclusions.

Measuring and Evaluating Counterterrorism

It is apparent throughout our analysis in this book that defining and measuring the effectiveness of counterterrorism measures is a formidable challenge. We could posit that the goal of American policy should simply be to minimize terrorist attacks, keep the threat in proportion, avoid oversimplification, think sensibly, and be consistent. But how would progress toward accomplishing these goals be calibrated? The world of terrorism and counterterrorism is one of subjective impressions as much as objective facts. Numerical results advertised or accepted as reliable measures of progress may be misleading. And there can be no accurate metrics without public consensus on goals. The means employed must be suited to the ends as well as compatible with each other and with American values. Alternative courses of action must be reevaluated as the threat changes. Both the September 2002 National Security Strategy of the United States of America and the February 2003 National Strategy for Combating Terrorism defined the goal of the United States as "a world in which terrorism does not define the daily lives of Americans and their friends."[12] The intent was to eliminate terrorism as a threat to the American way of life, although in reality not even the catastrophic attacks on 9/11 threatened the American way of life. Terrorism does, however, define the daily lives of many others, including the many Syrians, Iraqis, Afghans, Somalis, Libyans, Nigerians, and other citizens of conflict-ridden states, whether they are considered friends of Americans or even just enemies of violent jihadists (Shia Muslims, Christians, or presumed apostates). At the time, accomplishment of the goal of protecting the American way of life was predicated on an expansive conception of a world with no terrorism "of global reach," an end that could presumably be brought about through the preemptive use of military force, or unilateral "anticipatory self-defense." Ironically, however, if taken in a narrow sense, the formulation of this ambition for the first term of the Bush administration could have implied recognition of the subjectivity of strategic meaning. That is, the perception of safety matters as much as safety.

Will the Future Be Different?

In an interview with NBC's *Today* show on the morning of his final State of the Union address, President Obama told the interviewer Matt Lauer that the United States did not face a single existential threat as his presidency approached its end.[13] What the president seemed to mean by this was that the United States was not currently facing any danger that literally threatened its continued survival. The commentator James Fallows, in a discussion of the term "existential threat," concluded that during the cold war the application of this term was not mere hyperbole.[14] The world in general and the United States in particular faced an existential threat from nuclear weapons. Throughout this period people in the United States and the Soviet Union were constantly reminded of the danger that they could be incinerated in minutes. But what President Obama seemed to be suggesting in his statement, said Fallows, is that although organizations like ISIS and their sympathizers are clearly capable of mounting terribly lethal acts of violence against ordinary civilians going about their daily lives, nothing in their current capacity suggests an ability to carry out the kind of total destruction that is an actual possibility with nuclear weapons—at least not against the United States. Countries are not obliterated by terrorism.

Of the nearly 157,000 terrorist attacks since 1970 thus far there have been no nuclear terrorist attacks and very few chemical, biological, or radiological attacks. Of those few, most were unsophisticated and not extremely deadly. Thus, in many ways the threat of nuclear terrorism represents an extreme version of the general challenges we face with counterterrorism policy: a type of attack that is very hard to predict because of its low probability but one that nevertheless could have a major impact. There is general agreement that a full-blown nuclear explosion could result in the death of 10 or even 100 times more people than were killed in any terrorist attack since 1970, including 9/11. Nevertheless, the political scientist John Mueller argues that even this level of destruction would not qualify as an existential threat to the survival of the United States: "The explosion of a single atomic bomb capable of destroying a few city blocks is taken to portend the demise of the entire city, the economy of the country, the country itself, the modern state system, civilization, the planet."[15]

Regardless of whether the potential use of nuclear material in a terrorist attack qualifies as an existential threat, what are the chances of that happening? When the terrorism research expert Brian Jenkins of the Rand Corporation was asked this question he stated, "I'm not nationally recognized in the field of prophecy."[16] The data reported here for the past half century show that despite fears that began as early as 1945, the threat has not materialized. Mueller supports the conclusion that such an outcome is very unlikely and adds that unwarranted anticipation has been costly: "Fears and anxieties [about nuclear weapons] . . . while understandable, have been excessive, and they have severely, detrimentally, and even absurdly distorted spending priorities while inspiring policies that have often been overwrought, ill conceived, counterproductive, and sometimes massively destructive."[17]

And what of the opposing view, that the risk of a nuclear strike of some sort by terrorists is a real and perhaps increasingly likely possibility? Certainly, this danger has been a major theme in the U.S. intelligence community. In June 2003 the U.S. government issued a warning that there was a high probability of an al Qa'ida nuclear attack sometime in the next two years.[18] The CIA in an official statement in September 2008 concluded that al Qa'ida was currently the number one nuclear attack concern of the United States.[19] In fact, as early as 1998 Osama bin Laden described the acquisition of weapons of mass destruction as a "religious duty," and there is evidence that he discussed nuclear weapons with Pakistani scientists in August 2001, although unclassified sources do not provide many details.[20] In November 2001 bin Laden and Zawahiri gave an interview in which they claimed that they had nuclear weapons.[21] Also, al Qa'ida has commissioned *fatwas*, or religious rulings, to support the right to kill 4 million Americans, later amended to 10 million Americans. However, when al Qa'ida training camps were captured in Afghanistan in 2001 no evidence of nuclear material was found, and the recovered documents contained no information that could be construed to indicate that al Qa'ida operatives had the necessary knowledge to obtain the materials essential for a bomb's construction, let alone to actually make one.[22]

More recently, the risk of nuclear terrorism has been raised in light of the ascendancy of ISIS. A 2016 story in the *Huffington Post* claimed that over the past five years, the FBI, in conjunction with local authorities in Moldova, interrupted four attempts by nuclear smugglers to sell radioactive materials to Middle Eastern extremists, including ISIS.[23] The author of the post, Joe Cirincione, argued that the risk of ISIS getting a nuclear bomb is far less than the possibility that they could get access to highly enriched uranium with which they could construct a "dirty" bomb.[24] An opinion piece by Alan Kuperman in the *New York Times* warned that if terrorists could get their hands on as little as 100 pounds of highly enriched uranium, an amount about the size of a soccer ball, they could potentially replicate the Hiroshima attack of 1945.[25] In March 2002, Henry Kelly, the president of the Federation of American Scientists, estimated that a dirty bomb set off at the National Gallery of Art in Washington, D.C., could force the "abandonment for decades" of forty city blocks, including the Supreme Court, the Library of Congress, and the Capitol.[26] Still not an existential threat, according to John Mueller, but worrying.

Even before the rise of ISIS, in 2009, President Obama called nuclear terrorism the most immediate and extreme threat to global security and announced his intention to reduce the supply of nuclear materials that might be acquired by terrorists. On the occasion of the

2016 Nuclear Security Summit, the White House issued a statement summarizing the official U.S. position, which assumes that terrorists have the capacity as well as the desire to build nuclear devices, if they acquire the necessary materials:

> It is almost impossible to quantify the likelihood of nuclear attack by extremist groups. But we know that roughly 2000 metric tons of nuclear weapons usable materials—highly enriched uranium and separated plutonium—are present in both civilian and military programs, and we know that terrorists have the intent and the capability to turn these raw materials into a nuclear device if they were to gain access to them. A terrorist attack with an improvised nuclear device would create political, economic, social, psychological, and environmental havoc around the world, no matter where the attack occurs.[27]

In contrast to an existential attack, however defined, what are the chances of a cataclysmic attack, which we will define here as simply a large-scale mass-casualty violent event? Since 1970, the coordinated attacks of 9/11 still represent the most destructive terrorist violence in the modern age. If we abandon trying to predict the likelihood of existential terrorist threats, how likely are additional attacks of the magnitude of 9/11? Serious researchers have actually tried to answer this question with statistics. Aaron Clauset and Ryan Woodard used data from a terrorism event database similar to the GTD to examine the number of terrorist acts committed between 1969 and 2007.[28] They found that the attacks on the Twin Towers killed six times as many people as any other terrorist attack in the database during that time period. On the basis of several different sets of statistical assumptions the researchers then calculated the likelihood of another terrorist attack of the magnitude of 9/11. After estimating a number of statistical models they concluded that there was an 11 to 35 percent probability of 9/11 happening between 1969 and 2007—not particularly unlikely. Note that the researchers were not saying that anyone could have predicted the timing or the devastation of the 9/11 attacks; they are merely saying that if 9/11 is placed on a continuum of least to most deadly past attacks, an attack with the deadliness of 9/11 is not that surprising.

The researchers then applied the same model to the future and came up with a likelihood of another attack with the deadliness of the 9/11 attacks falling between 20 and 50 percent, depending on which model was used and assuming that the average number of attacks worldwide per year, approximately 2,000, stayed the same. Realizing that the odds of things holding steady were not good, the researchers tried factoring in such destabilizing scenarios as rising food prices or conflicts escalating or de-escalating in two of the current hot spots for terrorism, Iraq and Afghanistan. In these cases the models became truly alarming, indicating that in the worst-case scenarios the likelihood of another event as deadly as 9/11 becomes nearly 95 percent.

Where does this leave us? How can we at once argue that high-consequence terrorist attacks are exceedingly rare and yet also argue that they are not that surprising? An analogy from seismology might help. On a recent day seismologists concluded that there had been 16 earthquakes in California with a magnitude of 1.5 or greater. The same seismologists claimed that California had experienced 148 earthquakes in the past seven days, 630 earthquakes in the past month, and 7,093 earthquakes in the past year. The largest of these, at Borrego Springs, had a magnitude of 5.2. If we turned years of earthquake data for California into a distribution, we would undoubtedly conclude that the vast majority of quakes are trivial in their effects—taking no lives and doing little property damage. And yet in the same distribution as these thousands of minor quakes that took no lives and caused minimal property damage we would also identify those rare events such as the 1906 San Francisco earthquake, magnitude 7.8, which took the lives of more than 3,000 from the quake itself and the massive fires it spawned. We would also be right to conclude that from a purely statistical viewpoint, another major earthquake in California would not be anomalous.

Critics are correct to emphasize that on the basis of past information, the future likelihood of an existential or even cataclysmic terrorist strike is quite low. And we can confirm that as devastating as terrorist attacks can be in terms of their toll in human life, for the past half century this toll has been far less serious than deaths caused by more mundane sources. For example, the Association for Safe International Road Travel estimates that worldwide nearly 1.3 million people die in road crashes each year, an average of 3,287 deaths per day.[29]

This means that more people die in road crashes in one day than died in the deadliest terrorist attack in nearly one half century. At the same time, statistical research on long-tailed distributions—those with one or two very extreme values—indicates that, from a probabilistic standpoint, attacks that reach the lethality of 9/11 are not that improbable. So, although we strongly agree with the warning that the existential threat of terrorism has often been grossly exaggerated, we also want to avoid being in the position of one prognosticator who concluded less than a year before 9/11 that "terrorists did not strike the United States and the fear mongering came to an abrupt end with the dawn of January 2, 2000."[30]

This tension between taking the terrorist threat seriously while not overestimating its likelihood or destructiveness was brought home to Americans, with the June 12, 2016 nightclub shooting in Orlando, Florida, which killed forty-nine people. It ranked as the second deadliest terrorist attack on U.S. soil since 9/11.

Interpreting Current Trends

In June 2016 the U.S. State Department released its congressionally mandated annual report on worldwide terrorism, which is based in part on the Global Terrorism Database.[31] According to the statistics cited in the report, worldwide the number of terrorist attacks and fatalities in 2015 exhibited the largest declines in more than a decade, following years of striking increases. Terrorist attacks dropped by 13 percent and deaths by 14 percent. While the fact that more than 28,000 deaths and 35,000 injuries resulted from nearly 12,000 terrorist attacks in 2015 can hardly be regarded as good news, these numbers are a welcome development given the record-breaking numbers that have been recorded annually since 9/11. Terrorist attacks and deaths in 2015 dropped substantially in some of the countries that have suffered the most in recent years. In Pakistan, for example, attacks were nearly cut in half and fatalities declined by more than one-third. Iraq and Nigeria also experienced considerable declines.

But not all of the news was good. Violence worsened in 2015 in conflict-ridden Afghanistan, which witnessed a 20 percent increase in attacks. Terrorist attacks also increased in several countries where they had previously been less common, such as Bangladesh and Egypt. Perhaps most troubling, the decades-old conflict between Turkey and the Kurdistan Workers' Party (PKK), which once showed signs of coming to an end, reignited, resulting in a large increase in terrorist attacks in Turkey.

Breaking down the 2015 data also reveals important developments in the number of attacks committed by the world's deadliest organizations. Some groups, like al-Shabaab in Somalia and the Pakistani Taliban, were considerably less active, while others—the Taliban in Afghanistan and Boko Haram in West Africa—carried out more attacks than in previous years. Notably, terrorist attacks carried out in Iraq by ISIS declined by 31 percent in 2015. Although fewer attacks are undeniably better than the alternative, number of attacks is not the only metric by which to gauge the strength of terrorist organizations. ISIS was considerably less active in Iraq in 2015, but the group's activity in Syria increased, and it managed to expand operations into several new countries as well as to attract the allegiance of numerous additional affiliates and allies. In 2015 and 2016 ISIS claimed credit for a number of high-profile attacks in the United States and Western Europe by individuals who asserted that they were "inspired" by the group—including the 2015 San Bernardino and the 2016 Orlando attacks. This suggests that although ISIS may be changing, it may nevertheless pose a serious threat for years to come.

Interpreting patterns of terrorism is a complex challenge because situations can, and often do, evolve in unexpected ways. Despite a welcome decrease in the total number of terrorist attacks and fatalities that occurred worldwide, trends are not universally positive. Nor is there a guarantee that global declines will continue. Nevertheless, these latest numbers provide a bit of good news in an area where it has been in short supply. In fact, one of the few causes for optimism for those studying worldwide terrorism is the observation that terrorist activity generally does not stay high in the same regions forever. Geographic hot spots of terrorism, like global terrorism trends, have changed over time. Western Europe was the predominant location for terrorist attacks in the 1970s; countries in Latin America (Central America, the Caribbean Basin, and South America) experienced a great deal of terrorism in the 1980s; terrorism in the Middle East–North Africa, South America, and South Asia was especially prevalent in the 1990s; and attacks were highly concentrated in certain countries in the Middle East–North Africa and South Asia in the first thirteen years of the twenty-first century.[32] What are the chances that terrorism will exhaust itself in the Middle East–North Africa and South Asia and that terrorism as a worldwide problem will then simply fade away as a major issue? Unfortunately, we conclude that the chances for the disappearance of terrorism as a public threat are remote.

For the last few decades, criminologists have argued that all crime requires just three elements: motivated offenders, suitable targets, and the absence of capable guardians.[33] This also could be said to apply to terrorism. History shows a steady stream of motivated terrorist offenders, but nobody is particularly good at predicting who the offenders will be in advance of attacks. Capable watchfulness to counter terrorism is an ongoing concern and, particularly in democratic societies, requires a constant balancing of security on the one hand and privacy and civil liberties issues on the other. This leads us to consider the long-term trends in suitable targets and opportunities for terrorism. And here there have been some notable changes.

The propensity of human beings to prefer living in cities has grown exponentially in recent years. According to United Nations statistics, the urban population of the world has grown rapidly since 1950, from 746 million to 3.9 billion in 2014.[34] Continuing population growth and urbanization are projected to add 2.5 billion people to the world's urban population by 2050. At the same time declining rural populations mean that for the first three decades of the twenty-first century, all net expected world population growth will be in urban areas. Again, according to United Nations statistics, in 1950, 30 percent of the world's population was urban, and by 2050, 66 percent of the world's population is projected to be urban.[35] This level of urban density has a whole host of benefits, but it also provides an unparalleled opportunity for terrorism and the mass destruction of human life. With urban centers come mass transportation hubs, shopping centers, and crowds as accessible targets. Attackers enjoy the anonymity provided by a large diverse and mobile urban population. We are reminded of the attention paid to "urban guerrilla warfare" in the 1960s and 1970s.

To illustrate the magnitude of the change, we can point out that in the mid-1800s, London was the most populous city in the world, and Soho was the most densely populated neighborhood in London.[36] At that time Soho had a density of about 400 people per acre. Fast forward 150 years to New York City, where the Twin Towers occupied approximately one acre of land, and on a typical workday such as September 11, 2001, each tower accommodated about 50,000 people. The point is even if al Qa'ida had existed in the mid-1800s, it would have been impossible for the organization to have taken the lives of nearly 3,000 people in a single day by blowing up two buildings.

Other demographic changes will substantially reshape the world, and some of the implications of these changes may increase terrorist threats. Although there is no known terrorist "type" or profile, some generalizations can be hazarded.[37] Statistically, terrorists, like common criminals, are overwhelmingly likely to be young men. Today, roughly nine out of ten children under the age of fifteen live in economically developing countries—the same countries that are likely to have the world's highest birth rates in the future. Indeed, World Bank statistics show that over 70 percent of the world's population growth between now and 2050 will likely occur in just twenty-four countries, all of which are low- or lower-middle income, with an average per capita income of under $4,000 per year.[38] Many of these countries are also prone to civil conflict, poor governance, and corruption.

This demographic tsunami will have effects well beyond the developing world. Because economic opportunities and jobs are likely to lag in developing countries in the years ahead, young aspirant workers will be drawn in growing numbers to the labor markets of the aging developed countries of Europe and North America. Looking back from some future point in time, it is quite possible that current levels of immigration in Western Europe and North America, already a contentious political issue in many countries in these regions, will be seen as extraordinarily low. As there is more civil conflict and insecurity in the developing world, both resentment of and attraction to the developed world will increase. With intensified civil violence comes the possibility of safe havens in politically unstable countries for groups using terrorism.

What are the implications of such developments for the future threat of terrorism? We have already seen that identifying the conditions that are conducive to terrorism is exceedingly complex. Despite appearances, deadly terrorist attacks in most parts of the world and for most time periods are rare, which complicates statistical analysis and makes formulating general policies difficult. The fact that the identity of those behind attacks is often uncertain or altogether unknown makes punishment difficult and complicates understanding of the threat. And the reality that many attacks are carried out by individuals or groups that are short-lived, inchoate, or rapidly evolving impedes consistent and rational policy responses and poses unique problems for prevention strategies. These characteristics of terrorism help explain the challenges governments face in countering it. Effective policy requires that these constraints be kept firmly in mind.

Notes

Chapter One

1. To access the data directly go to https://www.start.umd.edu/gtd/.

2. For definitions of Islamism, Salafism, and jihadism, see Shadi Hamid and Rashid Dar, "Islamism, Salafism, and jihadism: A primer," Brookings Institution Markaz Blog, July 15, 2016.

3. One example among many is the controversy surrounding a DHS and FBI intelligence assessment of the sovereign citizen movement leaked to the press in February 2015 (see "Sovereign Citizen Extremist Ideology Will Drive Violence at Home, During Travel, and at Government Facilities," U.S. Department of Homeland Security, Office of Intelligence and Analysis, 2015). See also, Jerome P. Bjelopera, "The Domestic Terrorist Threat: Background and Issues for Congress" (Washington: Congressional Research Service, 2013).

4. Mitchell D. Silber and Arvin Bhatt, "Radicalization in the West: The Homegrown Threat" (New York: New York Police Department, NYPD Intelligence Division, 2007) (http://sethgodin.typepad.com/seths_blog/files/NYPD_Report-Radicalization_in_the_West.pdf).

5. Scott Shane, *Objective Troy: A Terrorist, a President, and the Rise of the Drone* (New York: Random House, 2015).

6. Other mass-casualty attacks in Baghdad since 2003 include an attack on November 23, 2006 that claimed 202 lives and an attack on September 14, 2005 when 160 were killed.

7. Although the term "terrorist organization" is used frequently—for example, by the U.S. government in its official list of "foreign terrorist

organizations"—we prefer to avoid it, since the conspiratorial organizations that use terrorism rarely do so exclusively. Where we do use the term we do not mean to imply that such groups necessarily employ only terrorism. We also leave open the possibility that states as well as nonstates can employ terrorism as a clandestine tool of deception.

8. Martha Crenshaw, "The Causes of Terrorism," *Comparative Politics* 13 (July 1981), pp. 379–99.

9. See descriptions of some of the reactions to the Countering Violent Extremism summit in Peter Beinart, "What Does Obama Really Mean by 'Violent Extremism'?," *The Atlantic,* February 23, 2015. See also Scott Shane, "Faulted for Avoiding 'Islamic' Labels to Describe Terrorism, White House Cites a Strategic Logic," *New York Times,* February 18, 2015.

10. Martha Crenshaw, "The Effectiveness of Terrorism in the Algerian War," in *Terrorism in Context,* edited by Martha Crenshaw (Pennsylvania State University Press, 1995).

11. Robert Pape, *Dying to Win: The Strategic Logic of Suicide Terrorism* (New York: Random House, 2005).

12. Max Abrahms, "Why Terrorism Does Not Work," *International Security* 31 (2006), pp. 42–78, and Max Abrahms, "The Political Effectiveness of Terrorism Revisited," *Comparative Political Studies* 45 (2012), pp. 366–93.

13. Andrew Kydd and Barbara F. Walter, "Sabotaging the Peace: The Politics of Extremist Violence," *International Organization* 56 (2002), pp. 263–96.

14. Peter Krause, "The Political Effectiveness of Non-State Violence: A Two-Level Framework to Transform a Deceptive Debate," *Security Studies* 22 (2013), pp. 259–94.

15. Robin Wright, "Chinese Detainees Are Men without a Country," *Washington Post,* August 24, 2005.

16. Alex P. Schmid and Albert I. Jongman, *Political Terrorism: A Research Guide to Concepts, Theories, Data Bases and Literature* (Transaction: Amsterdam and New Brunswick, 1988).

17. Gary LaFree, Laura Dugan, and Erin Miller, *Putting Terrorism in Context: Lessons from the Global Terrorism Database* (London: Routledge, 2015).

18. Ivan Sascha Sheehan, "Assessing and Comparing Data Sources for Terrorism Research," in *Evidence-Based Counterterrorism Policy,* edited by Cynthia Lum and L. W. Kennedy (New York: Springer, 2011), pp. 13–40.

19. John Mueller and Mark G. Stewart, *Chasing Ghosts: The Policing of Terrorism* (Oxford University Press, 2016).

20. Ibid., p. 246.

21. Gary LaFree and Laura Dugan, "How Does Studying Terrorism Compare to Studying Crime?" in *Criminology and Terrorism,* edited by Mathieu DeFlem (Oxford: Elsevier), pp. 53–74.

22. Ariel Merari, "Academic Research and Government Policy on Terrorism," *Terrorism and Political Violence* 3 (1991), p. 88. A more recent collection of accounts of progress in conducting primary research is Adam Dolnik, editor, *Conducting Terrorism Field Research: A Guide* (London: Routledge, 2013).

23. Brent L. Smith, Kelly R. Damphousse, Freedom Jackson, and Amy Sellers, "The Prosecution and Punishment of International Terrorists in Federal Courts: 1980–1998," *Criminology and Public Policy* 1 (2002), pp. 311–38.

24. See Public Interest Declassification Board, "Transforming the Security Classification System: Report to the President from the Public Interest Declassification Board," November 2012 (www.archives.gov/declassification/pidb/recommendations/transforming-classification.pdf).

25. The Boston College Belfast Project was an oral history project to collect recorded interviews with some participants in the Northern Ireland conflict who had been promised confidentiality. In 2010 an interview with Brendan Hughes was released after he died as per the agreement with Boston College. However, the name of Dolours Price was leaked by a reporter who had overheard an interview that she granted to a fellow reporter. In response, the U.K. government asked the U.S. Department of Justice to issue subpoenas for the interviews of Brendan Hughes and Dolours Price and subsequently for all interviews related to the abduction and death of Jean McConville, a request that the courts upheld. See April Witteveen, "Boston College Oral History Project Faces Ongoing Legal Issues," *Library Journal,* March 12, 2015, and Beth Mcmurtrie, "After Battle To Get Boston College's 'Belfast' Records, Prosecutors Now Largely Dismiss Their Value," *The Chronicle of Higher Education*, September 30, 2015.

26. For details on the GTD see LaFree, Dugan, and Miller, *Putting Terrorism in Context.*

27. For example, Amy B. Zegart, *Spying Blind: The CIA, the FBI, and the Origins of 9/11* (Princeton University Press, 2007), and Eric Dahl, *Intelligence and Surprise Attack: Failure and Success from Pearl Harbor to 9/11 and Beyond* (Georgetown University Press, 2013).

28. For an example of applying broader theoretical frameworks from political science, see Frank Foley, *Countering Terrorism in Britain and France: Institutions, Norms, and the Shadow of the Past* (Cambridge University Press, 2013). See also Zegart, *Spying Blind*, and Dahl, *Intelligence and Surprise Attack.*

Chapter Two

1. Nassim Nicholas Taleb, *The Black Swan: The Impact of the Highly Improbable* (New York: Random House, 2007), p. xvii.

2. United Nations Office on Drugs and Crime, *Global Study on Homicide 2013: Trends, Contexts, Data* (Vienna: United Nations, 2014).

3. Homicide figure: Federal Bureau of Investigation, "Uniform Crime Report, Crime in the United States, Expanded Homicide Data," 2010 (www.fbi.gov/about-us/cjis/ucr/crime-in-the-u.s/2010/crime-in-the-u.s.-2010/offenses-known-to-law-enforcement/expanded/expandhomicidemain). Robbery figure: Federal Bureau of Investigation, "Uniform Crime Report, Crime in the United States, Robbery Data," 2010 (www.fbi.gov/about-us/cjis/ucr/crime-in-the-u.s/2010/crime-in-the-u.s.-2010/violent-crime/robberymain).

4. Ian S. Lustick, *Trapped in the War on Terror* (University of Pennsylvania Press, 2006); John Mueller, *Overblown: How Politicians and the Terrorism Industry Inflate National Security Threats, and Why We Believe Them* (New York: Simon & Schuster, 2009); N. Chang, *Silencing Political Dissent: How Post–September 11 Anti-Terrorism Measures Threaten Our Civil Liberties* (New York: Seven Stories Press, 2009); John Mueller and Mark G. Stewart, *Chasing Ghosts: The Policing of Terrorism* (Oxford University Press, 2016).

5. While it is true that the level of reporting on terrorist threats and possible attacks increased dramatically in the spring of 2001, according to the 9/11 Commission Report (pp. 262–63) the threats received "contained few specifics regarding time, place, method, or target." The available intelligence did not even specify whether the attacks would be aimed at U.S. interests abroad or at specific locations in the U.S. homeland; see *The 9/11 Commission Report: Final Report of the National Commission on Terrorist Attacks upon the United States* (New York: W. W. Norton, 2004).

6. There are 233 attacks in the GTD that result in the number of fatalities being recorded as fractions. Fatality numbers for coordinated attacks are often reported by news media as a cumulative number, making it difficult to record how many exact fatalities were caused by each prong of the attack making up a coordinated attack. These 233 attacks that make up only 0.19 percent of the data were counted as attacks with at least one fatality in this instance.

7. Brian Michael Jenkins, "International Terrorism: A New Mode of Conflict," in *International Terrorism and World Security* (London: Croom Helm, 1975), p. 15. By 2006, however, Jenkins had revised the assessment to argue that terrorists now want both a lot of people watching and a lot dead. See Brian Michael Jenkins. *The New Age of Terrorism*. Santa Monica, CA: RAND Corporation, 2006 (www.rand.org/pubs/reprints/RP1215.html, p. 119).

8. "Iraq Empties Mass Graves in Search for Cadets Killed by ISIS," *New York Times*, April 7, 2015.

9. These cases illustrate the sometimes complex overlap between terrorism and genocide. The common definition of genocide is the deliberate and systematic destruction of a racial, political, or cultural group. The GTD defines terrorism as political violence directed by nonstate actors. In the case

of the Hutu-Tutsi conflict there was evidence of attacks planned by individuals at the top levels of government and the military, but also widespread participation of ordinary citizens. The GTD endeavors to include the latter but to exclude the former as "state terrorism."

10. The Multinational Force in Lebanon was an international peacekeeping force created in August 1982 following the 1981 U.S.-brokered ceasefire between the PLO and Israel to end their involvement in the conflict between Lebanon's pro-government and pro-Syrian factions. See "The Reagan Administration and Lebanon, 1981–1984," U.S. Department of State. Office of the Historian.

11. Steve Rothaus, "Pulse Orlando shooting scene a popular LGBT club where employees, patrons 'like family,'" *The Miami Herald*, June 12, 2016. Retrieved June 15, 2016.

12. "President Barack Obama and FBI say no clear evidence extremists directed Orlando killer," *The Sydney Morning Herald*, June 13, 2016. Retrieved June 13, 2016.

13. "Docs: Pulse gunman Omar Mateen taunted at job for being Muslim," *CBS News*, July 18, 2016. Retrieved July 20, 2016.

14. Alan Blinder, Jack Healy, and Richard A. Oppel, Jr. "Omar Mateen: From Early Promise to F.B.I. Surveillance," *New York Times*, June 12, 2016. Retrieved June 13, 2016.

15. Thomas, Joscelyn. "Orlando terrorist swore allegiance to Islamic State's Abu Bakr al Baghdadi," *The Long War Journal*, June 20, 2016. Retrieved July 3, 2016.

16. The GTD includes the Littleton case in a marginal category because GTD analysts ranked it as a terrorist attack but still had concerns about whether there was sufficient evidence that the act was aimed at attaining a political, economic, religious, or social goal.

17. The eleventh deadliest attack is also connected to an individual who acted alone: the December 2012 shooting at a Sikh temple in Oak Creek, Wisconsin, by white supremacist Wade Michael Page. The attack began when Page entered the Sikh temple and opened fire. At least six people were killed and four others wounded before Page was killed by a responding police officer. Page was a member of numerous white supremacist organizations, including the National Alliance and the Northern Hammerskins.

18. One recent high-profile U.S. domestic attack that is not included in table 2-3 is the Boston Marathon bombings of April 15, 2013. The three individuals killed in the Boston attacks do not place this incident in the top ten deadliest, even though the attacks injured 264 more individuals, many of them quite seriously.

19. Michel Foucault, *The Order of Things: An Archaeology of the Human Sciences* (New York: Random House: 1970), p. xv.

20. Although these estimates get much more complex when we factor in groups that have been affiliated with al Qa'ida, such as the Taliban, al Qa'ida

in Iraq, and the Islamic State of Iraq and Syria. See National Consortium for the Study of Terrorism and Responses to Terrorism, "Al-Qaida's Fatal Terrorism Under Osama bin Laden," background report, May 2, 2012 (www.start .umd.edu/sites/default/files/files/publications/br/AQAttacks_20120501.pdf).

21. Aaron Clauset, Cosma Rohilla Shalizi, and M. E. J. Newman, "Power-Law Distributions in Empirical Data," *Society for Industrial and Applied Mathematics Review* 51, no. 4 (June 2007), pp. 661–703; Chris Anderson, *The Long Tail: Why the Future of Business Is Selling Less of More* (New York: Hyperion, 2006).

22. Clauset, Shalizi, and Newman, "Power-Law Distributions in Empirical Data."

23. Aaron Clauset and Frederick W. Wiegel, "A Generalized Aggregation-Disintegration Model for the Frequency of Severe Terrorist Attacks," *Journal of Conflict Resolution* 54, no. 1 (2010), pp. 179–97.

24. In earlier work, Martha Crenshaw noted that before 9/11 international relations scholars by and large agreed that terrorism was not consequential enough to be a national security problem. See Martha Crenshaw, "Terrorism, Strategies, and Grand Strategies," in *Attacking Terrorism: Elements of a Grand Strategy*, edited by Audrey Kurth Cronin and James M. Ludes (Georgetown University Press, 2004).

25. On the difficulties of obtaining tactical intelligence, see Erik Dahl, *Intelligence and Surprise Attack: Failure and Success from Pearl Harbor to 9/11 and Beyond* (Georgetown University Press, 2013).

26. Ron Suskind, *The One Percent Doctrine: Deep inside America's Pursuit of Its Enemies since 9/11* (New York: Simon & Schuster, 2006).

27. See 9/11 Commission, *The 9/11 Commission Report: Final Report of the National Commission on Terrorist Attacks upon the United States* (New York: W. W. Norton, 2004); 9/11 Commission staff reports, excerpted witness testimony, and excerpts from the joint inquiry report, collected in Steven Strasser and Craig R. Whitney, *The 9/11 Investigations* (New York: PublicAffairs, 2004); and *Joint Inquiry into Intelligence Community Activities before and after the Terrorist Attacks of September 11, 2001: Report of the U.S. Senate Select Committee on Intelligence and U.S. House Select Permanent Committee on Intelligence*, December 2002.

28. Richard A. Clarke, *Against All Enemies* (New York: Free Press, 2004).

29. Ibid., p. 238.

30. Thomas H. Kean, Lee H. Hamilton, and Benjamin Rhodes, *Without Precedent: The Inside Story of the 9/11 Commission* (New York: Knopf, 2006).

31. For Senator Lindsey Graham's remarks, see *Congressional Record*, July 24, 2003, pp. S9887–S9888.

32. Edward Wyatt, "Publisher Names 9/11 Charities," *New York Times*, July 21, 2005.

33. Lustick, *Trapped in the War on Terror*; Mueller, *Overblown*.

34. Barbara Lee, "Why I Opposed the Resolution to Authorize Force," *San Francisco Chronicle–SFGate,* September 23, 2001.

35. Stephen M. Walt, "Beyond bin Laden: Reshaping U.S. Foreign Policy," *International Security* 26, no. 3 (Winter 2001–02), p. 56.

36. Emanuel Adler, "Damned If You Do, Damned If You Don't: Performative Power and the Strategy of Conventional and Nuclear Defusing," *Security Studies* 19, no. 2 (2010), pp. 199–229.

37. Bob Woodward, *Bush at War* (New York: Simon & Schuster, 2002), especially pp. 30–31 and 45. Woodward recounts that Bush's chief speechwriter, Michael Gerson, included the sentence "This is an act of war" in the first draft of the president's speech to the nation on the evening of September 11. The president ordered the sentence removed because he wanted to reassure the public. However, on the morning of September 12, after a meeting of the National Security Council, the president told reporters, "The deliberate and deadly attacks which were carried out yesterday against our country were more than acts of terror. They were acts of war" (Woodward, pp. 30–31, 45).

38. For a comparison of the war on drugs and the war on terror, see Michael Kenney, *From Pablo to Osama: Trafficking and Terrorist Networks, Government Bureaucracies, and Competitive Adaptation* (Pennsylvania State University Press, 2007).

39. Employing this line of discourse opened up avenues of criticism from competing analogies, such as Vietnam, thus generating more controversy.

40. President George W. Bush, Commencement Speech, United States Military Academy, West Point, New York, June 1, 2002 (https://georgewbush -whitehouse.archives.gov/news/releases/2002/06/20020601-3.html).

41. Russ Feingold, "Statement of U.S. Senator Russ Feingold on The Anti-Terrorism Bill from the Senate Floor, October 25, 2001," Electronic Privacy Information Center (https://epic.org/privacy/terrorism/usapatriot /feingold.html).

42. See Privacy and Civil Liberties Oversight Board, "Telephone Records Program Conducted under Section 215 of the USA Patriot Act and on the Operations of the Foreign Intelligence Surveillance Court," report, January 2014 (www.nsa.gov/about/civil-liberties/resources/assets/files/pclob_report _on_telephone_records_program.pdf).

43. Muzaffar Chishti and Claire Bergeron, "DHS Announces End to Controversial Post-9/11 Immigrant Registration and Tracking Program," Migration Policy Institute website, May 17, 2011.

44. See Martha Crenshaw, editor, *The Consequences of Counterterrorism* (New York: Russell Sage Foundation, 2010).

45. See Suskind, *The One Percent Doctrine.*

46. Martha Crenshaw, "The Obama Administration and Counterterrorism," in *Obama in Office: The First Two Years,* edited by James Thurber (Boulder, Colo.: Paradigm Publishers, 2011).

47. The statistics are available from the White House: www.whitehouse
.gov/the-press-office/2016/07/01/executive-order-united-states-policy-pre
-and-post-strike-measures.

48. "U.S. Policy Standards and Procedures for the Use of Force in Counterterrorism Operations Outside the United States and Areas of Active Hostilities" (www.whitehouse.gov/sites/default/files/uploads/2013.05.23_fact
_sheet_on_ppg.pdf).

49. Secretary of Defense Chuck Hagel, report on funding of Guantanamo Bay Detention Center, sent to Representative Adam Smith, Committee on Armed Services, June 27, 2013 (http://democrats.armedservices.house
.gov/index.cfm/files/serve?File_id=ac9bd462-786e-42ef-ae54-1da2
ceb6c3c9).

Chapter Three

1. John Mueller, *Overblown: How Politicians and the Terrorism Indus-
try Inflate National Security Threats, and Why We Believe Them* (New
York: Free Press, 2006), and Ian Lustick, *Trapped in the War on Terror*
(University of Pennsylvania Press, 2006). See also John Mueller and Mark G.
Stewart, "The Terrorism Delusion: America's Overwrought Response to
September 11," *International Security* 37 (Summer 2012), pp. 81–110.

2. Risa Brooks, "Muslim 'Homegrown' Terrorism in the United States:
How Serious Is the Threat?" *International Security* 36 (2011), pp. 7–47.

3. U.S. Senate, Select Committee on Intelligence, 2014. *Committee Study
of the Central Intelligence Agency's Detention and Interrogation Program*
together with Foreword by Chairman Feinstein and Additional Minority
Views, December 9, 2014, S. Report 113–288, 113th Cong., 2nd sess. (Government Printing Office).

4. See John Brennan, "CIA Comments on the Senate Select Committee
on Intelligence Report on the Rendition, Detention, and Interrogation Program" and "CIA Comments" June 2013, released publicly in December
2014 (https://www.cia.gov/library/reports/CIAs_June2013_Response_to
_the_SSCI_Study_on_the_Former_Detention_and_Interrogation
_Program.pdf).

5. Jose A. Rodriguez and Bill Harlow, *Hard Measures* (New York:
Threshold Editions, 2012).

6. Michael Morell and Bill Harlow, *The Great War of Our Time: The
CIA's Fight against Terrorism from Al Qa'ida to ISIS* (New York: Hachette,
2015), p. 271.

7. Project on National Security Reform, "Toward Integrating Complex
National Missions: Lessons from the National Counterterrorism Center's
Directorate of Strategic Operational Planning," report, February 2010 (http://
graphics8.nytimes.com/packages/pdf/world/201002pnsrReport.pdf).

8. U.S. Senate, Select Committee on Intelligence, *Attempted Terrorist Attack on Northwest Airlines Flight 253*, Report 111–199 (Government Printing Office, May 2010).

9. Dennis C. Blair, "Remarks by the Director of National Intelligence Mr. Dennis C. Blair," Alfred M. Landon Lecture Series on Public Issues, Kansas State University, Manhattan, Kansas, February 22, 2010 (www.dni .gov/files/documents/Newsroom/Speeches%20and%20Interviews /20100222_speech.pdf).

10. See Thomas Hegghammer and Petter Nesser, "Assessing the Islamic State's Commitment to Attacking the West," *Perspectives on Terrorism* 9 (2015) (www.terrorismanalysts.com/pt/index.php/pot/article/view/440/html). Their dataset covers January 2011 through June 2015, and the dataset is compatible with Hegghammer's "Jihadi Plots in the West" dataset, covering 1990 to 2010, in Thomas Hegghammer, "Should I Stay or Should I Go? Explaining Variation in Western Jihadists' Choice between Domestic and Foreign Fighting," *American Political Science Review* 107 (2013). See also 1995 to 2012 data analyzed in Petter Nesser, *Islamist Terrorism in Europe* (Oxford University Press, 2016).

11. Erik Dahl, *Intelligence and Surprise Attack: Failure and Success from Pearl Harbor to 9/11 and Beyond* (Georgetown University Press, 2013).

12. Jeff Gruenewald, Joshua D. Freilich, Steven M. Chermak, and William S. Parkin, "Research Highlight: Violence Perpetrated by Supporters of al-Qa'ida and Affiliated Movements (AQAM): Fatal Attacks and Violent Plots in the United States," Research Brief to the Resilient Systems Division, Science and Technology Directorate, U.S. Department of Homeland Security (College Park, Md.: START, 2014) (www.start.umd.edu/pubs/START _ECDB_ViolencePerpetratedbySupportersofAQAM_ResearchHighlight _June2014.pdf).

13. Martha Crenshaw, Margaret Wilson, and Erik Dahl, The Failed and Foiled Plots Dataset (FFP) 1993–2016, compiled with support from START and the Center for the Study of Terrorism and Behavior. Subsequent references to our data are drawn from this dataset (for further information e-mail Martha Crenshaw, crenshaw@stanford.edu).

14. Our approach is thus unlike that used in Gruenewald and others, "Research Highlight" (the 2014 START report), which counts each target and location as a separate plot. We argue that a plot can have multiple targets possibly in multiple locations that are part of the same plan of attack. As a partial consequence the START Report contains over twice as many "plots" in its dataset. Our inclusion requirements also differ. We are more restrictive in our requirement that the perpetrators intend to commit acts of violence in the service of jihadist causes than the 2014 START report. For example, we do not include the 2002 Beltway sniper shootings by John Allen

Muhammed and Lee Boyd Malvo, which the START report lists as fifteen independent plots.

15. Material support provisions were introduced in the 1990s, strengthened in the Patriot Act, and later revised in the Intelligence Reform and Terrorism Prevention Act of 2004. Constitutional challenges to the provision have not been successful.

16. Norman Abrams, "The Material Support Terrorism Offenses: Perspectives Derived from the (Early) Model Penal Code," *Journal of National Security Law & Policy* 1 (2005), p. 7.

17. Greg Miller and Karen DeYoung, "Al-Qaeda Airline Bomb Plot Disrupted, U.S. Says," *Washington Post,* May 7, 2012.

18. This definition also differentiates our study from Gruenewald and others, "Research Highlight" (the 2014 START report), which includes as "failed" plots those stopped by law enforcement action during their final stages.

19. Gruenewald and others, "Research Highlight" (the START Report) includes "perpetrator desistance" prior to the final stages of the plan as plot foiling. We would consider this a failed rather than a foiled plot.

20. Max Abrahms, "The Political Effectiveness of Terrorism Revisited," *Comparative Political Studies* 45 (2012), pp. 366–93; Peter Krause, "The Structure of Success: How the Internal Distribution of Power Drives Armed Group Behavior and National Movement Effectiveness," *International Security* 38 (Winter 2013–14), pp. 72–116; Peter Krause, "The Political Effectiveness of Non-State Violence: A Two-Level Framework to Transform a Deceptive Debate," *International Security* 22 (Summer 2013), pp. 259–94.

21. "Al-Qaeda in the Arabian Peninsula Releases Statement on Jihadist Website Claiming Responsibility for Attempted Christmas Day Terrorist Attack," Memri–Jihad and Terrorism Threat Monitor, Special Dispatch Series 2717, December 28, 2009 (www.memrijttm.org/al-qaeda-in-the-arabian-peninsula-releases-statement-on-jihadist-website-claiming-responsibility-for-attempted-christmas-day-terrorist-attack.html).

22. Ellen Nakashima, "At Least 60 People Charged with Terrorism-Linked Crimes This Year—a Record," *Washington Post,* December 25, 2015.

23. Like the GTD, we include military targets but would exclude attacks on combatant targets that are purely tactical—for example, to secure territory or obtain weapons—and not designed to inspire terror.

24. Our FFP database shows a higher proportion of military targets than we find in the GTD, where military targets are fourth most common, behind private citizens and property, business, government and police. See Gary LaFree, Laura Dugan, and Erin Miller, *Putting Terrorism in Context: Lessons from the Global Terrorism Database* (London: Routledge, 2015), p. 106.

25. These results are generally similar to findings on failed and foiled plots as reported by Jeff Gruenewald and others, "Research Highlight."

26. See LaFree, Dugan, and Miller, *Putting Terrorism in Context,* p. 119.

27. Gruenewald and others, "Research Highlight," pp. 14–15.

28. See 18 U.S. Code, § 2332.

29. Gruenewald and others, "Research Highlight," p. 10.

30. Ibid.

31. See "Lone Wolf and Autonomous Cell Terrorism," special issue edited by Jeffrey Kaplan, Heléne Lööw, and Leena Malkki, *Terrorism and Political Violence* 26 (2014), pp. 1–256.

32. Gruenewald and others, "Research Highlight," p. 9.

33. The concept of "lone wolf" is often loosely used, sometimes to mean small groups or pairs of individuals. We discuss the concept further in chapter 4.

34. Michael Schwirtz and William K. Rashbaum, "Attacker with Hatchet Is Said to Have Grown Radical on His Own," *New York Times,* October 24, 2014.

35. Molly Hennessy-Fiske, "Jason Abdo, Former AWOL Soldier, Sentenced in Ft. Hood Bomb Plot," *Los Angeles Times,* August 10, 2012; see also U.S. Attorney's Office, Western District of Texas, "Naser Jason Abdo Sentenced to Life in Federal Prison in Connection with Killeen Bomb Plot," FBI website, August 10, 2012 (www.fbi.gov/sanantonio/press-releases/2012/naser-jason-abdo-sentenced-to-life-in-federal-prison-in-connection-with-killeen-bomb-plot).

36. Since his intent was property damage, we could reasonably exclude him, but his actions risked harming people. See U.S. Attorney's Office, Eastern District of Virginia, "Man Pleads Guilty to Shooting Military Buildings in Northern Virginia," press release, FBI website, January 26, 2012 (www.fbi.gov/washingtondc/press-releases/2012/man-pleads-guilty-to-shooting-military-buildings-in-northern-virginia).

37. James Dao, "A Muslim Son, a Murder Trial, and Many Questions," *New York Times,* February 16, 2010.

38. Manny Fernandez, "Fort Hood Suspect Says Rampage Was to Defend Afghan Taliban Leaders," *New York Times,* June 4, 2013.

39. Brenda Goodman, "Defendant Offers Details of Jeep Attack at University," *New York Times,* March 8, 2006. See also "Mohammed Taheri-Azar's letter to the police," IPT—The Investigative Project on Terrorism (www.investigativeproject.org/documents/case_docs/248.pdf).

40. Some plots involved the assistance of more than one foreign government.

41. The progression is not necessarily linear; sometimes targets and methods are selected before an attempt to acquire capabilities.

42. Ed Pilkinton and Nicholas Watt, "NSA Surveillance Played Little Role in Foiling Terror Plots, Experts Say," *The Guardian,* June 12, 2013.

43. Human Rights Watch, "Illusion of Justice: Human Rights Abuses in US Terrorism Prosecutions," 2014 (www.hrw.org/report/2014/07/21/illusion

-justice/human-rights-abuses-us-terrorism-prosecutions). Similarly, see critical press investigations such as Eric Lichtblau, "Once Last Resort, F.B.I. Stings Become Common in ISIS Fight," *New York Times,* June 8, 2016.

44. Patrick James, Michael Jensen, and Herbert Tinsley, "Understanding the Threat: What Data Tells Us about U.S. Foreign Fighters," START, September 2015 (www.start.umd.edu/pubs/START_PIRUS_WhatDataTellUs AboutForeignFighters_AnalyticalBrief_Sept2015.pdf).

45. U.S. House of Representatives, Homeland Security Committee, *Final Report of the Task Force on Combating Terrorist and Foreign Fighter Travel,* September 2015 (https://homeland.house.gov/wp-content/uploads /2015/09/TaskForceFinalReport.pdf).

46. Cathy Burke, "Director Comey: Homegrown Extremists the 'Highest Priorities for the FBI,'" *Newsmax,* July 8, 2015 (www.newsmax.com /Newsfront/James-Comey-FBI-americans-joined/2015/07/08/id/654118 /#ixzz3zzoBXA8W).

47. Hegghammer, "Should I Stay or Should I Go?," p. 5.

48. Soufan Group, "Foreign Fighters: An Updated Assessment of the Flow of Foreign Fighters into Syria and Iraq," December 2015 (http://soufangroup .com/wp-content/uploads/2015/12/TSG_ForeignFightersUpdate3.pdf). A 2016 report of the Institute for Strategic Dialogue, a London think tank, examines anti-ISIS foreign fighters (Horizon Series No. 1, "Shooting in the Right Direction," www.strategicdialogue.org/wp-content/uploads/2016/08 /ISD-Report-Shooting-in-the-right-direction-Anti-ISIS-Fighters.pdf).

49. James, Jensen, and Tinsley, "Understanding the Threat."

50. Adam Goldman, Jia Lynn Yang, and John Muyskens, "The Islamic State's suspected inroads into America," *Washington Post,* December 18, 2015.

51. Hegghammer and Nesser, "Assessing the Islamic State's Commitment to Attacking the West."

52. Hegghammer, "Should I Stay or Should I Go?"

53. Scott Shane, "Ohio Man Trained in Syria Is Charged with Planning Terrorism in U.S.," *New York Times,* April 16, 2015. Thus the *Washington Post* list of ISIS sympathizers did not include him.

54. See U.S. Attorney's Office, Eastern District of North Carolina, "North Carolina Resident Daniel Patrick Boyd Sentenced for Terrorism Violations," FBI website, August 24, 2012 (www.fbi.gov/charlotte/press-releases /2012/north-carolina-resident-daniel-patrick-boyd-sentenced-for-terrorism -violations).

55. See U.S. Department of Justice, "Ohio Man Pleads Guilty to Conspiracy to Bomb Targets in Europe and the United States," 2008 (www .justice.gov/archive/opa/pr/2008/June/08-nsd-492.html).

56. Hegghammer and Nesser, "Assessing the Islamic State's Commitment to Attacking the West."

57. Rukmini Callimachi, Katrin Bennhold, and Laure Fourquetnov, "How the Paris Attackers Honed Their Assault through Trial and Error," *New York Times,* November 30, 2015.

58. However, the 2015 Homeland Security Committee Task Force combined training and acquiring combat experience in a single category.

59. Hegghammer, "Should I Stay or Should I Go?," p. 10.

60. Hegghammer and Nesser, "Assessing the Islamic State's Commitment to Attacking the West."

61. James, Jensen, and Tinsley, "Understanding the Threat."

62. "Bellingcat" [pseudonym], "The Other Foreign Fighters: An Open-Source Investigation into American Volunteers Fighting the Islamic State in Iraq and Syria" (www.bellingcat.com/wp-content/uploads/2015/08/The -Other-Foreign-Fighters.pdf).

63. Ellen Nakashima, "At Least 60 People Charged with Terrorism-Linked Crimes This Year—a Record," *Washington Post,* December 25, 2015. See also the FBI's list of terrorism-related events from 2004 to the present, "Terrorism," Federal Bureau of Investigation website (www.fbi.gov/collections/terrorism).

64. See reports from the Terrorism Trials Database at the Center on Law and Security at the Fordham Law School, for example "Case by Case: ISIS Prosecutions in the United States, March 1, 2014—June 30, 2016," Center on National Security at Fordham Law (http://static1.squarespace .com/static/55dc76f7e4b013c872183fea/t/577c5b43197aea832bd486c0 /1467767622315/ISIS+Report+-+Case+by+Case+-+July2016.pdf).

Chapter Four

1. Brian J. Phillips, "What Is a Terrorist Group? Conceptual Issues and Empirical Implications," *Terrorism and Political Violence* 27 (2015), pp. 225–42.

2. Listing a group can also create political problems if the listed group later becomes a potential asset to American policy objectives. For example, the Kurdistan Workers' Party, the PKK, was placed on the FTO list in 1997 as a result of its separatist violence within Turkey. However, by 2014 the United States found Kurdish forces to be an indispensable local ally in the fight against ISIS in Iraq and Syria. As the PKK became an asset to American national security, the Turkish government launched a campaign to destroy it as a domestic terrorist threat.

3. Phillips, 2015, p. 237.

4. Kim Cragin and Sara A. Daly, *The Dynamic Terrorist Threat: An Assessment of Group Motivations and Capabilities in a Changing World* (Santa Monica, Calif.: Rand, 2004).

5. Raffaello Pantucci, "A Typology of Lone Wolves: Preliminary Analysis of Lone Islamist Terrorists" (London: International Centre for the Study

of Radicalisation and Political Violence, 2011); Petter Nesser and Anne Stenersen, "The Modus Operandi of Jihadi Terrorists in Europe," *Perspectives on Terrorism* 8 (2014); Gary LaFree, "Lone-Offender Terrorists," *Criminology and Public Policy* 12 (2013), pp. 59–62; and Jeff Gruenewald, Steven Chermak, and Joshua Freilich, "Distinguishing 'Loner' Attacks from Other Domestic Extremist Violence: A Comparison of Far-Right Homicide Incident and Offender Characteristics," *Criminology and Public Policy* 12 (2013), pp. 65–91.

6. Brent L. Smith, Paxton Roberts, Jeff Gruenewald, and Brent Klein, "Geospatial and Temporal Patterns of Lone Actor Terrorism," presentation at the annual meeting of the START Center, Bethesda, Md., September 19, 2014.

7. Although there were two brothers, the case was generally treated as a lone-offender case by researchers and policymakers; see for example, Pat Sherman, "UCSD Professor Says Boston Marathon Was 'Lone Wolf' Terrorism," *La Jolla Light,* April 21, 2013.

8. For the start of the debate see Marc Sageman, *Leaderless Jihad: Terror Networks in the Twenty-First Century* (University of Pennsylvania Press, 2008); Bruce Hoffman, "The Myth of Grass-Roots Terrorism: Why Osama bin Laden Still Matters," *Foreign Affairs* 87 (May–June 2008); and Marc Sageman and Bruce Hoffman, "Does Osama Still Call the Shots? Debating the Containment of al Qaeda's Leadership," *Foreign Affairs* 87 (July–August 2008).

9. See Martha Crenshaw, "The Debate over 'Old' vs 'New' Terrorism," in *Jihadi Terrorism and the Radicalisation Challenge: European and American Experiences,* 2nd ed., edited by Rik Coolsaet (London: Ashgate, 2011).

10. Ami Pedahzur, "Social Network Analysis in the Study of Terrorism and Political Violence," *PS: Political Science and Politics* 44 (2011), pp. 45–50.

11. Petter Nesser, *Islamist Terrorism in Europe: A History* (Oxford University Press, 2016).

12. Guido W. Steinberg, *German Jihad: On the Internationalization of Islamist Terrorism* (Columbia University Press, 2013).

13. Barak Mendelsohn, *The al-Qaeda Franchise: The Expansion of al-Qaeda and Its Consequences* (Oxford University Press, 2016).

14. Jacob Shapiro, *The Terrorist's Dilemma: Managing Violent Covert Organizations* (Princeton University Press, 2013).

15. See Global Terrorism Database, "Incident Summary" of March 11, 2004, Madrid attack (www.start.umd.edu/gtd/search/IncidentSummary.aspx?gtdid=200403110006).

16. Fernando Reinares, "The Evidence of Al-Qa'ida's Role in the 2004 Madrid Attack," *CTC Sentinel,* March 22, 2012.

17. See Nic Robertson, Paul Cruickshank, and Tim Lister, "Documents Give New Details on Al Qaeda's London Bombings," April 30, 2012, CNN (report

on documents obtained in 2012 by German authorities) (www.cnn.com /2012/04/30/world/al-qaeda-documents-london-bombings/index.html).

18. International Crisis Group, "Islamic Parties in Pakistan," Asia Report 216, December 12, 2011. The case of Lashkar-e-Taiba points to another challenge in identifying perpetrators: banned militant groups sometimes simply change their names.

19. Gary LaFree, Martha Crenshaw, and Sue-Ming Yang, "Trajectories of Terrorism: Attack Patterns of Foreign Groups That Have Targeted the United States, 1970–2004," *Criminology & Public Policy* 8 (August 2009), pp. 445–73.

20. Wendy Pearlman, "Spoiling Inside and Out: Internal Political Contestation and the Middle East Peace Process," *International Security* 33 (Winter 2008–09), pp. 79–101.

21. Paul Staniland argues for the importance of prior social ties in explaining cohesion in *Networks of Rebellion: Explaining Insurgent Cohesion and Collapse* (Cornell University Press, 2014).

22. See "Al Qaeda in the Islamic Maghreb," Mapping Militant Organizations (website), Stanford University (http://web.stanford.edu/group/mapping militants/cgi-bin/groups/view/65). The website is maintained by Martha Crenshaw.

23. Andrew Lebovich, "The Hotel Attacks and Militant Realignment in the Sahara-Sahel Region," *CTC Sentinel*, January 19, 2016. For a short description of al-Murabitoun, see "Profile: al-Murabitoun," BBC News, January 16, 2016 (http://www.bbc.com/news/world-africa-34881170).

24. Tim Craig and Haq Nawaz Khan, "Pakistani Taliban Splits into Two Major Groups amid Infighting," *Washington Post*, May 28, 2014.

25. On splits within al Qa'ida well before the emergence of ISIS, see Vahid Brown, "Cracks in the Foundation: Leadership Schisms in Al-Qa'ida from 1989–2006," Combating Terrorism Center at West Point, January 2, 2007 (www.ctc.usma.edu/posts/cracks-in-the-foundation-leadership-schisms -in-al-qaida-from-1989-2006); Assaf Moghadam and Brian Fishman, editors, *Fault Lines in Global Jihad: Organizational, Strategic, and Ideological Fissures* (London and New York: Routledge, 2011).

26. The fact that governments do try to sow distrust and discord in the ranks of the adversary indicates the assumption of some organization. If we assumed that the actors behind terrorism were completely unstructured, then it would not make sense to try to divide them.

27. The relationships are depicted in organizational diagrams and timelines on the website maintained by Martha Crenshaw, which traces the organizational evolution of violent nonstate actors in distinct conflict theaters. It includes "maps" of both global al Qa'ida and global ISIS connections (http:// web.stanford.edu/group/mappingmilitants/cgi-bin/).

28. Murtaza Hussain, "Militant Leader Talks About Break with Al Qaeda and Possible Syrian Rebel Merger," *The Intercept*, Aug. 23, 2016

(https://theintercept.com/2016/08/23/militant-leader-talks-about-break-with-al-qaeda-and-possible-syrian-rebel-merger/).

29. See "Al-Qaeda Fighters Kill Syrian Rebel Leaders: The Islamic State of Iraq and the Levant Attack and Kill Commanders of Rivals in Escalation of Infighting among Rebels," *Al Jazeera,* February 2, 2014 (www.aljazeera.com/news/middleeast/2014/02/al-qaeda-fighters-kill-syrian-rebel-leader-2014229511898140.html).

30. See Martha Crenshaw, "Conclusion," in *Dynamics of Political Violence: A Process-Oriented Perspective on Radicalization and the Escalation of Political Conflict,* edited by Lorenzo Bosi, Charles Demetriou, and Stefan Malthaner (Farnham, U.K., and Burlington, Vt.: Ashgate, 2014), pp. 296–98.

31. Michael G. Findley and Joseph K. Young, "More Combatant Groups, More Terror?: Empirical Tests of an Outbidding Logic," *Terrorism and Political Violence* (2012), pp. 706–21.

32. See Gabriel Weimann, *Terror on the Internet* (Washington, D.C.: United States Institute of Peace Press, 2006), an early book recognizing this phenomenon, and Gabriel Weimann, "New Terrorism and New Media," report (Washington, D.C.: Wilson Center, 2014).

33. Aaron Y. Zelin, *The State of Global Jihad Online: A Qualitative, Quantitative, and Cross-Lingual Analysis* (Washington, D.C.: New America Foundation, January 2013). Studies of jihadis' use of Twitter include Nico Prucha and Ali Fisher, "Tweeting for the Caliphate: Twitter as the New Frontier for Jihadist Propaganda," *CTC Sentinel,* June 25, 2013, and Jytte Klausen, "Tweeting the Jihad: Social Media Networks of Western Foreign Fighters in Syria and Iraq," *Studies in Conflict & Terrorism* 38 (2015), pp. 1–22. Twitter permits the sharing of content among jihadists in different locations across a variety of social media platforms in real time.

34. J. M. Berger, "Tailored Online Interventions: The Islamic State's Recruitment Strategy," *CTC Sentinel,* October 23, 2015.

35. J. M. Berger and Jonathon Morgan, "The ISIS Twitter Census: Defining and Describing the Population of ISIS Supporters on Twitter," Outlook Series, Brookings, March 6, 2015 (www.outlookseries.com/A0982/Security/3619_ISIS_Twitter_census_population_supporters.htm), p. 2.

36. For an analysis of the impact of foreign fighters on ISIS organization in Syria and Iraq, see Scott Gates and Sukanya Podder, "Social Media, Recruitment, Allegiance and the Islamic State," *Perspectives on Terrorism* 9 (2015).

37. See Peter R. Neumann, "Victims, Perpetrators, Assets: The Narratives of Islamic State Defectors," report (London: International Centre for the Study of Radicalization and Political Violence, 2015) (http://icsr.info/wp-content/uploads/2015/09/ICSR-Report-Victims-Perpetrators-Assets-The-Narratives-of-Islamic-State-Defectors.pdf), which describes the experiences

of fifty-eight defectors from the Islamic State and stresses the importance of publicizing their disillusionment.

Chapter Five

1. Even in this situation attribution may not be straightforward. For example, in 2011 an attack listed in the GTD and attributed to the Provisional IRA involved an explosive device detonated in a bank in Londonderry by individuals who reportedly shouted that they were members of the Provisional IRA. This attack happened several years after formal overtures for peace and major declines in the number of attacks attributed to the Provisional IRA. The incident points out that in long-lasting organizations such as the PIRA there are no doubt individuals who are opposed to peaceful solutions, and so ongoing violence may be committed by dissident actors and splinter groups even after the central administration has brokered some type of peace. So in cases like this do we conclude that the PIRA was responsible or do we assign responsibility to some perhaps unnamed splinter group or even an individual acting alone?

2. "FBI: ISIS inspired California student in campus stabbings," CBS News, March 17, 2016.

3. "House Homeland Security Chairman Believes Suspect Trained in Russia," CNN, April 21, 2013.

4. Peter Foster, "Boston bomber: FBI 'Dropped the Ball' over Tamerlan Tsarnaev," *Telegraph* (London), April 21, 2013.

5. Alan Cullison, "Dagestan Islamists Were Uneasy about Boston Bombing Suspect," *Wall Street Journal,* May 9, 2013.

6. Will Englund and Peter Finn, "Conflict in the Caucasus, Reflected in Suspect's YouTube Playlist," *Washington Post,* April 20, 2013.

7. "After the Marathon Bombing: Terrible Swift Sword," *The Economist,* April 27, 2013. However, according to another source, on the day of the 2012 Boston Marathon, a year before the bombings, a post on Dzhokhar's Twitter feed mentioned a Quran verse often used by radical Muslim clerics and propagandists. Still, the article concludes that the two brothers were on "two separate paths." See Jenna Russell, Jenn Abelson, Patricia Wen, Michael Rezendes, and David Filipov, "Two Brothers, Two Paths," *Boston Globe,* April 19, 2013.

8. The original 1993 data that became the Global Terrorism Database were lost in an office move and were never recovered.

9. Wright, "Why Do Terrorists Claim Credit?"; see also Aaron M. Hoffman, "Voice and Silence: Why Groups Take Credit for Acts of Terror," *Journal of Peace Research* 47 (2010), pp. 615–26.

10. John Monahan and Laurens Walker, *Social Science Methods in Law: Cases and Materials* (New York: Foundation Press, 1985).

11. Illinois Committee on the Study of the Workings of the Indeterminate-Sentence Law and of Parole, *A Study of the Indeterminate Sentence and Parole in the State of Illinois* (Northwestern University Press for American Institute of Criminal Law and Criminology, 1928).

12. Michael Hakeem, "The Validity of the Burgess Method of Parole Prediction," *American Journal of Sociology* 53 (1948), pp. 376–86.

13. John Monahan and Jennifer Skeem, "Risk Redux: The Resurgence of Risk Assessment in Criminal Sanctioning," *Federal Sentencing Reporter,* 26, 158–66. doi: 10.1525/fsr.2014.26.3.158 (2014); Joel Alan Dvoskin, editor, *Using Social Science to Reduce Violent Offending* (Oxford University Press, 2012).

14. *aerial highjackers:* Monahan and Walker, *Social Science Methods in Law,* p. 208; *illegal aliens:* ibid., p. 216; *high-risk prison inmates:* Richard Berk, Brian Kriegler, and Jong-Ho Baek, "Forecasting Dangerous Inmate Misconduct: An Application of Ensemble Statistical Procedures," *Journal of Quantitative Criminology* 22 (2006), pp. 131–45; *drug couriers:* Edwin Zedlewski, *The DEA Airport Surveillance Program: An Analysis of Agent Activities,* in John Monahan and Laurens Walker, *Social Science Methods in Law: Cases and Materials* (New York: Foundation Press, 1985); *domestic-violence risks:* Richard A. Berk, Yan He, and Susan B. Sorenson, "Developing a Practical Forecasting Screen for Domestic Violence Incidents," *Evaluation Review* 29 (2005), pp. 358–83; *rape victims:* A. W. Burgess and L. L. Holmstrom, "Rape Trauma Syndrome," *American Journal of Psychiatry* 131 (1974), pp. 981–86.

15. Joshua B. Hill, Daniel J. Mabrey, and John M. Miller, "Modeling Terrorism Culpability: An Event-Based Approach," *Journal of Defense Modeling and Simulation: Applications, Methodology, Technology* 10, no. 2 (April 2013).

16. To further complicate matters if indeed the attacks can be traced directly to Muammar Qaddafi, the Libyan head of state, the attack could technically be seen as state terrorism and thus would be excluded from most definitions of terrorism.

17. See Central Intelligence Agency, "Terrorist Bombing of Pan Am Flight 103" (https://www.cia.gov/about-cia/cia-museum/experience-the-collection/text-version/stories/terrorist-bombing-of-pan-am-flight-103.html).

18. Jake Tapper, "Ambassador Susan Rice: Libya Attack Not Premeditated," ABC News, September 16, 2012 (http://abcnews.go.com/blogs/politics/2012/09/ambassador-susan-rice-libya-attack-not-premeditated/).

19. See Mark Landler, Eric Schmitt, and Michael D. Shear, "Early E-Mails on Benghazi Show Internal Divisions," *New York Times,* May 15, 2013.

20. Michael Morell, *The Great War of Our Time: The CIA's Fight against Terrorism from al Qa'ida to ISIS* (New York: Hachette, 2012), pp. 206–07, 219–23.

21. Adam Entous, Siobhan Gorman, and Margaret Coker, "CIA Takes Heat for Role in Libya," *Wall Street Journal,* November 1, 2012.

22. Tom Dannenbaum, "Bombs, Ballots, and Coercion: The Madrid Bombings, Electoral Politics, and Terrorist Strategy," *Security Studies* 20 (2011), pp. 303–49. See especially pp. 340–43, "Government Myopia in the Midst of Tragedy."

23. Morell, *The Great War of Our Time,* p. 119.

24. Fernando Reinares, "After the Madrid Bombings: Internal Security Reforms and Prevention of Global Terrorism in Spain," *Studies in Conflict & Terrorism* 32 (2009), pp. 367–88.

25. "Perry: U.S. Eyed Iran Attack after Bombing," United Press International, June 6, 2007.

26. Morell, *The Great War of Our Time,* pp. 38–39.

27. "U.S. Seeking F.B.I.'s Return to Yemen, Says State Dept.," *New York Times,* August 21, 2001.

28. Josh Gerstein, "Court Could Halt USS Cole Trial," *Politico,* February 17, 2016 (www.politico.com/blogs/under-the-radar/2016/02/court-could-halt-uss-cole-trial-219382).

29. Spencer S. Hsu, "Judge Orders Sudan, Iran to Pay $75 Million to Family of USS Cole Victim," *Washington Post,* March 31, 2015.

30. See Jim Gilmore, producer, "The Man Who Knew," *PBS Frontline,* broadcast October 3, 2002 (www.pbs.org/wgbh/pages/frontline/shows/knew/could/).

31. Martha Crenshaw, "Will Threats Deter Nuclear Terrorism?" in *Deterring Terrorism: Theory and Practice,* edited by Andreas Wenger and Alex Wilner (Stanford University Press, 2012).

32. Keir A. Lieber and Daryl Press, "Why States Won't Give Nuclear Weapons to Terrorists," *International Security* 38 (Summer 2013), pp. 80–104.

33. Philip Baxter, "The False Hope of Nuclear Forensics? Assessing the Timeliness of Forensics Intelligence," *Public Interest Report* 68 (Spring 2015).

Chapter Six

1. Stockholm International Peace Research Institute (SIPRI), 2015; this conclusion is based on the SIPRI Military Expenditure Data; downloaded on August 10, 2016: www.sipri.org/databases/milex/.

2. Gordon Adams and Cindy Williams, *Buying National Security: How America Plans and Pays for Its Global Role and Safety at Home* (London: Routledge, 2010).

3. John Mueller and Mark G. Stewart, "The Terrorism Delusion: America's Overwrought Response to September 11," *International Security* 37 (2012), p. 103.

4. Barack Obama, "Remarks by the President at the National Defense University," May 23, 2013 (www.whitehouse.gov/the-press-office/2013/05/23/remarks-president-national-defense-university). By "war" the president was clearly referring to military expenditures in the global war on terrorism.

5. Sendil Mullainathan and Richard H. Thaler, "Waiting in Line for the Illusion of Security," *New York Times*, May 29, 2016.

6. Greg Miller and Karen De Young, "Obama Administration Plans Shake-Up in Propaganda War against ISIS," *Washington Post*, January 8, 2016.

7. Robert J. Art and Louise Richardson, editors, *Democracy and Counterterrorism: Lessons from the Past* (Washington: U.S. Institute of Peace, 2007), pp. 16–17.

8. Cynthia Lum, Lesley Kennedy, and Alison Sherley, "The Effectiveness of Counter-Terrorism Strategies: A Campbell Systematic Review" (Washington: Campbell Collaboration, 2009).

9. Ibid., p. 10.

10. Laura Dugan and Erica Chenoweth, "Moving beyond Deterrence: The Effectiveness of Raising the Benefits of Abstaining from Terrorism in Israel," *American Sociological Review* 77 (August 2012), pp. 597–624.

11. Chairman, Joint Chiefs of Staff, *Counterterrorism*, Joint Publication 3–26 (Government Printing Office, October 14, 2014), pp. 1–5.

12. Ibid., p. viii.

13. Antony J. Blinken, "New Frameworks for Countering Terrorism and Violent Extremism," remarks at the Brookings Institution, Washington, D.C., February 16, 2016. Transcript available at www.brookings.edu/wp-content/uploads/2016/02/20160216_cve_blinken_transcript.pdf.

14. Department of Justice, Office of Public Affairs, "Launch of Strong Cities Network to Strengthen Community Resilience against Violent Extremism," September 28, 2015.

15. Matt Bai, "Kerry's Undeclared War," *New York Times*, October 10, 2004.

16. George W. Bush, "President's Remarks at Victory 2004 Rally in Hobbs, New Mexico," October 11, 2004 (https://georgewbush-whitehouse.archives.gov/news/releases/2004/10/text/20041011-2.html).

17. Dick Cheney, "Vice President Cheney's Remarks at a BC '04 Rally in Medford, New Jersey" (https://georgewbush-whitehouse.archives.gov/news/releases/2004/10/text/20041011-4.html).

18. Richard W. Stevenson, "Bush Faults Kerry on Terrorism Remarks," *New York Times*, October 12, 2004.

19. Ibid. See also "Bush Campaign to Base Ad on Kerry Terror Quote," CNN.com, October 11, 2004.

20. ZZAKI, "New Pentagon Report Uses Language Kerry Used in 2004 That Bush-Cheney Called 'Dangerous' and 'Naïve,'" *ABC News Blogs*, August 10, 2008 (http://blogs.abcnews.com/politicalpunch/2008/08/new-pentagon-re.html).

21. John Kerry, "Remarks at the UNITY 2004 Conference in Washington, DC," August 5, 2004, American Presidency Project (http://www.presidency.ucsb.edu/ws/?pid=29716).

22. Dick Cheney, "VP's Remarks in Dayton, Ohio," August 12, 2004 (https://georgewbush-whitehouse.archives.gov/news/releases/2004/08/20040812-3.html).

23. ZZAKI, "New Pentagon Report."

24. U.S. Department of Defense, *National Defense Strategy* (Government Printing Office, June 2008).

25. These include the White House, "National Security Strategy of the United States of America," September 2002 (text at www.state.gov/documents/organization/63562.pdf); White House, "National Strategy for Combating Terrorism," February 2003 (text at www.cia.gov/news-information/cia-the-war-on-terrorism/Counter_Terrorism_Strategy.pdf); Chairman of the Joint Chiefs of Staff, "National Military Strategic Plan for the War on Terrorism," February 2006 (http://archive.defense.gov/pubs/pdfs/2006-01-25-Strategic-Plan.pdf); White House, "National Security Strategy II," March 2006 (https://georgewbush-whitehouse.archives.gov/nsc/nss/2006/); White House, "National Strategy for Combating Terrorism II, September 2006 (https://georgewbush-whitehouse.archives.gov/nsc/nsct/2006/); White House, "9/11 Five Years Later: Successes and Challenges," report, September 2006 (https://georgewbush-whitehouse.archives.gov/nsc/waronterror/2006/); Strategic Communication and Public Diplomacy Policy Coordinating Committee, "U.S. National Strategy for Public Diplomacy and Strategic Communication," June 2007 (www.au.af.mil/au/awc/awcgate/state/natstrat_strat_comm.pdf), which included countering terrorism as one of its main objectives and established a Counterterrorism Communications Center in the Department of State; in October 2007 the White House released Department of Homeland Security, "The National Strategy for Homeland Security, October 2007" (www.dhs.gov/national-strategy-homeland-security-october-2007); see also, from the Obama administration, White House, "National Strategy for Counterterrorism," June 2011 (www.whitehouse.gov/sites/default/files/counterterrorism_strategy.pdf), and White House, "National Security Strategy," February 2015 (www.whitehouse.gov/sites/default/files/docs/2015_national_security_strategy.pdf).

26. President George W. Bush, 9/11 Address to the Nation, September 11, 2001, p. 2 (www.americanrhetoric.com/speeches/gwbush911addressto thenation.htm).

27. Ibid.

28. George W. Bush, "Address to Joint Session of Congress and the American People," September 20, 2001, p. 2 (http://georgewbush-whitehouse.archives.gov/news/releases/2001/09/20010920-8.html).

29. Catherine C. Gorka, "The Flawed Science behind America's Counter-Terrorism Strategy," white paper (Washington: Council on Global

Security, October 2014); Eric Schmitt and Thom Shanker, "U.S. Officials Retool Slogan for Terror War," *New York Times,* July 26, 2005.

30. White House, "The National Security Strategy of the United States of America," March 2006.

31. Barack Obama, "Barack Obama Speaks to the Muslim World from Cairo, Egypt," June 4, 2009 (http://lybio.net/barack-obama-speaks-to-the -muslim-world-from-cairo-egypt/speeches/).

32. Boaz Ganor, "Identifying the Enemy in Counterterrorism Opera-tions—A Comparison of the Bush and Obama Administrations," *Interna-tional Law Studies* 90 (2014); Gorka, "Flawed Science."

33. White House, "Empowering Local Partners to Prevent Violent Ex-tremism in the United States," August 2011 (www.whitehouse.gov/sites /default/files/empowering_local_partners.pdf).

34. Barack Obama, "Remarks by the President at the National Defense University," May 23, 2013 (www.whitehouse.gov/the-press-office/2013/05 /23/remarks-president-national-defense-university).

35. White House, "National Security Strategy," February 2015.

36. Ibid., p. 7.

37. The text of Rumsfeld's memo was leaked to the press; see "Rums-feld's War-on-Terror Memo," *USA Today,* Washington/Politics, October 16, 2003 (usatoday.com/news/washington/executive/rumsfeld-memo.htm). Note the assumption that madrassas and radical clerics are the causes of terrorism.

38. Lee Hamilton, Bruce Hoffman, Brian Jenkins, Paul Pillar, Xavier Raufer, Walter Reich, and Fernando Reinares, *State of the Struggle: Report on the Battle against Global Terrorism* (Washington: Council on Global Terrorism, 2006), p. 67.

39. Dylan Matthews, "Twelve Years after 9/11, We Still Have No Idea How to Fight Terrorism," *Washington Post, Wonkblog,* September 11, 2013.

40. William Martel, *Victory in War: Foundations of Modern Military Policy* (Cambridge University Press, 2007), p. 1.

41. Cynthia Lum, Lesley Kennedy, and Alison Sherley, 2009.

42. Daniel Byman, "Scoring the War on Terrorism," *National Interest* 72 (Summer 2003).

43. Daniel Byman, *The Five Front War: The Better Way to Fight Global Jihad* (New York: Wiley, 2008), p. 52.

44. Pew Research Center, "Views of Government's Handling of Terror-ism Fall to Post-9/11 Low," December 15, 2015 (www.people-press.org /2015/12/15/views-of-governments-handling-of-terrorism-fall-to-post-911 -low/).

45. Alex P. Schmid and Rashmi Singh, "Measuring Success and Fail-ure in Terrorism and Counter-Terrorism: US Government Metrics of the

Global War on Terror," in *After the War on Terror: Regional and Multilateral Perspectives on Counter-Terrorism Strategy,* edited by Alex P. Schmid and Garry F. Hindle (London: Royal United Services Institute, 2009), pp. 33–61.

46. President George Bush, "War Update, Fort Bragg, N.C., June 28, 2005" (www.presidentialrhetoric.com/speeches/06.28.05.html).

47. George W. Bush, "Speech at the National Endowment for Democracy, Washington, DC, October 6, 2005" (www.presidentialrhetoric.com/speeches/10.06.05.html).

48. Raphael Perl, *Combating Terrorism: The Challenge of Measuring Effectiveness,* CRS Report RL32522 (Congressional Research Service, 2007).

49. Ibid., p. 11.

50. Ibid., p. 6.

51. Nadav Morag, "Measuring Success in Coping with Terrorism: The Israeli Case," *Studies in Conflict and Terrorism* 28 (2005), pp. 307–20.

52. U.S. Department of Justice, Office of the Inspector General, *Audit of the Federal Bureau of Investigation Annual Financial Statements Fiscal Year 2015,* February 2016, p. 8 (https://oig.justice.gov/reports/2016/a1607.pdf).

53. For example, Jack Gibbs, *Crime, Punishment, and Deterrence* (Amsterdam: Elsevier, 1975).

54. Martha Crenshaw, "Will Threats Deter Nuclear Terrorism?," in *Deterring Terrorism: Theory and Practice,* edited by Andreas Wenger and Alex Wilner (Stanford University Press, 2012).

55. Jessica Stern and J. M. Berger, *The State of Terror* (New York: HarperCollins, 2015).

56. An early example is Martha Crenshaw, *Revolutionary Terrorism: The FLN in Algeria, 1954–1962* (Stanford, Calif.: Hoover Institution Press, 1978).

57. Gene Sharp, *The Politics of Nonviolent Action* (Boston: Porter Sargent, 1973).

58. Clark McCauley, "Jujitsu Politics: Terrorism and Responses to Terrorism," in *Psychology of Terrorism,* edited by Paul R. Kimmel and Chris E. Stout (New York: Praeger, 2006).

59. John Duckitt and Kirstin Fisher, "The Impact of Social Threat on Worldview and Ideological Attitudes," *Political Psychology* 24 (2003), pp. 199–222.

60. Edwin M. Lemert, *Social Pathology* (New York: McGraw-Hill, 1951), p. 77.

61. Tom R. Tyler, "Multiculturalism and the Willingness of Citizens to Defer to Law and Legal Authorities," *Law and Social Inquiry* 25 (2000), pp. 983–1019.

62. Alex S. Wilner, "Targeted Killings in Afghanistan: Measuring Coercion and Deterrence in Counterterrorism and Counterinsurgency," *Studies in Conflict and Terrorism* 33 (2010), pp. 307–29; Patrick B. Johnston, "Does Decapitation Work? Assessing the Effectiveness of Leadership Targeting in Counterinsurgency Campaigns," *International Security* 36 (2012), pp. 47–79.

63. Daniel Byman, "Why Drones Work: The Case for Washington's Weapon of Choice," *Foreign Affairs* 92 (2013), p. 32; Megan Smith and James Igoe Walsh, "Do Drone Strikes Degrade al Qa'ida? Evidence from Propaganda Output," *Terrorism and Political Violence* 25 (2013), p. 311.

64. Wilner, "Targeted Killings in Afghanistan"; Austin Long, "Whack-a-Mole or Coup de Grace?; Johnston, "Does Decapitation Work?"; Bryan Price, "Targeting Top Terrorists: How Leadership Decapitation Contributes to Counterterrorism," *International Security* 36 (2012), pp. 9–46.

65. Patrick B. Johnston and Anoop K. Sarbahi, "The Impact of US Drone Strikes on Terrorism in Pakistan," *International Studies Quarterly* (2016), pp. 1–17.

66. Long, "Whack-a-Mole or Coup de Grace?"; Price, "Targeting Top Terrorists."

67. Audrey Kurth Cronin, "Why Drones Fail: When Tactics Drive Strategy," *Foreign Affairs* 92 (2013), pp. 44–54.

68. Jenna Jordan, "Attacking the Leader, Missing the Mark: Why Terrorist Groups Survive Decapitation Strikes," *International Security* 38 (Spring 2014), pp. 7–38.

69. Eric van Um and Daniela Pisoiu, "Dealing with Uncertainty: The Illusion of Knowledge in the Study of Counterterrorism Effectiveness," *Critical Studies on Terrorism* 8 (2014), p. 5.

70. Alex P. Schmid and Albert J. Jongman, *Political Terrorism: A New Guide to Actors, Authors, Concepts, Databases, Theories and Literature* (Amsterdam: North-Holland, 1988), p. 177.

71. Andrew Silke, "The Devil You Know: Continuing Problems with Research on Terrorism," *Terrorism and Political Violence* 13 (2001), pp. 1–14.

72. Lum, Kennedy, and Sherley, "The Effectiveness of Counter-Terrorism Strategies," p. 3.

73. Gary LaFree, Laura Dugan, and Raven Korte, "The Impact of British Counter Terrorist Strategies on Political Violence in Northern Ireland: Comparing Deterrence and Backlash Models," *Criminology* 47 (2009), pp. 501–30.

74. Kieran McEvoy, *Paramilitary Imprisonment in Northern Ireland: Resistance, Management, and Release* (Oxford University Press, 2001), pp. 105–06.

75. Kevin J. Kelley, *The Longest War: Northern Ireland and the I.R.A.* (London: Zed Books, 1980), p. 155.

76. Tony Geraghty, *The Irish War* (Johns Hopkins University Press, 2000).

77. Colm Campbell and Ita Connolly, "A Model for the 'War against Terrorism'? Military Intervention in Northern Ireland and the 1970 Falls Curfew," *Journal of Law and Society* 30 (2003), pp. 341–75.

78. M. L. R. Smith and Peter R. Neumann, "Motorman's Long Journey: Changing the Strategic Setting in Northern Ireland," *Contemporary British History* 19 (2005), p. 413.

79. L. W. Sherman, D. Gottfredson, D. MacKenzie, J. Eck, P. Reuter, and S. Bushway, *Preventing Crime: What Works, What Doesn't, What's Promising: A Report to the United States Congress* (Washington: National Institute of Justice, 1997).

80. Dugan and Chenoweth, "Moving beyond Deterrence."

81. Vladimir Bejan and William S. Parkin, "Examining the Effect of Repressive and Conciliatory Government Actions on Terrorism Activity in Israel," *Economics Letters* 133 (2015), pp. 55–58.

82. Donald Rumsfeld, *Known and Unknown: A Memoir* (New York: Penguin, 2011).

83. David Easton, *A Framework for Political Analysis* (Englewood Cliffs, N.J.: Prentice-Hall, 1965).

Chapter Seven

1. Martha Crenshaw, editor, *The Consequences of Counterterrorism* (New York: Russell Sage Foundation, 2010).

2. Cass R. Sunstein, "Terrorism and Probability Neglect," *Journal of Risk and Uncertainty* 26 (March 2003), pp. 121–36.

3. In December 2015, an NBC–Wall Street Journal poll of 1,000 U.S. residents found that 40 percent of Americans ranked national security and terrorism as the top priority for the federal government—up 19 points from when this question was last asked in April 2014. When asked "which one or two events defined 2015?" respondents concluded that the Paris and San Bernardino attacks ranked ahead of all other issues that year in importance, including the conclusion of the nuclear deal with Iran. See the NBC News–Wall Street Journal Survey, December 6–9, 2015, Study #15564 (www.nbcnews.com/meet-the-press/nbc-wsj-poll-terror-fears-reshape-2016-landscape-n479831).

4. Drew Desilver, "More Than a Decade Later, 9/11 Attacks Continue to Resonate with Americans," Pew Research Center, May 14, 2014 (www.pewresearch.org/fact-tank/2014/05/14/more-than-a-decade-later-911-attacks-continue-to-resonate-with-americans/).

5. Samuel Walker, *Popular Justice: A History of American Criminal Justice* (Oxford University Press, 1980), p. 3.

6. John Mueller and Mark G. Stewart, *Chasing Ghosts: The Policing of Terrorism* (Oxford University Press, 2016), p. 249.

7. Robert Jervis, "Do Leaders Matter and How Would We Know?" *Security Studies* 22 (2013), pp. 153–79.

8. About half of the more than 2,500 groups identified in the GTD are associated with a single attack only. Even groups that manage to develop a high degree of organization and maintain this organizational structure over a period of time can be hard to trace. ISIS provides an excellent example of the complexities of keeping up with organizational evolution and group identity over time, as the group has operated under five different names since its beginnings in 2002.

9. Robert Powell, "Defending against Terrorist Attacks with Limited Resources," *American Political Science Review* 101 (August 2007), pp. 527–41.

10. Charles Manski, *Public Policy in an Uncertain World: Analysis and Decisions* (Harvard University Press, 2013).

11. Charles Manski, "Policy Analysis with Incredible Certitude," *Economic Journal* 121, no. 554 (2011), pp. F261–89.

12. White House, "National Security Strategy of the United States of America," September 2002 (text at www.state.gov/documents/organization /63562.pdf) and White House, "National Strategy for Combating Terrorism," February 2003 (text at www.cia.gov/news-information/cia-the-war -on-terrorism/Counter_Terrorism_Strategy.pdf). See also Raphael F. Perl, *CRS Report for Congress: National Strategy for Combating Terrorism: Background and Issues for Congress: November 1, 2007* (Library of Congress, Congressional Research Service, 2007), p. 4.

13. James Fallows, "On 'Existential' Threats: A Word That Has Replaced Thought," *The Atlantic*, February 20, 2015 (www.theatlantic.com /international/archive/2015/02/on-existential-threats/385638/).

14. Ibid.

15. John Mueller, *Atomic Obsession: Nuclear Alarmism from Hiroshima to al-Qaeda* (Oxford University Press, 2009), p. x.

16. Brian Jenkins, "Will Terrorism Go Nuclear?," address to the Los Angeles World Affairs Council, April 2, 2009 (www.lawac.org/speech-archive /pdf/2009/Jenkins_926.pdf).

17. Mueller, *Atomic Obsession*, p. xi.

18. Rolf Mowatt-Larssen, "Al Qaeda Weapons of Mass Destruction Threat: Hype or Reality? A Timeline of Terrorists' Efforts to Acquire WMD," paper, Harvard University, Belfer Center for Science and International Affairs, January 2010 (http://belfercenter.ksg.harvard.edu/publication /19852/al_qaeda_weapons_of_mass_destruction_threat.html?breadcrumb =%2Fexperts%2F1961%2Frolf_mowattlarssen).

19. Reported in Jenkins, "Will Terrorism Go Nuclear?," p. 3.

20. Gary Ackerman and Ryan Pereira, "Jihadists and WMD: A Re-Evaluation of the Future Threat," *CBRNe World* (October 2014), pp. 27–34a

(www.cbrneworld.com/_uploads/download_magazines/Jihadists.pdf); Jenkins, "Will Terrorism Go Nuclear?," p. 7.

21. Jenkins, "Will Terrorism Go Nuclear?," p. 7.

22. Ibid.

23. Joe Cirincione, "The Risk of a Nuclear ISIS Grows," *Huffington Post,* March 23, 2016 (www.huffingtonpost.com/joe-cirincione/the-risk-of-a-nuclear-isi_b_8259978.html).

24. Ibid. A dirty bomb is a nuclear weapon improvised from radioactive nuclear waste material and conventional explosives that would spread contamination widely.

25. Alan Kuperman, "Obama: The Anti-Anti-Nuke President," *New York Times,* op-ed, March 25, 2016.

26. Reported in Steven Brill, "Is America Any Safer?" *The Atlantic,* September 2016, p. 49 (www.theatlantic.com/magazine/archive/2016/09/are-we-any-safer/492761/).

27. White House, "Fact Sheet: The Nuclear Security Summits: Securing the World from Nuclear Terrorism," March 29, 2016 (www.whitehouse.gov/the-press-office/2016/03/29/fact-sheet-nuclear-security-summits-securing-world-nuclear-terrorism).

28. Aaron Clauset and Ryan Woodard, "Estimating the Historical and Future Probabilities of Large Terrorist Events," *Annals of Applied Statistics* 7 (2013), pp. 1838–65.

29. See Association for Safe International Road Travel, "Annual Global Road Crash Statistics" (asirt.org/initiatives/informing-road-users/road-safety-facts/road-crash-statistics).

30. Larry C. Johnson, "The Future of Terrorism," *American Behavioral Scientist* 44 (2001), pp. 894–913.

31. U.S. State Department, "Country Reports on Terrorism 2015," press release, June 2, 2016, on release of new country reports (www.state.gov/r/pa/prs/ps/2016/06/258013.htm).

32. Gary LaFree, Laura Dugan, and Erin Miller, *Putting Terrorism in Context: Lessons from the Global Terrorism Database* (London: Routledge, 2014).

33. Larry E. Cohen and Marcus Felson, "Social Change and Crime Rate Trends: A Routine Activity Approach," *American Sociological Review* 44 (1979), pp. 588–608.

34. United Nations, Department of Economic and Social Affairs, Population Division (2014). World Urbanization Prospects: The 2014 Revision, Highlights (ST/ESA/SER.A/352). (esa.un.org/unpd/wup/Publications/Files/WUP2014-Highlights.pdf), p. 1.

35. Ibid., p. 1.

36. Steven Johnson, *The Ghost Map: The Story of London's Most Terrifying Epidemic—and How It Changed Science, Cities, and the Modern World* (New York: Penguin, 2006).

37. Despite the fact that there is no single profile of a terrorist, the social scientists Diego Gambetta and Steffen Hertog, in *Engineers of Jihad: The Curious Connection between Violent Extremism and Education* (Princeton University Press, 2016), have called attention to the apparent preponderance of engineers among jihadists.

38. Based on data made available at World Bank, "Population Estimates and Projections" (database) (data.worldbank.org/data-catalog/population -projection-tables).

Index